MAGIC IN THE MODERN WORLD

THE MAGIC IN HISTORY SERIES

FORBIDDEN RITES
A Necromancer's Manual of the Fifteenth Century
Richard Kieckhefer

CONJURING SPIRITS
Texts and Traditions of Medieval Ritual Magic
Edited by Claire Fanger

RITUAL MAGIC
Elizabeth M. Butler

THE FORTUNES OF FAUST
Elizabeth M. Butler

THE BATHHOUSE AT MIDNIGHT
An Historical Survey of Magic and
Divination in Russia
W. F. Ryan

SPIRITUAL AND DEMONIC MAGIC
From Ficino to Campanella
D. P. Walker

ICONS OF POWER
Ritual Practices in Late Antiquity
Naomi Janowitz

BATTLING DEMONS
Witchcraft, Heresy, and Reform in the
Late Middle Ages
Michael D. Bailey

PRAYER, MAGIC, AND THE STARS IN THE
ANCIENT AND LATE ANTIQUE WORLD
*Edited by Scott Noegel, Joel Walker,
and Brannon Wheeler*

BINDING WORDS
Textual Amulets in the Middle Ages
Don C. Skemer

STRANGE REVELATIONS
Magic, Poison, and Sacrilege in
Louis XIV's France
Lynn Wood Mollenauer

UNLOCKED BOOKS
Manuscripts of Learned Magic in the Medieval
Libraries of Central Europe
Benedek Láng

ALCHEMICAL BELIEF
Occultism in the Religious Culture of
Early Modern England
Bruce Janacek

INVOKING ANGELS
Theurgic Ideas and Practices, Thirteenth to
Sixteenth Centuries
Edited by Claire Fanger

THE TRANSFORMATIONS OF MAGIC
Illicit Learned Magic in the Later Middle Ages
and Renaissance
Frank Klaassen

MAGIC IN THE CLOISTER
Pious Motives, Illicit Interests, and Occult
Approaches to the Medieval Universe
Sophie Page

REWRITING MAGIC
An Exegesis of the Visionary Autobiography of a
Fourteenth-Century French Monk
Claire Fanger

The Magic in History series explores the role magic and the occult have played in European culture, religion, science, and politics. Titles in the series bring the resources of cultural, literary, and social history to bear on the history of the magic arts, and they contribute to an understanding of why the theory and practice of magic have elicited fascination at every level of European society. Volumes include both editions of important texts and significant new research in the field.

MAGIC IN THE MODERN WORLD

STRATEGIES OF REPRESSION

AND LEGITIMIZATION

EDITED BY EDWARD BEVER
AND RANDALL STYERS

THE PENNSYLVANIA STATE UNIVERSITY PRESS
UNIVERSITY PARK, PENNSYLVANIA

Library of Congress Cataloging-in-Publication Data

Names: Bever, Edward Watts Morton, editor. | Styers, Randall, editor.
Title: Magic in the modern world : strategies of repression and legitimization /
    edited by Edward Bever and Randall Styers.
Other titles: Magic in history.
Description: University Park, Pennsylvania : The Pennsylvania State University
    Press, [2017] | Series: The magic in history series | Includes bibliographical
    references and index.
Summary: "A collection of essays on various aspects of the position of magic in the
    modern world. Essays explore the ways in which modernity has been defined in
    explicit opposition to magic and superstition, and the ways in which modern
    proponents of magic have worked to legitimate their practices"—Provided by
    publisher.
Identifiers: LCCN 2016052617 | ISBN 9780271077772 (cloth : alk. paper) |
    ISBN 9780271077789 (pbk. : alk. paper)
Subjects: LCSH: Magic. | Magic—History.
Classification: LCC BF1611 .M34 2017 | DDC 133.4/30903—dc23
LC record available at https://lccn.loc.gov/2016052617

CONTENTS

Edward Bever and Randall Styers

The place of magic in the modern world has long been a source of anxiety and confusion for intellectuals and social theorists. Since the rise of the modern social sciences in the nineteenth century, scholars of various sorts have formulated theories of social evolution that have assumed the inexorable decline of all forms of magical supernaturalism. In the early twentieth century, Max Weber offered a definitive formulation of the "disenchantment" of modernity (*Entzauberung*—in a literal translation, "getting the magic out"), arguing that capitalist rationalization entailed a decline in all forms of supernaturalism.[1] Theories of secularization and rationalization asserted that if religion could survive at all, its role in the modern social order would be only as a thin source of personal inspiration and moral guidance. But, these theories assumed, magic and other alternative forms of supernaturalism would surely shrivel and fade, brought low by their primitive irrationalism and unredeemable ignorance.

Yet reports of magic's imminent demise have proved to be greatly exaggerated. Edward B. Tylor, the founding figure of modern anthropology, offered a social typology that by its very structure indicated that modern culture was moving away from superstition and magical thinking. But at the same time, Tylor was compelled by facts on the ground to explain magic's stubborn persistence, styling it as a cultural survival. Even as he charted a course of social evolution that directed society away from supernaturalism of all types, Tylor lamented that these earlier forms of thought persisted in the contemporary world with alarming tenacity. As Tylor explained, magic "belongs in its main principle to the lowest known stages of civilization, and the lower races, who have not partaken largely of the education of the world, still maintain it in vigour."[2] Despite his conviction that modernity would expel the demons that had heretofore bedeviled humankind, he recognized that magical beliefs persisted and could be found even in modern nations, where not only did older practices survive but new superstitions continued to evolve.

Like Tylor, the other leading British intellectualist anthropologist, James George Frazer, was also distressed by the florescence of the turn-of-the-century spiritualist subculture in England. Fraser described in stark and vivid terms the deep "menace to civilization" he saw in the persistence of magical thinking, pointing to

> a solid stratum of intellectual agreement among the dull, the weak, the ignorant, and the superstitious, who constitute, unfortunately, the vast majority of mankind. . . . It is beneath our feet—and not very far beneath them—here in Europe at the present day. . . . This universal faith, this truly Catholic creed, is a belief in the efficacy of magic. . . . We seem to move on a thin crust which may at any moment be rent by the subterranean forces slumbering below. From time to time a hollow murmur underground or a sudden spurt of flame into the air tells of what is going on beneath our feet.[3]

Despite the fervent hopes of these and other scholars that this "subterranean" force would gradually fade away, magic and supernaturalism seem even stronger today than they did in the late nineteenth century. Not only do supernatural heroes and villains pervade literature, film, and other forms of popular entertainment, but esoteric traditions also inform the daily lives of a significant portion of the population. Wiccans and other Pagans meet to celebrate and exploit the occult powers they believe permeate nature. Many communities have storefront "readers" and "advisers," while almost every bookstore has a thriving "New Age" section. The Internet has fostered the formation and spread of supernaturalist communities and subcultures around the globe. Much of this supernaturalism is explicitly fictional, a benign mechanism to envision alternative ways of being in the world to compensate for the drab, rationalized routines of modern life. But there are also many who take supernaturalism much more seriously, finding in their beliefs, practices, and communities a vital sense of identity and meaning that forms a potent alternative understanding of the nature of the self and its relationship to the broader world.

In sharp contrast to the optimistic naturalism of modernist intellectuals, recent scholars have rejected the entire notion of the disenchantment and secularization of modern society. Recognizing that just as religion continues to adapt and thrive in the modern world, so, too, magic and supernaturalism of all sorts not only survive but prosper in modernity, a range of important thinkers including Bruno Latour and Michael Taussig have challenged the ideologies and self-presentations shaping modernity. Such scholars have moved from viewing the persistence of magic in modernity as a dilemma to be resolved to recognizing that "magic *belongs to* modernity."[4]

Peter Pels, for example, has recently affirmed the deep inter-implication of magic and the modern—their surprising symbiosis—arguing for "*the supplementarity of magic and modernity,* that is, the way in which many modern discourses position magic as their antithesis, reinventing it in the process. Thus, if modern discourse reconstructs magic in terms that distinguish it from the modern, this at the same time creates the correspondences and nostalgias by which magic can come to haunt modernity." The very effort to expel or repress magic makes it essential to the formulation of the modern. In this vein, it is impossible to understand the nature of modernity without taking into account its magical foil. In addition, Pels identifies specific mechanisms through which modernity itself has been structured by its own distinctive forms of magic, "those enchantments that are produced by practices culturally specific to modern states, economies, and societies—practices labeled as representation, commodification, and discipline."[5] Far from moving beyond magic, the modern world is fueled by complexly ambiguous flows of power very much like the ones it has sought so eagerly to disclaim. Magic is not alien to modernity, because without magic there could be no modernity.

This volume charts a different course, exploring a complex double gesture at the heart of modernity.[6] One set of essays examines the dynamics through which modernity has sought to expunge or repress magic, and in that process illustrates central aspects of the constructive labor required for moderns to maintain the fiction of a new mode of disenchanted rationality. These essays explore such topics as the neurocognitive mechanisms through which modern "rational" consciousness is generated and maintained, the intellectual process by which proponents of both magical and scientific traditions rationalize evidence to fit with accepted orthodoxy, and the cultural process by which superstition was pathologized as a cognitive lapse in order to serve the emergent social and political order. The second group of essays here examines the remarkable cultural ingenuity demonstrated by modern proponents of magic. Many denizens of the modern world deeply dissatisfied with the thin and sterile norms of modern subjectivity have opted for an overt embrace of various forms of magic, and these evolving forms of esotericism, supernaturalism, and magic often demonstrate extremely complex cultural creativity as they draw on strands of history, alternative epistemologies, and novel interpretations of experience. But given the stigma attached to magic, its proponents have regularly confronted deep questions concerning the legitimacy of their practices. Olav Hammer has identified three basic strategies employed by modern esoteric movements in their quest for legitimacy: a claiming of tradition, an appropriation of the rhetoric of scientific method and verification, and a reliance on the evidence of experience.[7] Essays in this volume examine proponents of magic who claim the support of tradition by redeploying John Dee's "Enochian" angel magic in novel fashion, invoking various forms of ancient Norse mythology, or simply assembling—Dan Harms's phrase—"a bricolage of mysticism, religion, history, and fiction." With the rise of modern science, particularly the forms it assumed over the course of the nineteenth century, the stigma surrounding magic intensified, and in response, other proponents of magic have engaged in complex negotiations with the methods and rhetoric of science or invoked identity and experience in innovative ways to support their magical worldviews.

Underlying both aspects of this double gesture is the need to come to terms with experiences that seem magical, whether to drive them away by denying their reality or to embrace them and affirm their validity. At the heart of this modern preoccupation with magic are complex dynamics concerning the construction of the modern self. In its many forms, magic explicitly foregrounds questions concerning the nature of the self and its boundaries, the capacities of the will, and the relation of the self to external powers. When magic is suppressed, the self is conceived and performed largely as physically isolated and internally directed; the self is constrained into narrow modes of agency and power. When magic is embraced, the self is seen in far more expansive terms as organically interconnected with—and permeated by—various aspects of the external world; the capacities of the self are understood as participating in a broad network of material and spiritual forces. The choice between suppressing and embracing magic turns on fundamentally different understandings of the nature of the self, its boundaries, and its powers.

The two sets of essays in this volume are divided not only thematically but roughly chronologically. The first four form a section titled "Magic and the Making of Modernity" because they focus primarily on the process by which early modern people defined their modernity in explicit opposition to magic and superstition. The last four, in contrast, focus more on the ways in which later modern proponents of magic have attempted to negotiate the relationship between their beliefs, traditions, and modernity, and this section is consequently titled "Magic in Modernity."

In the first essay, Randall Styers traces the way in which the notion of "superstition" was redefined from the medieval to the modern period. From antiquity through the Middle Ages, superstition was most commonly understood as a mode of excessive or misdirected religiosity. But through the theological debates of the Reformation and also in debates concerning the persecution of witches, superstition was framed in increasingly psychological, rather than theological, terms. Superstition was seen as a delusion, one that needed to be explained in purely cognitive terms.

By the twentieth century, psychological theorists were invoking magic in order to promote psychological and social maturity. Superstition and magic were attributed to a familiar set of causes: faulty observation and analysis, overinvestment of subjective desires, sublimated and projected desires, lapses in causal thinking, and errors in determining probability. For the majority of nineteenth- and twentieth-century social theorists, superstition and magical thinking posed a serious threat to the good order of society, a theme that persists in numerous texts by more recent behavioral and cognitive psychologists.

The three other essays in this section explore specific instances of the general processes Styers surveys. In the second essay, Edward Bever examines a famous set of dreams that René Descartes experienced on the evening of November 10, 1619, in the midst of his efforts to formulate a new system of knowledge. Bever's analysis of these dreams leads him to conclude that they are particularly significant because of the light they shed on the psycho-cultural stigmatization of magic in the modern world. Bever argues that the practice of magic generally centers on a manipulation of the nervous system and that magical beliefs can be understood as rational (or verbal) representations of associational-imagic processes and their products. In this light, the renunciation of magic serves to exclude these representations from the conscious formulation of deliberate action and to inhibit their function as mental mediating structures.

The study of Descartes's dreams thus illuminates both the central role of his philosophy in fostering broader rationalizing cultural changes and also the mechanisms through which the repression of magic was implemented on the psycho-physiological level. As Bever asserts, Descartes's dreams, and his responses to them, demonstrate the considerable effort required to constitute "modern" rational consciousness, a process that requires the masking or repression of imagination, intuition, and feeling—all modes of cognition central to the creation and apprehension of magical experiences. Thus the repression of magic actually requires a type of manipulation of the nervous system quite similar to that involved in the practice of magic—the types of rationality formalized by Descartes offer modern selves techniques that foster the illusion of an autonomous consciousness isolated from materiality. Descartes's dreams demonstrate that the very effort to repress magic has the unintended effect of making more magic.

Turning from the psychological to the physical aspects of magical beliefs, Benedek Láng explores an issue central to our understanding of the empirical claims of both magic and science, the issue of falsification. Numerous medieval and early modern texts prescribed specific methods and procedures to achieve specific practical effects, and these texts were circulated by a range of educated practitioners. Yet even though it seems to modern eyes that many of these mechanisms were obviously false, the scribes and compilers did not seem to recognize this failure. Láng argues that it is productive for contemporary scholars to ask why medieval and early modern claims seemed so immune to falsification, and he seeks to understand how historical actors might have resolved the discrepancy between their expectations and the actual results of their procedures.

With this task clarified, Láng considers the various factors that could allow both magical and naturalistic claims to resist falsification. He then turns to consider the ways in which the notion of an *experimentum crucis*—a decisive experiment with the power to demonstrate the falsity of a theory—is a myth not only in the history of magic but also in the history of science. Prior convictions can influence perception, and detailed prescriptions cannot ensure that an experiment will always be performed in an identical fashion. Experiments are deemed decisive only in retrospect, only after a choice has already been made among competing theoretical explanations. So, Láng concludes, the question of why theories persist even when experiments fail to confirm them is a proper inquiry not only for the history of magic but also for the history of science. His essay thus illuminates not only the resistance of premodern intellectuals to falsification of their beliefs, but also the veneration by modern intellectuals of sweeping ontological claims based on fragmentary and frequently ad hoc experimental evidence.

In the last of the essays in the first section, Adam Jortner looks at the interpretation of witchcraft and magic that permeated early nineteenth-century America. This understanding of magic appeared in a large number of genres—sermons, tracts, lectures and speeches, and popular entertainments such as novels, theater, traveling exhibitions, and stage magic. Jortner argues that the way of understanding magic and related topics—nature, human freedom, and the divine—conveyed in these sources contributed to the creation of the social and political structures of the Jeffersonian and Jacksonian United States, as it linked philosophical and religious issues of epistemology to the social and political anxieties aroused by the process of democratization. Opinion leaders in the new Republic shared an Enlightenment-inspired dogma that magic was antithetical to reason and a great social threat, since reason was seen as the essential basis of republican citizenship.

Jortner's essay offers a fertile case study in the ways in which modern notions of rationality are linked to issues of social order and authority. Jeffersonian opponents of superstition and supernaturalism felt compelled to use invective because so many of their peers—particularly those on the margins of social power, like women, slaves, native peoples, and unschooled immigrants—seemed rather less strictly wedded to a newly narrowed notion of rationality. The assault on magic and witchcraft was framed as a key component of the defense of freedom and civilization against tyranny and savagery—magic was seen as the enemy of liberty. Healthy intellectual habits needed to be instilled in the populace in order to produce a well-regulated citizenry. But the very process of seeking to expunge magic had the inadvertent consequence of making magic a prevalent theme both in cultural debates and in the popular imagination.

The first of the four essays in the "Magic in Modernity" section, by Egil Asprem, explores the dynamics of change in modern occultism. Asprem focuses particularly on the ways in which magical concepts of the Elizabethan natural philosopher John Dee and his collaborator Edward Kelly were transformed into modern "Enochian" angel magic. Dee recorded an intricate magical system and a version of the "language of Adam," and since the seventeenth century his magical diaries have inspired new and evolving fields of ritual magic. Asprem first details the key components of the magical materials that Dee claimed to have received in communications with the archangels Michael and Gabriel, a body of material formed before mathematics was seen as key to reading the book of nature and before the rise of mechanistic philosophy. Asprem then explores the reception and reinterpretation of Dee's magical corpus by various later magical communities, a process shaped by the contingencies of partial transmission and culminating, by the end of the nineteenth century, in a new occult system developed by the Order of the Golden Dawn, a system of "Enochian" magic that dramatically reworked the meaning of Dee's original materials.

Throughout the twentieth century, Enochian ritual magic continued to evolve in the hands of figures such as Aleister Crowley, Anton LaVey, and later New Age thinkers. Asprem argues that the persistence of ritual magic in modern culture can most profitably be understood by exploring the ways in which its practitioners seek various forms of cultural legitimacy by translating esoteric concepts into secular terms. As he explains, both disenchanted and reenchanted perspectives are in play within modern occult milieus, and both can serve as discursive strategies to help in the negotiation of various domains of culture. To this end, Asprem focuses on the struggles over the authenticity of Enochian magic that played out over the twentieth century, as the gap between the Enochian magic of the Golden Dawn and the original system of John Dee became increasingly apparent. Particularly in examining recent debates among practitioners concerning the metaphysical status of the supernatural entities with whom the Enochian rituals seek to interact, Asprem argues that modern occultism is neither a simple reaction against secularized rational culture nor merely a practice that has accommodated itself to that culture. Instead, he concludes that a central factor in magic's survival in modernity is its demonstrable cultural flexibility. Modern magicians are adept at improvising and at creating meaning with a vast array of cultural materials.

Erik Davis explores the interplay between magic and science in modernity in his biographical study of Jack Parsons (1914–1952), a cofounder of the Jet Propulsion Laboratory whose discoveries helped launch the U.S. space program. Parsons was also an enthusiastic follower of Aleister Crowley's "magickal religion of Thelema." In exploring Parsons's complex career—and particularly the ways in which Parsons negotiated the relationship between his scientific endeavors and his occultism—Davis examines the distinctively modern relationship between technology and the occult. Jack Parsons offers Davis a potent example of the interplay between modern rationality and the mystical aspects of modern occultism. While Parsons claimed to keep his science and his occultism distinct, the two endeavors did not remain cleanly separated, and Davis charts numerous complex interchanges between these two aspects of Parsons's life. In fact, Davis argues, magic finds its place in modernity as a boundary condition, "as this very code switching itself—a pragmatic, relativistic, and in some ways naturalist fluctuation between science and the holy."

Parsons's life exemplifies this magical flicker between science and the supernatural. Davis explores the ways in which Aleister Crowley himself adapted certain aspects of "scientific" method in the Thelemic system (particularly in his focus on quantification and his skeptical reluctance to make ontological claims about the existence of astral and other spiritual phenomena) and Crowley's insistence on a mode of pragmatic relativism that emphasized practice, experience, and results. Deeply influenced by the principles of Thelema, Parsons sometimes insisted on the difference between his scientific and his magical endeavors, but sometimes he mixed the two. Thus, Davis asserts, we can understand Parsons's magic only if we understand his science. Just as Parsons's scientific work was characterized by an extremely imaginative or intuitive experimental method, so also his occultism was characterized by a critical analysis of its experiential results. As Davis explains, Parsons found a practical resonance between his scientific investigations and his occult practice, a resonance that highlights the constructed—and constructive—nature of the modern divide between the scientific and the spiritual.

Megan Goodwin focuses on the relationship between modern practitioners and the premodern tradition that inspires them in her essay on contemporary

Norse Neopaganism. *Seiðcraft*, Norse magical practice, originated in a culture deeply invested in the performance of a hypervirile masculinity, and the practice of *seiðr* was deeply gendered: the majority of practitioners were women, and it was considered unmanly for men to engage in it. Contemporary Norse Neopagan groups have emerged in the shadow of these traditions, and the practice of *seiðr* remains contested in these communities. Some more conservative (or orthodox) Neopagans discourage or forbid men from engaging in the practice, viewing *seiðr* as effeminate, while more moderate groups accept male practitioners. As Goodwin argues, it is impossible to understand the cultural dynamics at play in the practice of *seiðr* without attending to the gendered genealogy of the practice. *Seiðr* has offered an opportunity for the deliberate performance of unmanliness, requiring its practitioners to negotiate cultural expectations for masculinity and offering space for reimagining fundamental aspects of personal identity within Norse Neopaganism.

For some practitioners, that transgression of expected gender norms has become a spiritual end in itself. Goodwin focuses particularly on Northern Tradition Paganism, a northern European Neopagan group founded by female-to-male transgender and intersex activist Raven Kaldera. Kaldera deploys the practice of *seiðr* in order to celebrate unmanliness as a religious vocation. He sees a deep link between his religious identity as a shaman and his bodily identity as transgender, and in both he works to challenge dominate understandings of sex and gender—unmanliness is an end in itself. Both in Kaldera's practice and in the other Neopagan permutations of the practice of *seiðr*, Goodwin demonstrates that the performance of gender and the performance of magic are both radically creative and culturally constrained.

Like Asprem's and Goodwin's essays, Dan Harms's discussion of the *grimoire* titled *The Necronomicon* explores the interplay between modern occultism and premodern traditions. Yet while Asprem's and Goodwin's subjects were based in actual historical traditions (regardless of the degree to which more recent practitioners may have refashioned them for their own purposes), Harms's topic involves what appears to be an ancient tradition that was invented out of whole cloth to legitimize a contemporary fabrication. The *Necronomicon* was first published in New York in 1977 and is perhaps the most popular modern exemplar of the genre. In an era in which magical texts could no longer be easily legitimized by attribution to past figures of spiritual authority or through a type of scientism, the author of the *Necronomicon* (identified only as Simon) used multiple strategies to establish the text's cultural authority. In a postmodern spiritual marketplace, older tactics of cultural legitimization give way to a broad array of new strategies in the text and its promotion.

The *Necronomicon* enlists horror fiction, a number of religious traditions, archaeology, and various portrayals of Satan in popular culture to support its claim to legitimacy. The author of the text draws connections to earlier grimoires, in both its ritual procedures and the iconography of its illustrations, and its initial marketing also made these parallels explicit. The text draws on the fictional work of H. P. Lovecraft, who first coined the term *necronomicon* in 1924 to designate an important collection of arcane knowledge, and the author repeatedly invokes Aleister Crowley's ceremonial magic and diverse Wiccan and Pagan tropes both ancient and modern. The *Necronomicon* also exploits the "dark aesthetic" that circulated in popular media in the 1970s. As Harms explains it, these various strategies of legitimization contributed to the text's positive reception in popular culture but simultaneously created barriers to its influence in more traditionalist occult circles. The *Necronomicon* represents a clear example of postmodern cultural construction; its appeal rests not so much on any particular belief system but on its ability to exploit a range of cultural symbols, anxieties, and desires.

While a collection of such diverse essays naturally presents an array of foci, approaches, and interpretations, certain common themes can be discerned, even if the contributors would not necessarily agree on all of them. In *The Magical Imagination: Magic and Modernity in Urban England, 1780–1914,* the historian Karl Bell has offered a critical overview of current scholarly perspectives on magic and modernity, and Bell's framework offers a useful template for drawing together the themes of this set of essays. Bell argues that the modern magical imagination should be understood in Lévi-Strauss's broad sense of the term *bricolage,* "a 'creative, associational . . . mode of thought,' a mentality defined by its acquisitive nature and adaptive capacity to fuse disparate elements . . . into a heterogeneous but somehow comprehensible system of its own."[8] The essays in this volume clearly reflect this aspect of modern magic. Davis's discussion of Parsons and Goodwin's discussion of Kaldera are perhaps the most vivid examples of this sense of bricolage, but it is also reflected in Asprem's and Harms's portrayals of their subjects.

Consequently, as Bell argues and as the essays collected here attest, modern magic can most profitably be understood not simply as false belief, anachronism, or make-believe, but as a potent resource conferring a sense of meaning and agency that, suitably adapted, can be as attractive amid the uncertainties of modern urban life as it is in more traditional or rural settings.[9] Magic's appeal stems not just from its offer of an illusion of control. Instead, even in the modern world, it exerts a powerful capacity to mobilize deep and complex mental processes and modes of making meaning, including not just fantastical but also pragmatic meaning. Its remarkable adaptive capability and deep roots in human cognitive processing allow magic to persist and flourish, defying, as both Bell and the present volume attest, the Whiggish interpretation of disenchantment running from the nineteenth-century intellectualists, through Weber, and on to Keith Thomas's 1971 *Religion and the Decline of Magic*. It has become increasingly clear that it is impossible to comprehend the nature of modernity without actively exploring the active magical undercurrents that permeate the contemporary world.

Following Joshua Landy and Michael Saler's *Re-Enchantment of the World*, Bell outlines three different interpretive approaches to the relationship between magic and modernity.[10] The first, the traditional "binary" approach, views magic and modernity as incompatible, so that the rise of modernity necessarily involves the suppression of magic, and any survival or resurgence of magic necessarily represents a repudiation of modernity. The second, "dialectic" approach (exemplified by a number of the essays included in Birgit Meyer and Peter Pels's 2003 *Magic and Modernity*) sees modernity as creating its own substitutes for traditional magic—namely, consumerism, advertising, mass entertainment, demagogic political movements, and spectator sports. The third approach, which Landy and Saler call "antinomial," builds on the recognition that "modernity embraces seeming contraries."[11] This perspective, they explain, recognizes

> that modernity is characterized by fruitful tensions between seemingly irreconcilable forces and ideas. Modernity is defined less by binaries arranged in an implicit hierarchy, or by the dialectical transformation of one term into its opposite, than by contradictions, oppositions, and antinomies: modernity is messy. . . . There is a growing awareness . . . that there are forms of enchantment entirely compatible with, and indeed at times *dependent* upon, those features of modernity usually seen as disenchanting the world.[12]

So, they argue, new forms of enchantment can be found in the mystery and wonder produced by modern science, the self-reflexivity and imaginative fantasy of modern literature, and the intensities produced in mass culture, spectator sports, and even ordinary language.[13] Like Landy and Saler, Bell favors this third perspective, arguing that it "liberates us from the binary notions of continuity and decline, dominance and marginalization, while at the same time it appreciates a more complicated interpretation of enchantment and modernity than that offered by dialectical transformation."[14]

It must surely be acknowledged that belief and disbelief coexist not only in modern culture but also within the psyche of most modern people—the psychologist Eugene Subbotsky has shown that even those who explicitly profess disbelief in magic often manifest belief implicitly through their actions.[15] As Bell puts it, various forms of modern occultism serve as "an intrinsic element in constructing and negotiating a sense of the modern 'self,' a way of reconciling the rational and the numinous in a more secular age."[16] Much of the most exciting recent historical and theoretical work on modern magic has aimed to explore the complex and vibrant inter-implication of magic and modernity—the unexpected ways in which modernity has fueled various new forms of enchantment and the culturally productive effects of these enchantments for modernity itself. Many of the essays in this volume richly reflect the insights of this new perspective.

It is at this point, however, that the present volume parts company with Bell, for its contributions suggest that the different approaches in Landy and Saler's typology are not as clearly separable or mutually exclusive as they first appear. Even as the essays collected here illustrate the inter-implication of magic and modernity, many of them also reaffirm the importance of focusing on the difference between cultural dominance and cultural marginalization, a central theme of the "binary" approach. Modern magic is constructed, legitimized, and practiced in a very different cultural context from earlier forms of magic. As the essays in the first section of this volume detail, the suppression of magic was an explicit goal of self-conscious modernizers, taken over from theologians and pursued through social, cultural, and psychological means for centuries. The results of this campaign are clearly evident in the more recent circumstances discussed in the second section: both in the struggle for legitimization of the Enochian magicians discussed by Asprem and also in Jack Parsons's split identity and institutional difficulties in the early twentieth century.

These essays certainly attest to the persistence of magic in modernity that so troubled Tylor and Frazer, and to the rich complexity of its relationship with various aspects of the modern social order emphasized by Pels, Landy and Saler, and Bell. Nevertheless, however much evidence we can find for magic's deep roots in the human psyche and its tenacious ability to emerge in creative new forms in modern contexts, the scene is framed, as it has been for centuries, by the pervasive and systematic campaign of dominant cultural elites, the guardians of official religious and intellectual truth, to marginalize magic by relegating it to the realms of fiction and delusion. This campaign has been sustained by continued religious opposition to marginal practices, the organizational needs of bureaucratic government and mass society, and the epistemological constraints of a knowledge system based on the consensus of printed sources and the idolization of dispassionate observation. Efforts to suppress magic serve to produce a population of predictable, rational workers and citizens who conform to the needs of the capitalist marketplace and the modern bureaucratic state.

The essays in this volume demonstrate that magic plays a crucial role in modernity, even as the dominant culture emphatically denies its validity. Despite the systematic and sustained employment of social and cultural power to promote officially sanctioned modes of knowledge, older forms of magic continue to develop, and new forms continue to emerge. Since modern rationality has been constructed in explicit contrast to magic, the efforts by proponents of magic to claim legitimacy in "scientific terms"—to legitimize their magic by recourse to a rhetoric of science and rationality that is the very source of their marginalization—are self-contradictory. Magic as a system posits an interconnection between the psyche and the physical world that is incompatible with controlled experimentation, and the moment phenomena considered magical are validated scientifically, they cease to be seen as magic and become part of the corpus of modern science. Similarly, modern historicism and information technologies render increasingly untenable the claim that contemporary magical subcultures are derived directly from age-old traditions.

Yet despite these difficulties in seeking to ground or legitimize modern magic, modernity itself remains inherently unstable. The modern concept of a rational, autonomous self is deeply artificial and constraining; it ignores vital realms of the human psyche, and it denies central dimensions of human interconnectedness. These fissures guarantee that alternative systems of knowledge will continually emerge, regardless of their official acceptability or historical validity. This dynamic illustrates both the power of modern culture and the poverty of the modern notion of the self.

NOTES

1. See Max Weber, *The Protestant Ethic and the Spirit of Capitalism,* trans. Talcott Parsons (New York: Scribner, 1958).

2. See Edward Burnett Tylor, *Primitive Culture: Researches into the Development of Mythology, Philosophy, Religion, Language, Art, and Custom,* 3rd American ed., vol. 1 (New York: Henry Holt, 1889), 16, 72, 112–13. For a classic overview of the notion of survivals, see Margaret T. Hodgen, *The Doctrine of Survivals: A Chapter in the History of Scientific Method in the Study of Man* (London: Allenson, 1936).

3. James George Frazer, *The Golden Bough: A Study in Magic and Religion,* abr. ed. (New York: Macmillan, 1922), 55–56; and James George Frazer, *Man, God, and Immortality: Thoughts on Human Progress* (London: Macmillan, 1927), 218–19.

4. See Peter Pels, "Introduction: Magic and Modernity," in *Magic and Modernity: Interfaces of Revelation and Concealment,* ed. Birgit Meyer and Peter Pels (Stanford: Stanford University Press, 2003), 3.

5. Ibid., 4–5.

6. Most of the essays gathered here were originally delivered at a conference sponsored by the Societas Magica at the University of Waterloo, Ontario, in the summer of 2008. We are

extremely grateful to the leadership of the society and the organizers of the conference, particularly Claire Fanger and David Porreca, for their efforts in facilitating such an engaging scholarly interchange and encouraging the publication of this volume. The essays compiled here represent only a portion of the papers delivered at the conference, which covered a wide range of historical contexts from biblical through modern times. We have focused this volume on a very specific subset of papers dealing with the relationship of magic to modernity, and we have supplemented them with two additional articles written expressly for inclusion here.

7. See Olav Hammer, *Claiming Knowledge: Strategies of Epistemology from Theosophy to the New Age* (Leiden: Brill, 2001).

8. Karl Bell, *The Magical Imagination: Magic and Modernity in Urban England, 1780–1914* (Cambridge: Cambridge University Press, 2012), 2.

9. Ibid., 4, 7.

10. See ibid., 18–20, discussing Joshua Landy and Michael Saler, "Introduction: The Varieties of Modern Enchantment," in *The Re-Enchantment of the World: Secular Magic in a Rational Age,* ed. Joshua Landy and Michael Saler (Stanford: Stanford University Press, 2009), 1–14.

11. Landy and Saler, "Introduction," 3.

12. Ibid., 6–7.

13. See ibid., 7–14, and the various essays in the volume.

14. Bell, *Magical Imagination,* 18–19.

15. See Eugene Subbotsky, *Magic and the Mind: Mechanisms, Functions, and Development of Magical Thinking and Behavior* (Oxford: Oxford University Press, 2010).

16. Bell, *Magical Imagination,* 19, discussing Alex Owen, *The Place of Enchantment: British Occultism and the Culture of the Modern* (Chicago: University of Chicago Press, 2004).

Part 1 | MAGIC AND THE MAKING OF MODERNITY

1

BAD HABITS, OR HOW SUPERSTITION DISAPPEARED IN THE MODERN WORLD

Randall Styers

In 1948, B. F. Skinner, the dean of behavioral psychology, published a short paper titled "'Superstition' in the Pigeon." In the paper, Skinner reported the results of experiments aimed at establishing conditioned behavioral responses in pigeons. Birds were brought to a stable state of hunger, and then a feeding mechanism began to operate at regular intervals (unrelated to the birds' behavior). Skinner recounted that after discovering the optimal interval for providing food, he was able to elicit conditioned responses in the large majority of birds—they began to repeat the random behaviors they were engaged in when the feeding mechanism first began to operate.

One of the most striking aspects of Skinner's brief report is the word he chose to designate this type of conditioned pigeon behavior: "superstition." As Skinner explained, "the bird behaves as if there were a causal relation between its behavior and the presentation of the food, although such a relation is lacking." The pigeon's response, he continued, has many analogies in human behavior, most notably in various human rituals for improving luck (in activities like card playing and bowling): "A few accidental connections between a ritual and favorable consequences suffice to set up and maintain the behavior in spite of many unreinforced instances."[1] Accidental correlations, Skinner concluded, are sufficient to establish and reinforce random behavior both in birds and in bowlers.

Skinner's framing of his pigeon experiment represents the culmination of an illuminating trajectory in modern thought. In his formulation, the term "superstition" is reduced to very simple content: it designates an error in causal reasoning, a compulsive repetition of habitual behavior despite the irrelevance of that behavior to the desired results. Superstition is understood here as a type of cognitive misfiring, and thus we can see that the ignoble pigeon and the human being share comparable propensities for error—there is a difference only in scale between the behavioral responses of the pigeon and the cardsharp.

This formulation of superstition has a complex lineage. From ancient writers through the medieval period, the dominant theological conceptualization of superstition centered on excessive or misdirected religiosity.[2] Aquinas defined superstition as "the vice opposed to the virtue of religion by means of excess ... because it offers divine worship either to whom it ought not, or in a manner it ought not."[3] As Keith Thomas demonstrates, the notion of superstition was used throughout the medieval period in an extremely elastic manner to designate ceremonies or practices meeting with the church's disapproval or falling outside its control.[4] In the sixteenth century, Martin of Arles could thus define superstition rather tautologically as "superfluous and vain religion, pursued in a defective manner and in wrong circumstances."[5]

This venerable understanding of superstition as misdirected or excessive religiosity began to shift in significant respects during the early modern era. The traditional understanding of superstition was redefined in the theological debates of the Reformation, as superstition was invoked as a prime polemical tool in the effort to delineate proper religious piety. Catholic reformers continued to use the label "superstition" most often in regard to practices seen as transgressing the boundaries of appropriate religious observance. But for Protestants the term came to serve as a sharp polemical weapon against central Catholic beliefs and practices, particularly the doctrine of transubstantiation.[6] Martin Luther denounced the impiety of priests who reverenced the words of consecration with "I know not what superstitious and godless fancies."[7] Jean Calvin complained that Catholics saw the words of consecration in the Roman sacrament "as a kind of magical incantation," a superstitious murmur that Calvin contrasted to the preached word of the Gospel. He mocked "superstitious worship, when men prostrate themselves before a piece of bread, to adore Christ in it." For Calvin, the performance of the Eucharist without assent to appropriate doctrine amounted to mimicry of the Lord's Supper as "a kind of magic trick."[8] Ulrich Zwingli declared the Catholic Eucharist "bread-worship."[9]

But in such accounts focusing on superstition as a religious ill, we find new elaborations of the causes of this type of error. Francis Bacon argued that it was better to be an unbeliever than to have an unworthy, superstitious notion of God. Superstition, he asserted, is to religion as an ape is to a human being. In his essay "Of Superstition," Bacon offered this explanation of the origins of superstition: "The causes of superstition are, pleasing and sensual rites and ceremonies; excess of outward and pharisaical holiness; over-great reverence of traditions, which cannot but load the Church; the stratagems of prelates for their own ambition and lucre; the favouring too much of good intentions, which openeth the gate to conceits and novelties; the taking an aim at divine matters by human, which cannot but breed mixture of imaginations: and lastly, barbarous times, especially joined with calamities and disasters."[10] Bestial superstitions, in Bacon's view, had their origins in a broad range of disreputable emotions—pride and self-seeking, but also sensuality, immoderation, and fear.

During the early modern era, a new set of themes assumed prominence in denunciations of superstition, particularly in arguments concerning the persecution of witches. In the debates over witchcraft, we find a growing number of opponents of the persecutions who begin to frame superstition in psychological, as opposed to theological, terms. A prime example of this tendency can be found in the work of Reginald Scot, one of the most important early English critics of the persecutions. Scot framed his 1584 *Discoverie of Witchcraft* in significant measure as a critique of the magical and superstitious practices of Catholicism, and he set about debunking claims concerning the power of witches and other superstitions and magical frauds. The crux of Scot's challenge to demonology was that the devil works only by deluding the human mind. Demonic agents exist only in a noncorporeal state, a state that removes them from nature and denies them the ability to affect the workings of natural causation; thus they are efficacious only through delusion.[11]

We find in opponents of the witchcraft persecutions, such as Scot and his contemporary Johann Weyer, the emergence of new, medicalizing arguments that people who confess to witchcraft are superstitiously deluded. Weyer offered various physical and psychological hypotheses to account for the behavior of alleged witches, much of which he attributed to physical illness and melancholia.[12] In contrast, as Scot framed it, witchcraft is largely trickery; both spiritual and demonic magic are illusory. Witchcraft is persuasive only to "children, fooles, melancholike persons and papists."[13] This view gained ground, and by the later seventeenth century, opponents of the witchcraft persecutions such as Balthasar Bekker were speaking of superstition no longer primarily as misdirected or improper religious belief but rather as faulty judgment or prejudice stemming from inadequate knowledge.[14] People who believed in superstitious magic were increasingly seen as feeble-minded and as suffering from an array of cognitive and emotional impairments.

Two interrelated shifts were taking place here. First, opponents of the witchcraft persecutions were offering a view of nature in which demonic forces were removed from the workings of causality; the parameters of causality were being redefined. At the same time, the discussion of "superstitious" beliefs was shifting from theological to psychological terrain. New notions of causality and rationality came to be articulated in explicit contrast to the superstition of the witch craze. As various early modern thinkers challenged the violent persecution of alleged witches, they began to formulate new medicalizing and pathologizing understandings of those prone to magical beliefs. Very closely related to this theme is the way in which the understanding of "magic" was reconfigured during the early modern period. While earlier theologians had understood magic as a sin involving the idolatrous worship of demons, it came increasingly to be viewed as a type of aberrational thinking, a delusion, a psychological malady. As we will see, in this emerging frame, even as the theological significance of magic and superstition began to recede, the boundary between the two became increasingly blurred.

Through the course of the seventeenth century, Europe's intellectual elites came increasingly to view witchcraft, magic, and religious enthusiasm as phenomena to be explained rationally. In Thomas Hobbes, the opposition to superstition assumed an overt concern with notions of social control. In his index of human passions in *Leviathan*, Hobbes summarized his understanding of the origin of religion and the distinction between religion and superstition: "Feare of power invisible, feigned by the mind, or imagined from tales publiquely allowed, RELIGION; not allowed, SUPERSTITION."[15] Hobbes here concurred with the ancient argument that religion originates in fear, and the ultimate distinction he drew between religion and superstition concerns public approbation. While Hobbes acknowledged that he could not rationally believe that there were actual witches, he supported their persecution on the grounds that that ridding society of "this superstitious fear of Spirits" would make the populace "much more fitted than they are for civill Obedience."[16]

John Locke argued that all sorts of superstitions, extravagances, and absurdities can emerge if human beings give too great a sway to faith and fail to give reason its proper role in assessing religious truth. Sensuality, lust, fear, and carelessness, Locke explained, deliver humanity into the hands of priests who, motivated by self-interest and profit, warp notions of God and religious practice into foolish rites, vice, and superstition.[17] Similar arguments can be found in the writings of Spinoza, Pierre Bayle, and many others.[18]

At the very time that such thinkers as Hobbes and Locke were demonstrating a new confidence in the capacity of reason, a newly rationalized perspective on the operations of the natural world was taking hold. Over the course of the seventeenth century, natural philosophers and scientists such as Descartes, Spinoza, Boyle, and Newton began to propound new mechanistic understandings of nature, and as the Enlightenment took shape, the mechanical philosophy taught that nature was a deterministic material system governed exclusively by natural laws. Any notion of causation deemed supernatural was expelled from consideration.

By the eighteenth century, numerous Enlightenment thinkers were engaged in an extended war against superstition, often as part of a much broader polemic against religion, and a number of closely interrelated themes predominated in their attacks. Let me address three of the most obvious. First, of course, for many Enlightenment thinkers, superstition epitomized excessive religiosity. Particularly as rationalized notions of natural religion became prominent, superstition was used as the foil for appropriately chastened and rationalized religion (as Locke framed it, "plain, spiritual and suitable worship," or, in the words of David Hume's Philo, "plain, philosophical assent" to true religious propositions).[19] This veneration of restrained, rational religion was a common theme in Enlightenment battles against religious intolerance, fanaticism, and priest-craft. From Herbert of Cherbury through figures like Voltaire and on to Kant, we find repeated attacks on the superstitious nature of religious ritual and the deployment of superstition to delineate the nature of appropriate rationalized religion.

Voltaire argued that Christianity was contaminated in its earliest days by pagan and Jewish superstition, and he mocked an array of contemporary practices (including the veneration of relics, religious ecstasies, visions, even belief in vampires). He stressed that there was no agreement as to what constitutes superstition. Each sect and nationality condemns the practices of other sects as superstition, and even sects with the fewest rites are superstitious to the extent that they maintain absurd beliefs. "It is therefore evident," he asserted, "that what is the foundation of the religion of one sect, is by another sect regarded as superstitious; the sole arbiter of this debate is raw force." In opposition to the divisive and violent fanaticism coming from superstition, Voltaire advocated a universal rational religion based on general notions of justice and probity; "nearly all that goes farther than the adoration of a supreme being, and the submission of the heart to his eternal orders, is superstition."[20] Voltaire's perspective would be reflected in the work of many subsequent Enlightenment thinkers.

This theme reached its definitive expression in Kant. Having demarcated the bounds of speculative reason, Kant sought to ground religion as a form of practical faith within the realm of practical reason. He argued that one of the prime objectives of his restrictions on speculative thought was to prevent idolatry ("a superstitious belief that we can please the Supreme Being by other means than by a moral sentiment"). The proper service of God is restricted to the performance of the moral duty, consisting "not in dogmas and rites, but in the heart's disposition to fulfill all human duties as divine commands."[21] Thus, Kant concluded, the true, moral service of God is "invisible . . . a service of the heart (in spirit and in truth). . . . Every initiatory step in the realm of religion, which we do not take in a purely moral manner but rather have recourse to as *in itself* a means of making us well-pleasing to God and thus, through Him, of satisfying our wishes, is a *fetish-faith.*"[22] In contrast, as Kant stated in *Religion Within the Limits of Reason Alone,* "The illusion of being able to accomplish anything in the way of justifying ourselves before God through religious acts of worship is religious *superstition.* . . . It is called superstitious because it selects merely natural (not moral) means which in themselves can have absolutely no effect upon what is not nature (i.e., on the morally good)."[23]

In a range of eighteenth-century thinkers culminating in Kant, we find an effort to sanitize religion, to get the magic and superstition out. As Euan Cameron points out in *Enchanted Europe,* Hume and other Enlightenment rationalists used the critique of superstition to attack not just marginal religious beliefs but also the distortions they found in the theological mainstream. Superstition served as a tool "to define by negation what was legitimate in the sphere of religion itself."[24] For these thinkers, Cameron explains, superstition came to mark a state of fanaticism, ignorance, and deceit—the antithesis of Enlightenment reason. But these polemics could also readily shift (as we see perhaps in Hume and more overtly in subsequent writers) to a broadside against all religion. The norms for religion within these formulations made acceptable religion increasingly vaporous.

A second central theme of the Enlightenment war on superstition was the effort to determine its psychological causes, whether in the emotions or in faulty reasoning. Voltaire offered various accounts of the ways in which natural events were mistakenly ascribed to supernatural causes, a delusion, he said, to which Europe was particularly prone during prior periods in which "the majority of our provincial population was very little raised above the Caribs and negroes."[25]

David Hume linked religious enthusiasm to the excessive piety of Protestant sects (characterized by excessive rapture and fanatical imagination), but he offered a different account of the origins of superstition, most vividly demonstrated, he says, by the credulous associations of "the ROMISH church." Hume argued that superstition arises from "weakness, fear, melancholy, together with ignorance."[26] In the face of invisible and unknown enemies, a wide array of absurd superstitious rites and practices are invoked to placate these powers.

Hume attributed superstition to mentally and emotionally feeble groups who had not properly cultivated and trained their faculties. Just as it is at the weakest and most timid periods of life that human beings are most addicted to superstition, so also, he argued, the weaker and more timid sex was most superstitious. Thus, he asserted, nothing is more destructive to superstition than "a manly, steady virtue, which either preserves us from disastrous, melancholy accidents, or teaches us to bear them."[27]

This insistence that superstition is born of ignorance and fear was prominent throughout the eighteenth century and beyond. It appeared in a litany of thinkers too long to catalogue (Shaftesbury, Anthony Collins, William Robertson, Baron d'Holbach, and many others). Time and again, they attributed superstition to ignorance, stupidity, and prejudice.

A third major aspect of the Enlightenment war on superstition was an overt concern with the social disruption caused by these dangerous mental tendencies and the use of the battle against superstition as part of a broader campaign for social discipline and control. We see this issue in Hobbes, and it reappears in the works of many Enlightenment writers, nowhere more vividly than in Hume. In his *Dialogues Concerning Natural Religion*, Hume catalogued the "pernicious consequences on public affairs" of vulgar superstition: "Factions, civil wars, persecutions, subversions of government, oppression, slavery; these are the dismal consequences which always attend its prevalency over the minds of men."[28] Hume argued that superstition promotes the concentration of power in the hands of impudent and cunning priests. Superstition enters into religion gradually, rendering the population "tame and submissive"; thus it is acceptable to the civil authorities and seems inoffensive until at last the priest becomes "the tyrant and disturber of human society, by his endless contentions, persecutions, and religious wars." An enemy of civil liberty, superstition renders the population "tame and abject, and fits them for slavery."[29] Other Enlightenment thinkers joined Hume in arguing that superstition was a tool of authoritarian social control. As Voltaire put it, "the superstitious man is to the knave, what the slave is to the tyrant."[30]

The Enlightenment war on superstition migrated readily to North America. As Adam Jortner demonstrates in his essay in this volume, by the time of the American Revolution, prominent leaders of the new Republic shared the notion that magic and superstition were antithetical to reason, and since reason was the basis of democratic governance, superstition had no legitimate place in the new nation. The dominant view among a range of social and political leaders in the decades following the Revolution was, as Jortner shows, that superstition and witchcraft "belonged to foreigners and slaves, Catholics and tyrants; to believe in such things would tear the nation from the sacred place of liberty down . . . to a state of monarchy or theocracy." In the early decades of the nineteenth century, theater, traveling exhibitions, sermons, and various types of American popular literature were devoted to debunking claims of superstitious supernaturalism in the interest of promoting a rational citizenry.

By the middle of the nineteenth century, as modern science consolidated its hold and new social-scientific scholarly disciplines began to emerge, superstition had already been cast in predominantly psychological terms. The effort to explain the causes and nature of superstition became a significant preoccupation of new social scientists seeking to promote various theories of social development. At the same time, new scholarly theories of magic began explicitly to frame magical thinking in a closely related manner. Comparable types of rational error or fallacy were seen as underlying both superstition and magical thinking, and any distinction between the two effectively collapsed as the terms were used in an increasingly interchangeable manner.

This tendency was pervasive among European social theorists. Feuerbach's 1851 *Lectures on the Essence of Religion* is a clear example. Feuerbach invoked magic as part of a broader attack on religion. Magic was only a more vivid demonstration of tendencies that Christians share with polytheists and idolaters to attempt to bend nature to the human will. Rejecting the claim of the influential Protestant theologian Friedrich Schleiermacher that human beings have "a special organ of religion, a specific religious feeling," Feuerbach argued that "we should be more justified in assuming the existence of a specific organ of superstition," "a special organ for superstition, ignorance, and mental laziness." In Feuerbach's view, "the source and strength of superstition are the power of ignorance and stupidity, which is the greatest power on earth, the power of fear and the feeling of dependency, and finally the power of the imagination."[31] In short, Feuerbach saw religion, magic, and superstition as comparable expressions of ignorance of the true causes of nature.

A similar sense of the porous boundary between magic and superstition informed nineteenth-century anthropological theory. In his 1871 *Primitive Culture*, Edward Burnett Tylor, the founding figure of modern anthropology, discussed magic in the context of cultural survivals. Tylor explained that most survivals could properly be described as "superstitions"; he preferred the more neutral term "survival" simply to avoid the stigma attached to "superstition." The very structure of Tylor's argument thus classified magic as a species of the genus superstition. While magical beliefs persist within modern society, Tylor said, the "modern educated world" rejects beliefs in the occult as "a contemptible superstition" and "has practically committed itself to the opinion that magic belongs to the lower level of civilization."[32] The study of these survivals was useful, he believed, in demonstrating the large role of ignorance, superstition, and conservatism in preserving various traces of the history of the human race.

We find a comparable collapsing in James George Frazer, particularly in his account of the transition from magic to religion in the course of social development. Frazer used the term *superstition* as synonymous with ignorance; those prone to ignorance and superstition persist in their belief in magic even as the pious and enlightened portions of society move toward new understandings of causality.[33]

This blurring of the differentiation between superstition and magic plays out in regard to each of the major Enlightenment concerns with superstition I discussed earlier. Let me briefly turn to examine how each of these three themes evolved in the nineteenth and twentieth centuries. First, magic and superstition were framed as comparable affronts to appropriately rationalized religion. For example, Robertson Smith argued that magic, but not religion, is born of fear. "In times of social dissolution," he explained, when human beings feel powerless, "magical superstitions based on mere terror, or rites designed to conciliate alien gods, invade the sphere of tribal or national religion." Thus magical superstition, built on the notion of "mysterious hostile powers" rather than "the prerogative of a friendly god," is "the barrenest of all aberrations of the savage imagination."[34] A range of modern theorists thus configured magic and superstition as sharing comparable irreligious tendencies to coerce desired outcomes, to overvalue material objects, and to engage in compulsively repetitive and sterile behavior. They were seen as comparable affronts to rationalized religion.

Second, the effort to explain the causes and nature of superstition and magical thinking became a major preoccupation of modern social scientists, particularly psychologists. This preoccupation appears in the work of such diverse thinkers as Alfred Lehmann, Freud, and Piaget. In numerous texts by more recent behavioral and cognitive psychologists, we find efforts to explain the prevalence of superstition and magical thinking in accounts of the emotional and cognitive lapses on which they are seen as being based. Superstition and magic, these theorists explain, arise from a familiar set of causes: faulty observation and analysis, the overinvestment of subjective desires (what Freud called the "omnipotence of thoughts"),[35] sublimated and projected desires, errors in causal thinking, even errors in determining probability. To cite just one example, the psychologist A. E. Heath said in 1948 that the proper calculation of probabilities could place beliefs accurately on a scale between mere superstition and reasonable expectation.[36] Both superstition and magic have repeatedly been condemned as comparable and related "pseudo-sciences."

Particularly in the late nineteenth and early twentieth centuries, American psychological literature sought to comprehend the nature of superstitious thinking in order to promote psychological and social maturity. One particularly interesting example is found in Stanley Hall, a founding figure in the development of psychology in America and the first president of the American

Psychological Association. Hall concluded his two-volume study *Adolescence* (1904–5) with a lengthy chapter titled "Ethnic Psychology and Pedagogy, or Adolescent Races and Their Treatment," in which he examined colonial policies directed at large new populations. Hall argued that preadolescent children are irrational savages who must simply be coerced along the path of proper development. Adolescents have progressed physically and mentally, but they too require authoritarian discipline to avoid the pitfalls of the excessive individualism afflicting American society. But while children and youths are on a normal developmental path, "most savages," Hall explains—"nearly one-third of the human race, occupying two-fifths of the land surface of the globe, now included in the one hundred and thirty-six colonies and dependencies of the world"—fester in a state of adolescent development. They demonstrate the cognitive disintegration of *dementia praecox* (an early psychological disorder related to schizophrenia). They are prone to arrested development in a stage of imitation and fixation on superficial resemblance and require authoritarian management similar to that used to constrain children and youth.[37]

The practices and beliefs of these primitive people, Hall explained, are "related to ours somewhat as instinct is related to reason," displaying a compulsiveness "so overmindful of higher and supernatural powers" that they cannot attain worldly prudence. Somewhat surprisingly, given these analogies, the primary target of Hall's invective was the colonial regimes that sought to coerce cultural homogeneity by dragging the "savages" precipitously out of this "magnified stage of boyhood." That colonialist effort was foolhardy, Hall said, both because the adolescent is incapable of meeting adult standards and because the modern West itself has much to learn from primitive cultures— both about the nature of adolescence and also about cultural variation that could actually revitalize the West. (A further reason to fight homogenization, Hall stated, was that the West could also benefit from the savages' genetic lines; they offered "stocks and breeds of men of new types and varieties, full of new promise and potency for our race, because heredity so outweighs civilization and schooling.")[38] Savage patterns of thought are present among us in our own children, but we moderns can also reap the benefit of the cultural and genetic diversity of primitive culture.

Fifteen years later, in 1920, Fletcher Dresslar, an influential American professor of health education, published a lengthy study of the nature of superstition in the context of a larger program of educational reform. Dresslar began by defining superstition as "a willingness and [an] . . . instinctive desire to believe in certain causal relations, which have not and cannot be proved to exist through a course of reasoning . . . or direct observation." This desire to believe arises, according to Dresslar, from innate human discomfort with ambiguity and uncertainty, so it constitutes a retrograde "form of emotional credulity," "our inheritance of the unreasonable." While these emotional tendencies might have had some benefit in earlier human development, modern education must seek to free human beings from these errors through a concerted program of education in "scientific method and scientific feeling." "We shall never attain unto rational living," Dresslar concluded, "until we are regenerated through the gospel of truthful learning; until we acquire the habit of fearless investigation, persistent thinking, and courageous belief. [We look for] the dawning of a better day for humanity, when the soul of man will be satisfied with the rational concept of law and order."[39]

If social scientists worked to explore superstition as a significant exemplar of cognitive misfiring or arrested development, the emerging field of the psychology of religion sought rather purposefully to exclude the study of superstition from its purview. So, for example, in the second lecture of his 1901–2 *Varieties of Religious Experience*—titled "Circumscription of the Topic"—William James pointedly excluded superstition from his discussion of religion: "it is certain that the whole system of thought which leads to magic, fetishism, and the lower superstitions may just as well be called primitive science as called primitive religion." Superstition, in James's view, was as much a matter of cognitive as of religious development, and in any event, "our knowledge of all these early stages of thought and feeling is . . . so conjectural and imperfect that further discussion would not be worth while."[40]

In a similar vein, Edwin Starbuck, who studied at Harvard under James, believed that a proper psychology of religion would distill the essential elements of religious experience by separating that experience from superstition. In a recent study of Starbuck's reformist agenda, Christopher White quotes a 1902 letter from Starbuck to James about the promise of the new psychology of religion: "a multitude of superstitions and crudities are doomed to fold their tents. People will be living in a new era of religious experience before they know it."[41]

In his 1912 *Psychological Study of Religion*, James Leuba (who studied with Stanley Hall at Clark University) also perfunctorily excluded superstition as irrelevant to the psychological study of religion. In Leuba's view, religion is born of anthropopathy, through which human beings develop interpersonal relations with unseen beings. Distinct from such tendencies are the mechanical behaviors that characterize human interactions with inanimate things and the magical behaviors aimed at producing concrete effects. Superstition, Leuba explained, is a subset of magic, though it is magic's most rudimentary form, based not on a notion of supernatural power but only on the principle of repetition ("something that has happened once is likely to happen again"). In superstition, "the effect is thought to follow upon the cause without the mediation of a force passing . . . from the magician." The "senseless superstitions of the savage" and of children arise from immature inclinations to concoct irrational prohibitions, or from irrational causal linkages formed in situations of heightened emotion. But superstition and magical thinking, Leuba concluded, are decisively distinct from religion. At the same time, they are also decisively distinct from science (which is based on an accurate acknowledgment of "definite and constant *quantitative* relations between causes and effects").[42] In Leuba's framing, superstition is too impersonal to lead to religion, and it is too cognitively primitive to lead to science.

Let me underscore two significant issues here. First, much of this literature made no differentiation at all between superstition and magic—one might be configured as a subset of the other, but the terms became relatively interchangeable within this network of thought. Second, irrationality had come to cover a vast terrain. A wide array of human perception, response, and desire was configured as superstitious and magical, and as psychological theorists worked to show how such irrationality arose from the repetition of behavior based on erroneously or irrationally formed causal linkages, almost all habitual human behavior became suspect, since habitual behavior often fails to demonstrate its instrumental basis. "Rationality" was configured as a very constricted ideal.

Some later psychological theorists would come to voice a more favorable understanding of the adaptive value of superstition and magical thinking. The most commonly identified benefits are enhanced confidence and reduced anxiety, a theme that builds on Bronislaw Malinowski's anthropological theory of magic. A prominent and influential example is Gustav Jahoda's 1969 *Psychology of Superstition*. Superstition, Jahoda asserted, might well have "positive survival value" in providing a "subjective feeling of predictability and control" and thereby reducing anxiety. He noted other adaptive values of superstition, such as supporting beneficial social norms and encouraging the repetition of behavior that has proved harmless. Jahoda saw superstition as a by-product of the adaptive human tendency to identify patterns in the natural environment. Thus, he concluded, superstition is "an integral part of the adaptive mechanisms without which humanity would be unable to survive."[43]

But for the majority of nineteenth- and twentieth-century thinkers, superstition and magical thinking posed a great threat to the good order of society. This is a venerable theme; we find versions of it rehearsed throughout the witchcraft persecutions and the Enlightenment, in the work of such thinkers as Feuerbach, Tylor, and Frazer, and in innumerable subsequent theorists.

A vivid recent example of this concern with social order can be found in the work of Theodor Adorno. In his essay "The Stars Down to Earth," analyzing a *Los Angeles Times* astrology column, Adorno argued that such superstition is indicative of broad, reactionary tendencies toward authoritarian irrationalism. While modern superstitious phenomena such as astrology may appear relatively benign, Adorno saw them as "a small test-tube scale" example of broader modern social phenomena that fuse irrational elements with "pseudo-rationality" and raise the specter of totalitarianism.[44]

One of the preeminent characteristics of modern astrology, Adorno asserted, is its underlying tendency toward authoritarianism. In Adorno's view, astrology works to breed and exploit dependency in its audience. Indeed, astrology offers its followers "an *ideology for dependence*" and caters to their flight from responsibility for changing their own lives or the social conditions within which they live. Astrology thus preaches social conformity and social contentment, "a conservative ideology, generally justifying the *status quo*." Through these tendencies, contemporary superstitions stand as a bitter harbinger of the totalitarian impulses lurking in the heart of modernity.[45]

Adorno was far from alone in these concerns. Many nineteenth- and twentieth-century psychological and social theorists shared these concerns about the disruptive potential of superstition and magical thinking, a theme that appears quite often in subsequent behavioral and cognitive psychology texts. Recent decades have seen a continued stream of texts from social scientists and cultural theorists indicting superstition and magical thinking (including quite a few pronouncing postmodernism a prime example of these invidious proclivities). Such rampant irrationality, its opponents claim, threatens the reasoned and orderly decision making on which the modern social order and capitalist economies depend.

The psychologist Stuart Vyse's 1997 *Believing in Magic: The Psychology of Superstition* is a prime example. First, note the title of Vyse's book; magic and superstition are merged conceptually. But, more interestingly, Vyse's text comes to ominous conclusions concerning the prevalence and dangers of superstition ("if you are not superstitious," he tells us, "then someone close to you is"). Rampant, superstitious irrationality, he says, threatens the rational and orderly decision making on which modern democracy depends. In this light, Vyse concludes his study with a section titled "What Can We Do About Superstition?" His answer: teach critical thinking and decision analysis, promote science education, and improve the public image of scientists.[46]

Vyse and numerous scholarly precursors use the notion of superstition as a tool for demarcating norms for appropriate rationality. The rationalist battle against superstition reveals both a distinctive notion of psychological development and new efforts to exert social control. Just like B. F. Skinner's pigeons, superstitious people are seen as prone to mindless and compulsive behavior, and social scientists have responded with a concerted new regime of behavioral reinforcement.

NOTES

1. B. F. Skinner, "'Superstition' in the Pigeon," *Journal of Experimental Psychology* 38 (1948): 168–72 (quotation on 172).

2. See Dale B. Martin, *Inventing Superstition: From the Hippocratics to the Christians* (Cambridge: Harvard University Press, 2004); and Euan Cameron, *Enchanted Europe: Superstition, Reason, and Religion, 1250–1750* (Oxford: Oxford University Press, 2010).

3. Thomas Aquinas, *Summa Theologica* II, Q. 92, part 1.

4. Keith Thomas, *Religion and the Decline of Magic* (New York: Scribner, 1971), 48–50.

5. Mary O'Neil, "Magical Healing, Love Magic, and the Inquisition in Late Sixteenth-Century Modena," in *New Perspectives on Witchcraft, Magic, and Demonology*, ed. Brian P. Levack, vol. 5 (New York: Routledge, 2001), 173, quoting Martino de Arles, *Tractatus de superstitionibus* (Rome: Vincentium Luchinum, 1559), 354.

6. See Thomas, *Religion and the Decline of Magic*, 52–77.

7. Martin Luther, "The Babylonian Captivity of the Church," in *Luther's Works*, vol. 36, ed. Abdel Ross Wentz (Philadelphia: Muhlenberg Press, 1959), 41.

8. Jean Calvin, *Institutes of the Christian Religion*, trans. John Allen, 6th ed. (Philadelphia: Presbyterian Board of Christian Education, 1935), 538 (4.14.15). And see ibid., 570–71 (4.17.36); Calvin, "Short Treatise on the Supper of Our Lord," in *Tracts and Treatises on the Doctrine and Worship of the Church*, vol. 2, trans. Henry Beveridge (Grand Rapids: William B. Eerdmans, 1958), 193; and W. T. Davison, *The Lord's Supper: Aids to Its Intelligent and Devout Observance* (London: Charles H. Kelly, 1895), 83n1.

9. Ulrich Zwingli, "On the Lord's Supper," in *Zwingli and Bullinger: Selected Translations*, trans. G. W. Bromiley, Library of Christian Classics, vol. 24 (Philadelphia: Westminster Press, 1953), 176–238.

10. Francis Bacon, "Of Superstition," in *The Essays, the Wisdom of the Ancients, and the New Atlantis* (London: Odhams Press, n.d.), 69–70.

11. Reginald Scot, *The Discoverie of Witchcraft*, ed. Montague Summers (1930; reprint, New York: Dover, 1972), bk. 3, chaps. 7–13, pp. 28–35; bk. 13, chap. 3, pp. 164–65; and see Stuart Clark, *Thinking with Demons: The Idea of Witchcraft in Early Modern Europe* (Oxford: Oxford University Press, 1997), 211–12. Scot's position reflected the earlier medieval Christian position that God alone could alter the course of nature and that witchcraft was an illusion or fantasy; for example, the *Canon Episcopi* (dating perhaps from the tenth century) asserted that tales of the exploits of witches were based only on illusion or phantasm inspired by the devil. See Gratian, "A Warning to Bishops: The *Canon Episcopi*, 1140," in *Witchcraft in Europe, 1100–1700: A Documentary History*, ed. Alan C. Kors and Edward Peters (Philadelphia: University of Pennsylvania Press, 1972), 28–31.

12. See Clark, *Thinking with Demons*, 117–18, 198–203; Gerhild Scholz Williams, "The Woman/The Witch: Variations on a Sixteenth-Century Theme (Paracelsus, Wier, Bodin)," in *The Crannied Wall: Women, Religion, and the Arts in Early Modern Europe*, ed. Craig A. Monson (Ann Arbor: University of Michigan Press, 1992), 119–37.

13. Scot, *Discoverie of Witchcraft*, bk. 16, chap. 2, p. 274.

14. See Balthasar Bekker, "The Enchanted World (1691)," in Kors and Peters, *Witchcraft in Europe*, 369–77; and G. J. Stronks, "The Significance of Balthasar Bekker's *The Enchanted*

World," in *Witchcraft in the Netherlands from the Fourteenth to the Twentieth Century*, ed. Marijke Gijswitjt-Hofstra and Willem Frijhoff (Rotterdam: Universitaire Pers Rotterdam, 1991), 149–56.

15. Thomas Hobbes, *Leviathan*, ed. Richard Tuck (Cambridge: Cambridge University Press, 1991), bk. 1, chap. 6, p. 42. See also bk. 1, chap. 12, pp. 82–86.

16. Ibid., bk. 1, chap. 2, pp. 18–19.

17. John Locke, *The Reasonableness of Christianity*, ed. I. T. Ramsey (Stanford: Stanford University Press, 1958), 57–59, 67–68.

18. See Randall Styers, *Making Magic: Religion, Magic, and Science in the Modern World* (New York: Oxford University Press, 2004), 42–44.

19. Locke, *Reasonableness of Christianity*, 68; and David Hume, *Dialogues Concerning Natural Religion*, in *Writings on Religion*, ed. Antony Flew (La Salle, Ill.: Open Court, 1992), 290–91.

20. Voltaire, "Superstition," in *A Philosophical Dictionary*, in *The Works of Voltaire*, trans. William F. Fleming, 42 vols. (Paris: E. R. DuMont, 1901), 14:30–32, 27–28.

21. Immanuel Kant, *Critique of Judgment*, trans. J. H. Bernard (New York: Hafner Press, 1951), 298–312, particularly 310–11.

22. Immanuel Kant, *Religion Within the Limits of Reason Alone*, trans. Theodore M. Greene and Hoyt H. Hudson (New York: Harper Torchbooks, 1960), 180–82 (emphasis in original).

23. Ibid., 78–79, 158–62 (emphasis in original).

24. Cameron, *Enchanted Europe*, 303.

25. Voltaire, "Enchantment," in *Works of Voltaire*, 8:228–29.

26. Hume, "Of Superstition and Enthusiasm," in *Writings on Religion*, 3–4, 7.

27. Hume, "The Natural History of Religion," ibid., 120, 178.

28. Hume, *Dialogues Concerning Natural Religion*, ibid., 283.

29. Hume, "A Note on the Profession of Priest," ibid., 5–8, 11–12.

30. Voltaire, "Superstition," 14:30.

31. Ludwig Feuerbach, "Twenty-Third Lecture," in *Lectures on the Essence of Religion*, trans. Ralph Manheim (New York: Harper & Row, 1967), 207–8, and "Twenty-Fourth Lecture," 219–23.

32. Edward Burnett Tylor, *Primitive Culture: Researches into the Development of Mythology, Philosophy, Religion, Language, Art, and Custom*, 3rd American ed., vol. 1 (New York: Henry Holt, 1889), 16–17, 72, 112–13.

33. See James George Frazer, *The Golden Bough: A Study in Magic and Religion*, abr. ed. (New York: Macmillan, 1922).

34. W. Robertson Smith, *Lectures on the Religion of the Semites: The Fundamental Institutions*, 3rd ed. (New York: Macmillan, 1927), 54–55, 154.

35. Sigmund Freud, *Totem and Taboo: Some Points of Agreement Between the Mental Lives of Savages and Neurotics*, trans. James Strachey (New York: W. W. Norton, 1989), 107.

36. A. E. Heath, "Probability, Science, and Superstition," in *The Rationalists Annual, 1948*, ed. Frederick Watts (London: Watts & Co., 1948), 39–46.

37. G. Stanley Hall, *Adolescence: Its Psychology and Its Relations to Physiology, Anthropology, Sociology, Sex, Crime, Religion, and Education*, 2 vols. (New York: D. Appleton, 1905), 2:648–50.

38. Ibid., 2:726, 650.

39. Fletcher B. Dresslar, *Superstition and Education* (New York: Johnson Reprint, 1966) (first published in 1920 by the University of California Press), 141, 145, 227, 231, 234.

40. William James, *The Varieties of Religious Experience: A Study in Human Nature* (Glasgow: Fountain Books, 1960), 50.

41. Quoted in Christopher White, "A Measured Faith: Edwin Starbuck, William James, and the Scientific Reform of Religious Experience," *Harvard Theological Review* 101 (2008): 433.

42. James H. Leuba, *A Psychological Study of Religion: Its Origin, Function, and Future* (1912; reprint, New York: AMS Press, 1969), 3–7, 159, 161, 165, 188–89.

43. Gustav Jahoda, *The Psychology of Superstition* (London: Allen Lane/Penguin Press, 1969), 134–35, 147.

44. Theodor W. Adorno, "The Stars Down to Earth: The *Los Angeles Times* Astrology Column," in *The Stars Down to Earth and Other Essays on the Irrational in Culture,* ed. Stephen Crook (New York: Routledge, 1994), 34–35.

45. Ibid., 38, 41, 51–59, 111–14.

46. Stuart A. Vyse, *Believing in Magic: The Psychology of Superstition* (New York: Oxford University Press, 1997), 209, 211–18.

2

DESCARTES'S DREAMS, THE NEUROPSYCHOLOGY OF DISBELIEF, AND THE MAKING OF THE MODERN SELF

Edward Bever

In 1958, the psychoanalyst Bertram Lewin published one of "the most sophisticated" contributions to the long-running discussion of the series of three
dreams that Descartes identified as a seminal influence his philosophy, which,
in turn, was a seminal influence on the "disenchanted" modern worldview.[1] In
Dreams and the Uses of Regression, Lewin started from Freud's "cardinal statement" that the function of dreams is to preserve sleep by presenting thoughts
that are potentially disturbing to consciousness in a way that keeps them from
waking the dreamer, and concluded that "when Descartes came to formulate
his scientific picture of the world, he made it conform with the state of affairs
in an ordinary successful dream."[2] To get from Freud's principle to this conclusion, Lewin analyzed Descartes's report of his experiences on the night the
dreams occurred, as transmitted by his first biographer, Adrien Baillet, from
an account now lost. Descartes described his first two dreams, which were
disturbing and from which he woke in distress, and the waking interlude after
each dream, during which he attempted to grapple with the dream's implications. The third and final dream, in contrast, was a pleasant one, and Descartes
slept soundly through it. As he awoke and reflected on it, he concluded that it
contained signs that pointed the way forward in his life and work.

From this account, Lewin concluded that Descartes's experiences that night
were the source of his "dualistic view of the world," in which "what the observer
is supposed to be and tries to be" corresponds exactly to the dreamer in a successful dream: a disembodied consciousness whose "only function . . . is to
observe and perceive."[3] What is particularly provocative about this conclusion
is its larger implications for our understanding of science and scientists in
particular, and of people who seek to understand and act rationally more generally: while there is no question that science and rationality have yielded a rich
understanding of and powerful control over the natural world, the emotional

attraction of the rational worldview as a habitual orientation lies in its insulating the observer from the affective meaning of what is observed, allowing him or her to exist in the world like a dreamer, observing without being disturbed by what is observed.

In order to understand how Lewin arrived at this conclusion, and to see what was particularly innovative about his approach, it is necessary to look a bit more closely at the context and content of Descartes's dreams and the waking periods between them. The dreams took place on the night of November 10, 1619, while the twenty-three-year-old Frenchman was staying in the vicinity of Ulm, where he had interrupted his journey to rejoin the Bavarian army because of inclement weather.[4] While secluded there for days in a "stove-heated room," he spent his time thinking about a new system of knowledge that he had been working on since making the acquaintance of the Dutch preacher, doctor, and aspiring scientist Isaac Beeckman the previous year.[5] During the day of November 10, Descartes reached what he recalled as a fever pitch of excitement at achieving a breakthrough, and he retired exhausted but exhilarated. Once asleep, however, he had a distressing dream in which he encountered frightening phantoms while walking on the street, was buffeted by a contrary wind, and felt lame on one side, unable to move where he wanted to go or even to stand up straight. He awoke feeling "a pain that caused him to fear that all this was the work of some evil spirit," and spent the next two hours contemplating good and evil and praying to God for forgiveness for his sins, which he felt "might be grievous enough to draw upon his head the bolts of divine vengeance." He finally drifted back to sleep, but was "immediately" awakened by a "sharp and piercing noise which he took for a clap of thunder, and opening his eyes, he perceived a large number of fiery sparks all around him in the room." He was frightened, but he had seen these before, so "he chose to have recourse to reasons from philosophy; and after having observed by alternately opening and closing his eyes . . . he drew from it conclusions favorable to his understanding . . . his fear was dissipated, and . . . in a reasonably tranquil condition . . . he fell asleep again." This time, Descartes had a pleasant dream involving books, a dictionary and a compendium of poetry, which he discussed with a man who appeared before him.[6] After the books and man disappeared, he began interpreting the dream to himself while still asleep, and he continued to do so while lying in bed with his eyes open after waking up.

As mentioned above, Lewin started from Freud's theory that the primary purpose of dreams is to protect sleep, and he judged that Descartes's first two dreams were failures because they did not prevent his slumber from being interrupted by the intrusion of what Lewin took to be some sort of somatic disorder, a "migrainous or convulsive" ailment that caused his bodily distress and perceptual distortions. His third dream, by contrast, was successful, "filled with interesting conversation about science, philosophy, inspiration, and poetry" that left his "body . . . at rest, but his observing and thinking faculties . . . pleasantly awake."[7] Descartes's own interpretation of his dreams focused on the nature and meaning of their manifest content, and he concluded that the first two were "warnings and threats concerning his past life, which can not have been . . . innocent in the eyes of God," while the third showed that "the Spirit of Truth . . . wanted to open unto him the treasures of all the sciences."[8] Similarly, numerous subsequent commentators have analyzed the symbolism of the dream elements and their relationship to various aspects of Descartes's background, personality, and philosophy according to their own interpretive schemes. Freud himself interpreted the dreams, without knowing the identity of the dreamer, as manifesting anxiety about sexual or other illicit feelings, while J. O. Wisdom postulated that they revealed a fear of impotence and castration.[9] Stephen Schönberger thought they expressed Descartes's desire to regain his mother, and Lewis Feuer and John Cole interpreted them as Descartes's validation of his youthful rebellion.[10] What was particularly innovative about Lewin's approach was that he, by contrast, focused on the structure of Descartes's experience and showed how its successful resolution of his problem with sleeping anticipated, and indeed structured, the resolution of his philosophical problems over the following months and even years. This interpretation was endorsed by a series of later commentators.[11]

While new interpretations of Descartes's dreams have continued to appear, Freudian psychology has fallen into considerable disrepute since the 1980s, particularly among medical doctors and psychologists.[12] In the area of dream research specifically, both neurobiological studies of the sleeping brain and content studies of dream reports by people in labs awakened periodically (as opposed to reports recorded after waking normally) indicate that Freud was wrong about many things. For example, real-time content studies show that most dreams are relatively mundane rather than bizarre fantasies, while neurobiology suggests that the elements of unreality in them reflect the balance of neurotransmitters and the deactivation of certain brain centers during sleep rather than any convoluted attempt to disguise information or repress the memory of it.[13] In the case of Descartes's dreams, it was already noted in the 1980s that despite Freud's own warning about the dangers of psychoanalyzing dead people, who can't supply free associations, numerous Freudians had gone ahead and analyzed the dreams by applying stock meanings to various elements in the dream reports, although the advances in both physiological and psychological dream research in the past generation seem to have fatally undermined the theoretical structure of psychoanalytic interpretations.[14]

Lewin's thesis could thus be regarded as at most a provocative but merely suggestive proposal.

However, several recent developments in our understanding of sleep and dreaming suggest that Lewin's interpretation has a more substantial basis than it may have seemed, and also that it hints at issues of greater significance than simply understanding the emotional motivation of self-styled rationalists.

As far as our understanding of sleep and dreaming goes, recent research suggests that the postmortems on Freudianism were somewhat premature. Freud may have gotten many things wrong, but he seems to have gotten some important things right. For a while, it appeared that dreams are nothing more than audio-visual rationalizations of random neurological noise produced by the brainstem and other autonomic systems performing restorative physiological processes during REM sleep, but it is now clear that dreaming is an autonomous process related to and affected by REM but also occurring outside it.[15] It appears to heavily involve the ventromesial forebrain, "the brain's 'I want it' system," and to reflect the brain's nightly reconfiguration of itself to integrate recent experiences into long-term memory.[16] Thus Freud seems to have been correct in thinking that "dreams are driven by strong emotion and primitive instincts" and that they "draw on memory, both recent experiences and those dating back to childhood."[17]

More specifically relevant to Lewin's discussion of Descartes's dreams, at least some dreaming does appear, as Freud hypothesized, to act as a hallucinatory substitute for volitional physical activity stimulated by "external stimuli above a certain threshold" or "the arousing effects of endogenous stimuli."[18] Therefore, while Freud's claim that the primary purpose of dreams is to protect sleep from troubling unconscious realizations by rehearsing them in disguised, symbolic form has been discredited, Lewin's assessment of Descartes's dreams as successes or failures seems to have some basis in physiological reality.[19] There is no doubt that the process of integrating new experiences into long-term memory sometimes involves working with disturbing material, whether recent, older, or both, and if this process is interrupted by the sleeper's waking up, the process can understandably be regarded as unsatisfactory and experienced as frustrating. In contrast, if the physiological processes of sleeping and dreaming proceed without interruption, they can be regarded as successful and experienced as satisfying, particularly if they follow several physiologically disturbed, psychologically disturbing episodes, as Descartes's dreams did.

In terms of the broader significance of Descartes's dreams, the philosopher's experiences on the night of November 10, 1619, were important not only because of their role in his psychological and philosophical development but also because they provide insights into the psycho-cultural basis of disbelief in magic in the modern world. In the balance of this chapter, I will highlight the links and parallels between social and psychological types of repression of magic, relating them to Descartes's dreams to illustrate how much work it takes to sustain the normal mode of consciousness of the modern Western skeptical intellectual self. I will first give a summary account of the cognitive processes involved in ritual effects, generally speaking, and then return to discussion of the reception and implications of Descartes's dreams for magic and the modern self.

The most important point about magical ritual from the cognitive perspective is that its claimed effects can very frequently be explained as the direct or indirect manipulation of someone's nervous system: either the practitioner's, some other, target person's, or, perhaps most frequently, both. For example, illness played a leading role in accusations of witchcraft, and disturbed interpersonal relations can have a strong influence on the onset and course of a wide variety of ailments through a range of connections between mind and body, psyche and soma. On the other side of the coin, healing is a frequent focus of charms and magico-religious rituals in general, and psychologically supportive therapeutic activities can have a similarly potent effect on the course and outcome of a wide variety of ailments. Divinatory rituals like scrying and the sieve and shears often induce a mildly altered state of consciousness or make use of ideomotor activity that facilitates the raising to conscious awareness of unconscious knowledge; incantations and spells can act as a form of neuro-linguistic self-programming that enables the practitioner to consciously cultivate the kind of hostile displays of emotion that occur spontaneously in witchcraft, as anthropologically defined; and some magic rituals involve protracted and demanding exercises that drive the practitioner into a dramatically altered state of consciousness, an ecstatic trance that enables him or her to perceive and interact with what seem to be autonomous intelligences or spirits and to manifest unusual abilities and powers.[20]

From the later Middle Ages on, in response to both perceived and actual resurgences of learned and popular magic, church and state, supported by an expanding segment of the social elite, increasingly reacted with measures to counteract magic in a variety of forms. The range of forms that repression took included judicial punishment, religious sanctions, communal pressure, and the intrapsychic inhibitions by which these were transformed from external imperatives into internal regulation.[21] This last process is obviously of particular concern here, for

> magical beliefs can be seen to be rational-verbal representations of associational-imagic processes and their products. Explicit renunciation

of these beliefs serves the purpose of excluding them from the conscious network of linguistic representations of the world and precludes their employment in the conscious formulation of deliberate actions, an exclusion from consideration that can become automatic through internalization so that not only are magical beliefs not actively incorporated into rational-linguistic cogitations, but also even the suggestion that they might be at work is processed via an alternative, resistant neural circuitry employed for unwanted evidence.[22]

Furthermore, "the repression of these concepts inhibits their function as mediating structures" through which the processes and output of the right frontal lobe, which is particularly involved with associational-imagic cognition and autonomic body processes, can be represented in the left frontal lobe, which is particularly associated with rational-linguistic cognition and relations with the external world, depriving the brain as a whole of the ability to bring this significant body of understanding into conscious awareness. Moreover,

> it is possible for the left frontal lobe to block information "that is *consciously* recognized as undesirable" from being transferred from the right hemisphere at all, . . . [while] the right frontal lobe . . . acts "to prevent information that has been *emotionally* recognized" as forbidden "from spreading across the corpus callosum, thereby preventing the . . . [inclusion in] information processing in the left half of the brain" . . . the inadmissible evidence from the right.[23]

Given the seminal role of Descartes's philosophy in the formation of the mechanistic worldview that is the basis of much of the modern Western educated outlook, the dream experiences, which played a seminal role in the formation of that philosophy, seem to have the potential to yield important insights into both the origins of the cultural changes his philosophy helped create and the mechanisms by which the larger campaign to repress magic was implemented on the psycho-physiological level.

I return now to the open issues surrounding Descartes's dreams, and will begin by discussing their significance in the suppression of magic and addressing the questions of whether he actually had the dreams recorded in the *Olympica*, a short unpublished manuscript that is our only record of them, and whether it is legitimate to treat Descartes's experiences as paradigmatic at all.

To start with the last question, there is a venerable psychoanalytic tradition, as we have seen, of exploring Descartes's dreams, but this is just one of the traditions in which evaluating the meaning and importance of the dreams has played a part. Anthony Grafton has observed that "great philosophers have primal scenes" in which "they play the starring roles . . . which their disciples and later writers tell and retell over the decades and even the centuries," and that "no philosopher in the Western tradition has left a more fascinating—or more puzzling—train of anecdote behind him than . . . Descartes": that concerning the three dreams.[24] Descartes began this tradition himself by recording his dreams and insisting that they were of providential rather than human inspiration. Yet his decision not to publish them and his defensive insistence that he had not been drinking before going to sleep (or during the previous three months, for that matter) betray an ambivalence about this supernatural claim that Baillet echoed in his account. Indeed, Descartes's dreams and his claims for them did open him to criticism. "Leibniz openly called him an 'Enthusiast' . . . Christiaan Huygens described the entire experience as 'a great weakness,'" and Pierre-Daniel Huet wrote a parody in 1693 that "claimed that the dreams were not 'revelations from Heaven' at all but just 'ordinary dreams' caused by tobacco or alcohol or melancholy."[25]

Later Cartesians tried to minimize the dreams' importance either by focusing on Descartes's waking reflections on them, trying to prove that they were entirely fabricated, or disregarding them, but "the dreams have never ceased to be a problem" for them.[26] "Biographers, psychologists, psychoanalysts, and historians" return regularly to the dreams, convinced that they "not only make a nice story . . . but actually shed light on the origins of" Descartes's "central intellectual enterprise."[27] Descartes's experiences in the "stove-heated room" have not played the usual role of a paradigm—as an exemplar that adherents of a tradition hold to be the embodiment of its central tenets—but they were presented as seminal by the founder of the tradition, and generations of commentators and critics have regarded them as a singular source of insight into the formulation and nature of the modern worldview. Exploring them in light of a new approach to understanding magic and disbelief would seem to be well within the bounds of established scholarly practice, part of a venerable intellectual tradition, in fact.

The second topic to be dealt with, the question of the dreams' authenticity, involves three separate issues. First, no copies of the dream reports that Descartes recorded at the time survive, so historians have had to rely on Baillet's transcription, supplemented by some notes taken by Leibniz, who also saw the originals, and references to the dreams in Descartes's later works. Second, the original reports are also suspect because they were not clinical records of the dreams or even casual accounts recorded immediately after waking, but instead were composed by Descartes sometime after the night he had them. Third, it has been asserted that Descartes never dreamed anything like the dreams at all, but instead consciously composed them as a literary device based on one or more of several models in the occult literature available to him at the time.[28]

Scholars have debated all three of these questions over the course of the last century, and there may never be universal agreement on them, but the most thorough and balanced analysis comes from the historian John Cole. His *Olympian Dreams and the Youthful Rebellion of René Descartes* devotes three substantial appendices to a careful consideration of the arguments about each of these three questions. To test the reliability of Baillet's transcription, Cole compared his translations of three known texts and found that even where Baillet was ostensibly paraphrasing, he was actually translating more or less verbatim, and so concludes that Baillet's "rule was to transcribe literally." With respect to the validity of Descartes's recollections as dream reports, Cole analyzed the various psychologists upon which the original challenge was based and subsequent dream research and concluded that "there is no psychologically valid reason to suspect the accuracy of the reports." As for the allegations that Descartes based his account of the dreams on a Rosicrucian model, Cole demonstrates that the alleged "exact parallel" involves strong selectivity and extensive misrepresentation, so that the "argument fails at every stage."[29] Cole thus "argues persuasively" on the basis of "the most exhaustive reading of the dreams" that "the historical judgment is that the surviving sources on the Olympian dreams are remarkably good."[30]

While the suggestion that Descartes consciously modeled his dream reports on one of the occult texts in circulation at the time does not seem to hold water, there is no question that he was aware of and interested in the occult sciences. Therefore, his dreams and his understanding of them may well have been influenced by such works. He wrote that the "Spirit who had aroused in him" the excitement that had preoccupied him in the days prior to the dream "had predicted these dreams before he had gone to bed"; that the dreams "could only have come from on high," since "his human mind had nothing to do with them"; that the contrary winds and pain in his first dream were "the work of some Evil Spirit who wanted to seduce him"; that the clap of thunder in his second dream was actually the "Spirit of Truth descending to take possession of him"; that the third dream signified that God "wanted to open unto him the treasures of all the sciences"; and that the last element of the last dream, a set of portraits Descartes was surprised to find as he leafed through the poetry anthology, was a premonition of a visit he would receive later that same day from an Italian painter.[31] At the time that Descartes had the dreams, interest in Rosicrucianism was at its height, and there is good evidence that Descartes was aware of and intrigued by it and other occult traditions. Indeed, he was in contact with at least one person strongly identified with Rosicrucianism who lived in Ulm at the time. There have even been suggestions that he was a member of the secret society himself, or, alternatively, that he was a Jesuit agent working against the Rosicrucians.[32]

Whatever Descartes's interests and allegiances at the time of his dreams, there is no question that by the time he began publishing his seminal philosophical works a decade later, he had become a firm opponent of all things occult. He was closely connected with Marin Mersenne, "one of the leading hammers of Rosicrucianism," and he himself asserted that "there exist no occult forces in stones or plants, no amazing and marvelous sympathies and antipathies, in fact, there exists nothing in the whole of nature which cannot be explained in terms of purely corporeal causes, totally devoid of mind and thought."[33] Because he believed in the total separation of mind and body, his philosophy had no room for magical causation or occult forces.[34]

The seminal role of Descartes's thought in defining the modern scientific worldview is beyond question.[35] His philosophy established the metaphysical foundations and procedural methods of mechanistic materialism, while his work on optics and meteors provided models of the new philosophy in action. By the time of his death, his ideas had acquired a widening circle of intellectual and aristocratic followers, and an even wider circle of opponents, whose vehement and variegated attempts to refute or transcend his philosophy even to this day attest to its foundational status. But what needs to be emphasized in the present context is that Descartes's influence was not simply that he taught modern Westerners to think different thoughts, but that he contributed mightily to a broader and deeper change during the early modern period that led modern Westerners to think their thoughts differently.[36] In the words of Carolyn Merchant, "The rise of mechanism laid the foundation for a new synthesis of the cosmos, society, and the human being, construed as ordered systems of mechanical parts subject to governance by law and to predictability through deductive reasoning. A new concept of the self as a rational master of the passions housed in a machinelike body began to replace the concept of the self as an integral part of a close knit-harmony of organic parts united to the cosmos and society."[37] What was crucial about this new sense of self was, in the words of Susan Bordo, that it "was not simply a philosophical or ideological superstructure but a mode of experiencing being human and being-in-the-world that permeated ordinary language, and even the most basic levels of perception."[38] Furthermore, what was crucial about this new mode of experiencing being human and being-in-the-world is that it is an artificial construct that requires "methodical self-discipline" in order to maintain "the inner domination of passion by thought."[39] Just how basic the impact of this new configuration of self was and what role "methodical self-discipline" played in it is suggested by consideration of the psycho-physiology of the dreams that helped give rise to it in the first place.

Let us return, then, to Descartes's experiences on the night of November 10, 1619. In particular, let us consider the second dream, because it was really the decisive one, the turning point in Descartes's nocturnal drama, in his life, and for the wider world. It came, as we have seen, after Descartes had gone to bed exhausted but elated by the progress he had made in his intellectual project after several days of intense thought, found himself paradoxically in a disturbing dream, awoke in real pain, afraid that he was being assailed by an evil spirit, and then ruminated on good and evil and prayed for two restless hours. As he finally drifted off, though, instead of falling into a sound sleep, he was jolted awake again by the loud crash that he took for thunder, apparently fulfilling his fear that his sins might indeed be "grievous enough to draw upon his head the bolts of divine vengeance."[40] As if to confirm this fear, when he opened his eyes, he saw "fiery sparks all around him in the room." Since he had seen them before, though, he decided "to find [scientific] reasons drawn from [natural] Philosophy, and he was able to reassure himself" about their natural origin.[41] "After having opened and closed his eyes in turn and observed what was represented to him, his terrors faded away, and he fell asleep again quite calmly." This time, he dreamed his happy dream, sleeping peacefully until he awoke serenely, already considering how the night's experiences validated his intended life course. If, as Lewin argued, Descartes's happy dream provided him with a general model of how the mind should relate to the world, along with specific reassurances about his life choices, it was Descartes's "recourse to philosophy" that provided the method for arriving at the truth that initiated his peaceful slumber after prayer and moralizing had failed.

Upon consideration, Descartes's second "dream" was hardly a dream at all: a single clap of thunder immediately upon falling asleep, and then a vision of sparks immediately after waking. What could have caused these unusual phenomena? There have been numerous attempts to explain them physiologically. The sound has been ascribed to some external noise magnified tremendously or, alternatively, to something called "exploding head syndrome" caused by "some sort of neural discharge."[42] The sparks have been explained as resulting from a muscular shock to the optic nerve; as "flicker symptoms" of a migraine, a nervous breakdown, convulsions, or some other disease; and as entopic "lightning streaks" caused by ocular motion and the normal illusion of light perceived even in the dark.[43] All of these explanations are speculative, though, since we have no way of knowing whether there was a sound outside Descartes's window, or whether he had a headache when he went to bed, or whether he woke up flicking his eyes around wildly. We do know one thing about these experiences, however: both of them occurred close to the threshold between waking and sleep, the hypnagogic phase, which occurs at sleep onset, and the hypnopompic phase, which begins as sleep ends but can include "phenomena occurring after the subject has woken."[44] These states, during which the brain goes through a complex series of neuro-electric and chemical changes, often involve dissociation, a desynchronization of different neurological systems that normally work in coordination that creates variable and unpredictable sensations, because "consciousness has some features characteristic of one state mixed with features characteristic of another."[45] Both aural and visual hallucinations in these states are usually more complex than what Descartes experienced, but some people report simple "crashing noises, bangs and explosions," while "a great many reports begin with references to moving clouds of bright colors . . . little luminous wheels, little suns," and "luminous points and streaks, which shift and change in remarkable ways." Similarly, while most hypnagogic experiences seem to start and change at random, with little clear meaning or connection to one another or to waking life, people in the hypnagogic state are very susceptible to suggestion from both external and internal stimuli, so it is quite possible that Descartes's perception of a sound he took to be thunder and sparks reminiscent of lightning were prompted by memories of his earlier thoughts about how his sins might draw down "upon his head the bolts of divine vengeance."[46]

In any case, what is important for us here is not so much what caused Descartes's perceptions but how he reacted to them. His reaction to the sound that "he took for thunder was terror," which woke him up. When he awoke, though, the sparks he saw do not seem to have intensified his fear, for he realized that he had seen them before and wondered if, instead of some sort of supernatural retribution, they might be the result of his own perceptual system. He resolved the question experimentally, by comparing what he saw when his eyes were open with what he saw when they were closed, and having come to "conclusions favorable to his understanding . . . his fear was dissipated."[47] Reassured by the conclusions generated by this model application of reason and experience, he was able to fall asleep again "quite calmly."[48]

That, at least, has been the traditional explanation of his final lapse into sleep. However, recent research into the biochemistry of sleep suggests that something else was going on as well. During sleep the level of aminergic neurotransmitters, which promote "exteroceptive focus, linear thinking, and rationality," drops, while the level of acetylcholine, which promotes "interoceptive focus, analogical thinking, and emotionality," remains steady at first and then, during REM sleep, rises sharply.[49] While Descartes was apparently just drifting off to sleep when he had the second "dream," the drop in aminergic neurotransmitters alone is enough to create a marked shift from exteroceptive to interoceptive focus, from linear to analogical thinking, and from rationality to emotionality, and it creates a "loosening of ego controls" and "a lessening of the internal-external distinction" as well.[50] Furthermore, if the sparks resulted from some sort of rapid eye movement, either because Descartes was already in REM sleep or because he did look around the room wildly as he awoke, this would have pushed the aminergic-cholinergic balance even further toward the cholinergic, or dreamy, side, for "bursts of acetylcholine . . . [and] neuronal discharge appear to be strictly and precisely related to eye movement," and "extreme eye movements . . . produce powerful changes in cholinergic output," pushing consciousness even further toward the analogical-emotional-interoceptive-interconnected mode.[51] More important from the present perspective is the potential for this process to work in the opposite direction: deliberate moderating control of eye movements appears to have the effect of inhibiting the discharge of acetylcholine, pushing the balance of neurotransmitters back toward the aminergic side and consciousness toward the linear-rational-exteroceptive-dualistic mode. J. Allan Hobson, a leading researcher into the neurology and biochemistry of sleep, provides evidence of this effect; he describes a patient who told him that "she could stop her visual hallucinations simply by counting the ceiling tiles in her bedroom. How could this work? By directing her eye movements voluntarily and by focusing her attention on a specific part of the visual world, and by using her cognitive apparatus to actively analyze and compute features of that world, she was able to tip the balance of power between internal (hence dreamlike) image generation and the external image generation of normal waking."[52] Similarly, Descartes's eye experiments seem to have pushed his nervous system away from the cholinergic, dreamlike state toward the aminergic, rational mode of cognition, bringing the fireworks to an end, enabling his reason to prevail over his passions, and setting the stage for his mind to finally enjoy the aware yet detached view of the world of a successful dreamer and of a successful scientist.

In addition to supporting Lewin's thesis, this analysis of Descartes's second dream and his reaction to it suggests three important insights into the modern self that they helped create. First of all, it shows that this self, the isolated, rational, sovereign consciousness charged with controlling the emotions and the body, is not the normative state of the human mind. The natural state of the human mind is actually constantly changing modes of consciousness brought about by steady, internally regulated rhythmic cycles punctuated by intermittent reactions to external events. Each has its own form or shading, and each plays its part in maintenance of the human animal. The sustenance of the modern self, as Descartes and other early adopters acknowledged and as Descartes's dream experiences illustrate, actually requires considerable mental and even physical effort, effort that is a form of what can be called "fine-tuning the nervous system" (since the process of achieving the dramatically altered trance states of consciousness mentioned above are already referred to as "tuning the nervous system").[53] Maintaining rational control over emotions and bodily functions means intervening in the operations of the nervous system to promote what we modern selves call normal waking consciousness whenever possible, and to induce it by force of will whenever necessary.

The second insight conveyed by Descartes's dreams involves what is "tuned out" when "normal waking consciousness" is "tuned in." As Hobson notes, the aminergic system that is tuned in "is generally reciprocal to the" cholinergic system, which promotes dreamlike sensory experiences, "emotion-based unconscious processing," and "the conscious experience of involuntary autonomic nervous system activation," or what are popularly called imagination, intuition, and gut feelings.[54] What is particularly important about this effect in the present context is that these are important elements in magic, and in fact much magical ritual works to "tune in" these faculties even as it explicitly calls upon some presumed external source of knowledge or power. In other words, "tuning in" our rational, everyday, normal waking consciousness means "tuning out" our ability to access information and influence through magic.

The final insight yielded by Descartes's dreams is related to this second one. Because rational and magical modes of cognition are incompatible, if magical effects, from an explanatory perspective, tend to involve control of the nervous system, then by the same logic to disbelieve in magic is actually to participate in it; it is a way of "fine-tuning" the nervous system to defend against it, like whistling while walking past a graveyard. Descartes did not undertake his eye experiments out of disinterested curiosity; he undertook them because he feared that his physical pain had been caused by an "evil spirit" and the thunderclap by a wrathful God, and the two hours in prayer and moral musings had failed to protect him from additional spiritual assaults. By taking control of his eyes, he succeeded in reestablishing control of his mind, and taking control of his mind enabled him to defeat the spirits that assailed him. The methods of science—rational analysis and systematic empirical investigation—thus provided the techniques that have enabled generations of educated modern Westerners to maintain the fiction that their conscious minds are sovereign rulers of an inner space that is essentially isolated from the surrounding world. Descartes's experiences on the night of November 10, 1619, may not have served as an explicit paradigm embraced by his followers, but they have constituted an implicit paradigm for the formation and maintenance of the modern, disenchanted way of thinking.

NOTES

1. Michael Keevak, "Descartes' Dreams and Their Address for Philosophy," *Journal of the History of Ideas* 53, no. 3 (1992): 394.

2. Bertram Lewin, *Dreams and the Uses of Regression* (New York: International Universities Press, 1958), 31, 50, 22.

3. Ibid., 18, 14.

4. A. C. Grayling, *Descartes: The Life and Times of a Genius* (New York: Walker & Co., 2006), 45, 57; John Cole, *The Olympian Dreams and the Youthful Rebellion of René Descartes* (Urbana: University of Illinois Press, 1992), 61–63; and Desmond Clarke, *Descartes: A Biography* (Cambridge: Cambridge University Press, 2006), 58.

5. Jacques Maritain, *The Dream of Descartes, Together with Some Other Essays*, trans. Mabelle L. Andison (Port Washington, N.Y.: Kennikat Press, 1969), 113; and Cole, *Olympian Dreams*, 79–82.

6. Lewin, *Dreams and the Uses of Regression*, 23–29, 32–33.

7. Ibid., 39, 42–44. For other discussions of the peacefulness during and after the third dream, see Marie-Louise von Franz, *Dreams: A Study of the Dreams of Jung, Descartes, Socrates, and Other Historical Figures* (Boston: Shambhala Publications, 1991), 121; and Lewis Feuer, "The Dreams of Descartes," *American Imago* 20 (1963): 22–23, which notes that Descartes enjoyed dreaming after that.

8. Quoted in Cole, *Olympian Dreams*, 37–38.

9. Owen Flanagan, *Dreaming Souls: Sleep, Dreams, and the Evolution of the Conscious Mind* (Oxford: Oxford University Press, 2000), 165–68; and J. O. Wisdom, "Three Dreams of Descartes," *International Journal of Psycho-Analysis* 28 (1947): 15, 17.

10. Stephen Schönberger, "A Dream of Descartes: Reflections on the Unconscious Determinants of the Sciences," *International Journal of Psycho-Analysis* 20 (1939): 57; Feuer, "Dreams of Descartes," 23; and Cole, *Olympian Dreams*, 182.

11. See Ben-Ami Scharfstein, "Descartes' Dreams," *Philosophical Forum*, new ser., 1, no. 3 (1969): 312; John Hanson, "René Descartes and the Dream of Reason," in *The Narcissistic Condition*, ed. Marie Coleman Nelson (New York: Human Sciences Press, 1977), 169, 176–77; and Allen Dyer, "The Dreams of Descartes: Notes on the Origins of Scientific Thinking," *Annual of Psychoanalysis* 14 (1987): 172–73, 175.

12. See Jonathan Redmond and Michael Shulman, "Access to Psychoanalytic Ideas in American Undergraduate Institutions," *Journal of the American Psychoanalytic Association* 56, no. 2 (2008): 391–408; thanks also to Christopher T. Bever, MD, professor of neurology at the University of Maryland School of Medicine, for sharing his insights on the subject with me.

13. Andrea Rock, *The Mind at Night: The New Science of How and Why We Dream* (New York: Basic Books, 2004), 31, 20, 50–51; Kelley Bulkeley, *An Introduction to the Psychology of Dreaming* (Westport, Conn.: Praeger, 1997), 75; and J. Allan Hobson, *The Dream Drugstore: Chemically Altered States of Consciousness* (Cambridge: MIT Press, 2001), 74–75.

14. Charles D. Minahen, "'Olympian Vertigo': Deconstructing Descartes's Reconstruction of the 'Trois Songes,'" *Symposium* 41, no. 2 (1987): 139n18.

15. William Domhoff, *The Scientific Study of Dreams: Neural Networks, Cognitive Development, and Content Analysis* (Washington, D.C.: American Psychological Association, 2003), 147–48; Bulkeley, *Psychology of Dreaming*, 57–58; and Ernest Hartmann, *Dreams and Nightmares: The New Theory on the Origin and Meaning of Dreams* (New York: Plenum Trade, 1998), 197.

16. Rock, *Mind at Night*, 46, 51–54, 71, 188; and Anthony Stevens, *Private Myths: Dreams and Dreaming* (Cambridge: Harvard University Press, 1995), 95–96.

17. Rock, *Mind at Night*, 132, 105.

18. Mark Solms, *The Neuropsychology of Dreams: A Clinico-Anatomical Study* (Mahwah, N.J.: Lawrence Erlbaum, 1997), 243–45; and Hartmann, *Dreams and Nightmares*, 14, 188–89.

19. For critiques of Solms's endorsement of Freud's "cardinal statement" about the primary purpose of dreams being to protect sleep, see Domhoff, *Scientific Study of Dreams*, 142; and Flanagan, *Dreaming Souls*, 125n4. Note that the analysis here does not concern itself with identifying the primary purpose of dreams, just with whether agitated dreams have a different psychological valence from placid ones.

20. Edward Bever, *The Realities of Witchcraft and Popular Magic in Early Modern Europe: Culture, Cognition, and Everyday Life* (Basingstoke: Palgrave, 2008), 11–39, 272–303, 221–30, 164–66, 185–212.

21. Ibid., 349–78.

22. Ibid., 377.

23. Ibid.

24. Anthony Grafton, "Descartes the Dreamer," *Wilson Quarterly* 20, no. 4 (1996): 36–37.

25. Keevak, "Descartes' Dreams," 375–77.

26. Ibid., 380–81.

27. Alan Gabbey and Robert E. Hall, "The Melon and the Dictionary: Reflections on Descartes' Dreams," *Journal of the History of Ideas* 59, no. 4 (1998): 651; and Grafton, "Descartes the Dreamer," 46.

28. Cole, *Olympian Dreams*, 189.

29. Ibid., 191–226, quotations on 201–2, 213, 217–21.

30. Ibid., 4; see also Gabbey and Hall, "Melon and the Dictionary," 655; and Stephen Gaukroger, *Descartes: An Intellectual Biography* (Oxford: Clarendon Press, 1995), 108–9.

31. Cole, *Olympian Dreams*, 37–39; Gaukroger, *Descartes*, 59; Maritain, *Dream of Descartes*, 17–19; Clarke, *Descartes*, 54–56, 61–62; Grayling, *Descartes*, 83; Lewin, *Dreams and the Uses of Regression*, 30; and Richard Kennington, "Descartes' 'Olympica,'" *Social Research* 28 (1961): 184.

32. Grayling, *Descartes*, 85–86.

33. Quoted in Clarke, *Descartes*, 79; see also Grayling, *Descartes*, 70; Morris Berman, *Coming to Our Senses: Body and Spirit in the Hidden History of the West* (New York: Simon & Schuster, 1989), 237–38, 240, 243, 246; Feuer, "Dreams of Descartes," 10–11; and Brian Eslea, *Witch Hunting, Magic, and the New Philosophy: An Introduction to Debates of the Scientific Revolution, 1450–1750* (Brighton, UK: Harvester Press, 1980), 111.

34. Eslea, *Witch Hunting*, 115; and Carolyn Merchant, *The Death of Nature: Women, Ecology, and the Scientific Revolution* (San Francisco: Harper San Francisco, 1990), 204–5.

35. Grafton, "Descartes the Dreamer," 38.

36. On the roots of the change, see Vwadek P. Marciniak, *Towards a History of Consciousness: Space, Time, and Death* (New York: Peter Lang, 2006), 225, 249.

37. Merchant, *Death of Nature*, 214.

38. Susan R. Bordo, *The Flight to Objectivity: Essays on Cartesianism and Culture* (Albany: State University of New York Press, 1987), 60; see also Marciniak, *Towards a History of Consciousness*, 225, 249.

39. Marciniak, *Towards a History of Consciousness*, 223, 249. See also Merchant, *Death of Nature*, 193, 195; and Hanson, "Descartes and the Dream of Reason," 162.

40. Lewin, *Dreams and the Uses of Regression*, 28.

41. Cole, *Olympian Dreams*, 35, quoting Baillet (bracketed words are Cole's).

42. Gregor Sebba, *The Dream of Descartes* (Carbondale: Southern Illinois University Press, 1987), 21, 53; and Grayling, *Descartes*, 61–62.

43. Wisdom, "Three Dreams of Descartes," 16; Sebba, *Dream of Descartes*, 21; Lewin, *Dreams and the Uses of Regression*, 29; Gaukroger, *Descartes*, 110; Scharfstein, "Descartes' Dreams," 309; Andreas Mavromatis, *Hypnagogia: The Unique State of Consciousness Between Wakefulness and Sleep* (London: Routledge & Kegan Paul, 1987), 15; and Cole, *Olympian Dreams*, 145–46, 266–67n26.

44. Mavromatis, *Hypnagogia*, 82.

45. Hobson, *Dream Drugstore*, 88–89, 153, 157.

46. Mavromatis, *Hypnagogia*, 34, 15, 19, 53.

47. Lewin, *Dreams and the Uses of Regression*, 29.

48. Cole, *Olympian Dreams*, 35.

49. Hobson, *Dream Drugstore*, 142–47, 91–92.

50. Ibid., 153–54; Mavromatis, *Hypnagogia*, 265, 267.

51. Hobson, *Dream Drugstore*, 91–92.

52. Ibid., 80–81.

53. Bever, *Realities of Witchcraft*, 211.

54. Hobson, *Dream Drugstore*, 91–92.

3

WHY MAGIC CANNOT BE FALSIFIED BY EXPERIMENTS

Benedek Láng

This essay reopens an old (and some might think naïve) question about the nature of experimental falsification, and I hope the reader will bear with me as I demonstrate the utility of revisiting this issue. The puzzle is the following: medieval texts on natural magic, talismans, divination, and angel magic report practical methods (often called experiments: *experimenta*) that the modern reader will find at best curious, if not unreal. The *Liber aggregationis* (Book of Collections) attributed to Albertus Magnus explains that certain herbs collected and prepared appropriately will ensure that their possessor is addressed only with friendly words, and can even become invisible. The book claims that the magnet has the property of revealing whether one's wife is chaste and that by using the tongue of the sea cow a person can prevent others from having bad opinions of him.[1] A tract on geomancy attributed to Gerard of Cremona provides divinatory tools that can be used if we want to learn whether the king will die.[2] The *De imaginibus* attributed to Thabit ibn Qurra recommends the use of talismans if one wants to destroy a city or to expel scorpions from the town.[3] Certain anecdotes written at the end of the fourteenth century tell a story in which Thomas of Pizan—doctor of astrology and medicine in the service of the French king, Charles V—successfully used planetary talismans engraved with the names of angels to expel the English army from French territory.[4]

These prescriptions are not curiosities or exceptions in the medieval literary corpus. Many such texts and stories were widespread in the Middle Ages as well as in early modern times: learned monks, court intellectuals, and university masters—that is, intelligent individuals capable of reflection—copied and collected them.[5] Even though we cannot exclude the possibility that some of these thinkers had a certain skepticism concerning certain methods, there is no reason to doubt that most of these texts were copied with a fairly strong conviction that the procedures outlined in them were valid. To be sure, in some cases, the author or scribe simply wished to create a beautiful and fascinating book that was meant not to be a manual for actual use but to entertain his sei-gneur, bishop, students, wife, or children. Yet even if this is true in some instances, most of the time the fact that they were copied in the same books with practical scientific texts, along with the marginal notes and other background information, indicates that these texts were generally meant for actual use.

The question I want to ask is this: why didn't the scribes and collectors see that it was impossible to become invisible with the help of herbs, that it was impossible to expel scorpions from Bagdad or destroy cities with the help of Thabit's *De imaginibus*, and that the magnet says nothing about the chastity of their wives?[6] How did these persons fail to recognize that the methods they were copying were nonsense? Did they not see that the mechanism of magic is obviously false, and that its falsity can be easily shown in practice with the help of simple experiments?

Before trying to address this question, however, certain metalevel consider-ations must be explored. Specifically, is such a question legitimate at all, or is it desperately naïve and anachronistic?

The answer depends on the perspective of the answerer. For a traditional positivistic—or rather Popperian—scholar, for example, such a question can be seen as legitimate but somewhat uninteresting. All of the experiments described above would be seen either as clearly falsified by simple counterevidence or as pseudoscientific in the sense that they avoid empirical falsification with the help of ad hoc hypotheses. Karl Popper had famous examples for both cases. He called astrology and Marxism pseudoscientific in the first sense: they make predictions that prove false in front of the tribunal of *empiria*, yet advocates of these "disciplines" avoid taking this falsification seriously:

> Astrology did not pass the test. Astrologers were greatly impressed, and misled, by what they believed to be confirming evidence—so much so that they were quite unimpressed by any unfavourable evidence. More-over, by making their interpretations and prophecies sufficiently vague they were able to explain away anything that might have been a refuta-tion of the theory had the theory and the prophecies been more precise. In order to escape falsification they destroyed the testability of their theory. It is a typical soothsayer's trick to predict things so vaguely that the predictions can hardly fail: that they become irrefutable.

The case with Marxism is quite similar:

The Marxist theory of history, in spite of the serious efforts of some of its founders and followers, ultimately adopted this soothsaying practice. In some of its earlier formulations . . . predictions were testable, and in fact falsified. Yet instead of accepting the refutations the followers of Marx re-interpreted both the theory and the evidence in order to make them agree. In this way they rescued the theory from refutation; but they did so at the price of adopting a device which made it irrefutable.[7]

In these two cases, the followers of the criticized disciplines systematically resisted counterevidence. Psychoanalysis, on the other hand, is pseudoscientific in Popper's second sense: "The psycho-analytic theories were in a different class. They were simply non-testable, irrefutable. There was no conceivable human behaviour which could contradict them."[8] The theories of this discipline— Popper argues—are constructed in such a way that they simply avoid any possible empirical falsification.

The post-Popperian period, however, reconsidered the question, and Popper's theories of falsification and of demarcation were seriously challenged. They received famous criticisms from theorists such as Imre Lakatos and Larry Laudan. On the one hand, Lakatos argued that many genuine scientific theories are immediately falsified after their birth. This does not mean, however, that scientists get rid of them; just the opposite: a constructive reaction to the falsificatory attempts can allow theories to develop in ways that enable them to conform to the *empiria* better. Thus newly introduced auxiliary hypotheses that make theories more resistant to empirical refutation is not a characteristic of pseudoscience; it is also an important constituent of scientific activity.[9] Laudan, on the other hand, famously called the whole issue of demarcation a pseudoproblem. He maintained the difference between good and bad, between reliable and unreliable science, but he rejected the notion of universal standards, necessary and sufficient conditions, according to which science and pseudoscience could be differentiated.[10] While Laudan's claims have been challenged by a number of philosophers, his argument that *purely epistemic* criteria cannot differentiate science from pseudoscience has been largely accepted. We can also mention Pierre Duhem, whose thesis of underdetermination undermined the theory of falsification half a century before it was formulated at all.[11] Duhem, a former practicing scientist himself, called attention to the fact that scientific theories never occur individually. Each theory consists of a group of interconnected theoretical claims and considerations, and when a given theory seems to be falsified by experimental results, one can never know precisely which part of the network of claims is responsible for the negative results.

Where exactly the scientist is required to emend his theory, or which part of it he has to get rid of, is—philosophically speaking—underdetermined.

In the 1960s, partly as a result of Thomas Kuhn's work, the philosophy of science underwent a historical turn, and questions concerning the falsifiability of earlier belief systems were disqualified. The argument was made that such questions fell into the error of presentism, or Whiggish history. In Kuhn's view, "Whig history" presupposed a cumulative and linear progress toward an ever-expanding field of solid knowledge; once they had made their contribution to the present collection of true and valid data, the old wrong ideas, falsified by the new science, would drop away. In other words, the presentist historian of science (or historian of magic) writes about the past in terms of the present, judging phenomena from the history of science in terms of present-day science, or even treating the past as a mere preparation for the present.[12] In the case of alchemy, for example, this attitude led to the famous evolutionary theory according to which alchemy was a partly mistaken, partly ridiculous, yet partly useful protochemistry (useful to the extent that it helped uncover phenomena now considered valid). In the past, magic suffered especially from the judgments of Whig history—from the investigation of magic either as a protoscience or purely as a dead end. The great historian of magic Lynn Thorndike is a frequent stalking horse for this error, and serves as well as other examples to show the way it works. Thorndike wrote, "in works of the fourteenth and fifteenth centuries might be found the germs of later scientific discoveries. We have seen the conception of gas already current among the alchemists, to say nothing of scholastic discussion of density and rarefaction. Various theories of attraction and gravitation have been put forward to explain the influence of the moon on tides or the suspension of our globe in mid-space. . . . We have heard a theory of the circulation of the spirits somewhat resembling the circulation of the blood."[13]

Similar Whiggism characterized the work of Karin Figala, who rationalized Isaac Newton's alchemical activity by claiming that it resembled early twentieth-century atomic theories, particularly the atomic shell model of Niels Bohr.[14] Even the famous thesis of Frances Yates was Whiggish when she defended hermetic magic as the *predecessor* of modern science.[15] For a contextualist scholar—someone who rejects Whiggish arguments—these are not acceptable approaches, since scientific (and other) enterprises should not be evaluated according to their afterlife but according to the standards of the given historical context.

The contextualist reaction to Whig history strongly informed the next generation of historians. Over the past forty years scholars have tended to follow the prescription Thomas Kuhn offered in his encyclopedia article on the history of science: "Insofar as possible (it is never entirely so, nor could history be written if it were), the historian should set aside the science he knows. His science should be learned from the textbooks and journals of the period he studies."[16] Such considerations have led to a healthy anti-Whiggish attitude in the history of science, cultural studies, and many other fields. It has made us more tolerant of cultures and epochs alien to our own. It has helped historians understand seemingly nonsensical scientific theories and reconstruct historically changing, dynamic categories (among them "science," "religion," and "magic"). And it has helped minimize ahistorical explanations in history writing.

Contextualism's impact on magic and witchcraft scholarship has been recently summarized by Stuart Clark. These two fields, he argues, "present, as few other historical subjects do, the challenge of interpreting and understanding things in the past *without any attempt whatsoever* to say whether anything about them *was* or *was not* real."[17] This agnosticism—advocated by most magic scholars in the past two or three decades—avoids making claims on past or present *reality* and concentrates instead on the practices and historical ontologies that enabled past certainties, without comparing them to our own sense of correct scientific procedure or evaluating them as true or false. Without this agnosticism, serious scholarship on magic would never have been born.

The importance of the anti-Whiggish approach in the history of science cannot be exaggerated, and the constant need for it in science education and the popularization of the history of science is undeniable. However, as several authors have argued in the past two decades, anti-Whiggism in professional history of science appears to have run its course.[18] As it gradually defeated the old positivistic attitude, historians realized something that Kuhn had already referred to in his article, namely, that it is not so simple to follow the anti-Whiggish agenda, and, what is more, that such a program is not always even desirable. First of all, historians can never forget about present-day science; they will be always a bit more interested in what became a successful trend in the history of science than in what proved to be a dead end. They will be more interested in Newton's kinematics than in Descartes's. Second, historians write for a present-day audience and use neologisms, modern categories that were not used and often did not even have equivalents in the past. They are interested in the history of Greek "mathematics" even though this discipline as a separate entity is not an antique category. They write about the "theory of evolution" as belonging to Darwin, even though Darwin hardly ever used this term. Third, historians do not even want to give up their right to approach the past through concepts rooted in the present. Histories of childhood, gender, women, and everyday life would not be legitimate themes in a dogmatic application of anti-Whiggism, as these are not genuine categories of many of the ages under study.

All in all, today an anti-anti-Whiggish position is popular in the history of science. Nothing is more alien to contemporary scholars than a return to Whiggism, but contemporary historians also warn against the harmful effects of doctrinaire contextualism, an approach that permits only the use of categories and questions raised in the period under study. Contemporary scholarship permits historians to ask *questions* inspired by the concerns of the present, but—in contrast to older Whiggish historians—insists that they refrain from giving *answers* distorted by the same concerns.[19]

What about anti-anti-Whiggism in scholarship on magic? Without implying that anti-Whiggism has run its course also in magic studies, and without implying that it is no longer needed in fields related to witchcraft, alchemy, astrology, and magic, I believe that the time has arrived when anti-anti-Whiggish questions can and should be raised. My inquiry into medieval and early modern magic is inspired by this understanding of anti-anti-Whiggism. I believe that one can freely raise the naïve question concerning falsifiability with which I began, even though there is clearly something anachronistic in such an inquiry. One only has to be careful when *answering* this question. This approach is fairly rare in magic scholarship. Recently, Edward Bever has asked, "what basis did early modern beliefs about witchcraft and magic have in reality?"[20] In contrast to his substantial investigations that integrate the results of psychology, neurophysiology, and cognitive science in the field of history of magic, in my considerably shorter study, I situate my basic question rather in the context of the history of science. My aim is not to reconstruct what might have happened in a magic experiment, but rather to imagine what the perception of the person who carried out the experiment might have been. I would like to understand how it was possible that historical actors did not see a given experiment as a falsification of related magic theories. I would like to explain for the *modern* reader how *historical* actors could have handled the discrepancy between what might have happened in an experiment from our *modern* perspective and what those historical actors expected.[21] What is shared in my analysis and that of Bever—apart from asking heterodox questions—is the conviction that medieval and early modern claims about magical efficacy should not be understood as imaginary but should be taken as "real."[22]

An Anti-Anti-Whiggish Approach to Magic Experiments

Arriving finally at the point where an attempt can be made to address my initial question, it must be noted that we are not looking for one single explanation for why theories of magic were not falsified by negative experiments, but rather for a group of interconnected answers. First, there is no reason to doubt that in many cases magical practices actually worked, producing the desired outcomes. In such cases, magical techniques were certainly regarded by the practitioners as valid methods that led to success. Women sometimes fell in love with someone who previously cast a love spell, armies sometimes occupied castles after someone used talismanic magic, and the number of scorpions sometimes decreased in a city after someone applied a method described in a book on talismans. Such instances were certainly viewed as positive cases confirming the efficacy of magic. One should not forget that the methods described in the widespread handbooks of natural and talismanic magic were not as foreign to medieval and early modern natural philosophy as they seem to be to modern natural science. The underlying assumptions behind the mechanism of talismans and magic stones, the occult virtue of herbs, and the healing power of animal substances formed part of the same correspondential worldview that was typical of many fields of medieval science.

Nevertheless, while we can assume that magical practices led to many positive results and thus produced confirming experiments, we should also assume that in many cases these techniques manifestly did not work. When trying to understand why such negative examples did not destroy the practitioners' belief in magic, we have to differentiate the various types of magic. Let us first consider ritual magic, which addresses spiritual powers (angels, demons, or spirits) through prayers and conjurations. To ask why the practitioner of such a method did not become disillusioned when his or her prayers to the spirits did not influence the earthly events is just as irrelevant as asking Christian believers whether they become atheists if their prayers remain unanswered by God. Faith in spiritual beings and entities obviously requires different kinds of proof from that needed for scientific convictions, not least because God, angels, and demons are usually seen as conscious beings, as opposed to the mechanical processes of science. It sounds fairly absurd to construct scientific experiments in order to test the efficacy of prayers and to count the percentage of those prayers that prove successful. Yet such an experimental approach to testing the percentage of successful prayers was actually proposed by the "science-manager" John Tyndall (1820–1893) in late nineteenth-century England, and—quite understandably—this proposal provoked a fairly heated debate and an important conflict between science and religion.[23] The proposed experiment was never carried out, not least because it seemed just as absurd in the nineteenth century as it does today to try to falsify religious beliefs with controlled experiments.[24]

If ritual magic does not seem to be a field where experiments might possess relevant falsificatory power, natural magic, which embraces a wide range of what is called "*experimenta* literature," would appear a more promising territory for experimental confirmation. Yet as we turn to this field, I should underscore a basic discrepancy between the medieval and the present scientific attitude. In medieval natural philosophy, eagerness to disqualify procedures that systematically failed to produce the expected results was not particularly common. The notion of "experiment" was not understood to be something involving a number of controlled experimental situations, but rather as commonly shared knowledge described by traditional philosophers and authorities.[25] Experience was used in scholarly arguments, but in a different manner from the present day.[26] For example, experience was called upon to prove the existence of demons, and quite understandably, since the existence of spiritual entities was indeed a commonly shared conviction in the Middle Ages.[27] The main source for the so-called *experimenta* literature in the Middle Ages was what ancient books and authorities claimed; actual experience, repeated experiments, and actual counterexamples did not play a considerable role in judging the authenticity of the recipes. The *experimenta* literature (which was the wider context of natural magical recipes) was a textual tradition that should be conceived not as a practical genre but as "theoretical literature that speaks about practice."[28]

As we reconstruct this notion of experiment, it becomes easier to understand why and how relatively fantastic convictions could be considered for centuries as sufficiently—and experimentally—confirmed scientific facts. Authors from Plutarch to the sixteenth century famously referred to the conviction that magnets will lose their power of attraction if they are rubbed with garlic. They did not see this as a claim that had to be proved, but rather they used this accepted "fact" as a "proof" for the theory of antipathies. A congenial worldview (in this case the theory of sympathies and antipathies) and a sufficiently strong textual tradition were more efficient means than practical tests for this conviction to gain epistemological status. Furthermore, several authors explicitly claimed that they had actually tried the magnet-garlic antipathy in practice, and they said it did work. The very same empirical approach that is assumed today to falsify the theory became its actual proof. As Daryn Lehoux has convincingly argued, this proof lost its status only in early modern times, when the generally accepted ontology of the world was transformed, and magnets and garlic were no longer seen as having antipathies and sympathies (instead, one came to be seen as having magnetic force and the other as being completely irrelevant as far as magnetism is concerned). Things are proved to be nonexistent and theories are proved to be false only when they change their status in the classificatory framework of a new worldview.[29]

The solution is not much more straightforward in the case of talismanic magic. A great variety of texts and archeological finds (talismans, amulets, rings containing stones, teeth, crosses, shells, hair, bones, and herbal and animal materials) show that belief in the general protective power of such objects was widely shared in many societies.[30] As long as only a general protective power is attributed to such objects, the belief in their efficacy can hardly be falsified. Nonetheless, when specific objects were claimed to be useful for specific goals (such as the destruction of a given city, the defeat of a given army, or the failure of a given business at a well-defined moment), we would expect a considerable rate of negative outcomes. Yet there is little indication that negative results discouraged their use or that skeptical attitudes emerged because of the malfunctioning talismans: popular stories were spread about their efficacy despite any negative results, and texts with talismanic content were copied by university students and professors, apparently in the assumption that the texts were effective.[31]

But what could have happened when magical methods produced results that undeniably contradicted the underlying magical theory? Even in such cases, it would be too "Whiggish" to expect the practitioners to abandon the theory, because various explanations could have saved the core hypotheses of magic from falsification. The argument could always be made that the operator was not properly prepared to perform the given magical procedure: he did not fast enough, or his bodily or spiritual chastity had not reached a satisfactory level. It was also possible to argue that the constellations at the moment of the experiment were not favorable. Or perhaps everything happened as it was described in the magic manuals, only the proper person was not involved. Instead of the democratic ideal of modern science, according to which an experiment carried out under the same specified conditions can be repeated by anyone with access to properly functioning laboratory equipment, regardless of gender, race, age, and so forth, in magic only properly initiated persons succeed.[32] Only adepts could perform the experiments properly, and pupils did not always possess the necessary abilities. If the given result was expected from a helping angel or demon, the argument could be made that the spirits were able, just not willing, to provide the requisite assistance. Finally, one could always say that the instructions—originating usually from texts written several hundred years earlier, often in a different Arabic or Jewish

culture—were not understood properly, or that the text was simply not copied or translated correctly. This last argument was more than plausible; the
Picatrix, for example, was translated from Arabic to Castilian, and then in a
second step from Castilian to Latin, and then further small Latin texts were
added to it, so the end result was fairly far from the Arabic original. If we add
to this picture the fact that many texts were first translated from Greek to
Arabic, or from Greek to Syriac and then from Syriac to Arabic, there is no
reason to be surprised by the corruption of the texts' content. We know,
furthermore, that scribes were not particularly keen on copying the material
correctly even if angels' names were at stake, and even if the importance of
transmitting the texts precisely, so as to make the prayers efficacious, was
explicitly emphasized.[33] Similarly, talismans of magic squares were also often
copied with many errors, even though all talismanic texts stressed the importance of correctly reproducing the figures and characters on the talismans.[34]
In short, the argument could always be made that the negative outcome of a
magic experiment was inconclusive because the experiment was not performed competently.

All of these arguments are hypothetical. To my knowledge, no explicit
records have survived on how practitioners interpreted failed magic experiments (although methodological problems regarding astrological prognostica-
tions were often spelled out, among them the often criticized idiosyncrasy of
astrological theories; the optical problems that make the observations of
celestial phenomena uncertain, according to some authors; and the famous
argument of Nicholas Oresme concerning the incommensurability of celestial
motion, which holds that it is impossible to predict the path of constellations in
a reliable manner, making it impossible, in turn, for the astrologer to formulate
stable astrological laws).[35] I do not claim that the assumptions, defensive arguments, and ad hoc hypotheses required to save magic theories occurred in
scholarly debates on the efficacy of magic; instead, I offer them as examples of
how the modern mind can grasp how belief in experiments that appear to us
nonsensical could have survived for centuries.

Nonfalsifying Experiments in the History of Science

One further example illustrates that the problems discussed here do not emerge
exclusively in the history of magic but also characterize the history of science.
The existence of the *experimentum crucis,* the crucial experiment that is meant
to provide a final decision between rival theories and to demonstrate the falsity

of all but one of them, is a myth not only in the history of magic but also in the history of science.

The example involves Galileo Galilei, whom posterity considers one of the founding fathers of experimental science. Galileo reported in his books three types of experiments: real experiments that he performed; imaginary experiments that he did not perform personally but whose outcomes seemed so persuasive and convincing that he did not feel obliged actually to complete them; and thought experiments that were not to be performed in practice at all.

In his 1638 book *Two New Sciences*, Galileo proposed the following experiment in hydrodynamics:

> I filled with water a glass ball that had an opening as narrow as a straw stem . . . and turned it over with its mouth downward. However, neither the water, although very heavy and suited to falling through air, nor the air, although very light and much inclined to rise in water, will agree, the former to falling out of the hole [of the ball], the latter to rising upon entering [therein]; but remain, both of them, stubborn and perverse [in their places]. On the contrary, as soon as we shall present to that hole a vessel containing red wine, which is only imperceptibly less heavy than water, we shall see it immediately rise slowly in red streaks through the water; and the water, with the same slowness, descend through the wine, without in the least mixing together, until finally the ball would be completely full of wine, and all the water would fall to the bottom of the vessel. Now, what should one say, and what arguments should be appealed to, except that there is between water and air an incompatibility that I do not understand.[36]

So we have wine in a container below, and water in a glass ball with a small opening on it above, turned carefully into the container. This is the initial situation, and—if we can believe Galileo—the two liquids will slowly change place.

Now, the question arises in the skeptical mind: did Galileo really perform this experiment, the outcome of which he admittedly did not understand?

Alexandre Koyré, the famous Galileo scholar, has shown that many famous experiments were never performed by the Italian scientist, and this water-wine experiment was one of them. In a 1960 article, Koyré claims that the two liquids have fairly similar density, and that therefore they have to mix:

> I confess that I share Salviati's perplexity. It is, indeed, difficult to put forward an explanation of the astonishing experiment he has just

reported; particularly, because, if we repeated it exactly as described, we should see the wine rise in the glass globe (filled with water), and water fall into the vessel (full of wine); but we should not see the water and the wine simply replacing each other; we should see the formation of a mixture.

What is the conclusion? Do we have to admit that red wines of the seventeenth century had properties no longer possessed by the wines of today—properties that made them, like oil, immiscible with water? Or can we suppose that Galileo, who undoubtedly never mixed water with his wine (for wine to him was "the incarnation of the light of the sun"), had never made the experiment; but, having heard of it, reconstructed it in his imagination, accepting the complete and essential incompatibility of water with wine as an indubitable fact?—Personally, I feel that the latter supposition is the right one.[37]

While acknowledging the elegant sense of humor with which Koyré interprets Galileo's text, let me call the reader's attention to the words Koyré is using here: we *should* see the wine rise in the glass globe, and water fall into the vessel; but we *should* not see the water and the wine simply replacing each other; we *should* see the formation of a mixture. Why does Koyré use *should* instead of *did*?

Did Koyré actually perform this experiment? Or he was so strongly convinced of the negative outcome of the experiment that he believed—even without executing it—that Galileo was so strongly convinced of the positive outcome of the experiment that Galileo merely described it without performing it?

In the late summer of 1973, James MacLachlan, another Galileo scholar, filled an aftershave bottle with water and inverted it over a goblet of red wine, and for more than an hour he "watched in fascination as a perfectly clear layer of water formed at the bottom of the goblet and became deeper and deeper!"[38] (A few hours later, the two liquids finally formed a mixture.) Precisely because the experiment had such an unexpected outcome, MacLachlan believed that Galileo had indeed seen in 1638 (or somewhat earlier) what MacLachlan himself saw in 1973. Thus the experiment was not an imaginary one for Galileo, but a real one.

But is that certain?

In 1995, Peter Dear, referring to this debate in his famous book *Discipline and Experience*, modestly mentions that the water-wine experiment was widely known in the seventeenth century. Among others, the famous Giambattista della Porta included it in his popular *Natural Magick*, describing it as a practical joke for making fun of one's friends in the pub. Using a specially made cup that basically mirrors the experimental setting described above (the cup consists of an inverted cone with a narrow hole at the apex, set into a hollow glass ball), a person pours water into the ball and wine into the cone. The two liquids do not mix, because the hole between the two parts of the cup is small. He then drinks from the wine and gives the cup to his friend, who drinks and gets the water. Now, if this friend decides next time to drink first, in order to have the wine, the practical joker should keep him talking and simply wait until the two liquids slowly change place, and then give the cup to the victim, who will again drink water.[39] Dear implies that Koyré and MacLachlan, Galileo scholars who are supposed to know the basic literature read by everyone in the seventeenth century, should have known about the content of della Porta's book. Precisely because the experiment was widely known, we cannot have the slightest idea whether Galileo performed it personally or only heard about it and described it without actually executing it. In either case, it seems that the experiment was real, if not for Galileo then at least for many of his drunken contemporaries, and it could be performed in the seventeenth century just as well as it can be in our time.

Or perhaps not?

Aftershave bottle in one hand and a glass of Australian cabernet sauvignon that I was ready to consecrate on the altar of experimental science in the other, I performed the experiment, and what happened? The two liquids did not replace each other; instead, they mixed, giving birth to what we could call a wine "spritzer." Or, more precisely, what I saw was that a uniform mixture developed above in the aftershave bottle, while a somewhat lighter layer, slightly more transparent than the red wine, formed in the bottom of the vessel.

The conclusion I drew from the negative result of my own experiment was by no means that Galileo and MacLachlan were wrong in claiming that the experiment was real and that Koyré was right to doubt it. I still believe those who have argued that the experiment can yield a positive outcome, and I am convinced that the problem with my attempt lay in my methodology and the materials I used: water in Budapest is fairly hard and contains high levels of chlorine, while the red wine I chose was not some high-quality Hungarian wine but cheap imported wine already mixed with water. In other words, I applied auxiliary hypotheses in order to convince myself that my experiment was not performed competently, and that therefore its negative outcome proves nothing.

I have cited this example for several reasons.

First, it demonstrates how earlier convictions may influence perception itself. In other words, we see what our theoretical background and beliefs allow us to see, even if we are cautious, well-prepared historians of science like Alexandre Koyré. There is probably not much difference between my confidence that the water-wine experiment can work, even though I did not manage to reproduce it, and the conviction of the medieval reader of Thabit ibn Qurra that scorpions can be expelled from a city with a talisman, even if that reader did not personally manage to prove it.

Second, this example shows that even a detailed description of an experiment is insufficient in itself and does not guarantee that the very same experiment can be repeated in a slightly different age or in a slightly different place, where the materials (the wine and the water) and the apparatus are a bit different.

Finally, this case shows something that has become a commonplace in modern philosophy of science and contemporary science studies[40] but has not yet become a widespread idea for the public: there is no such a thing as a crucial experiment. Experiments seem to be crucial, that is, to provide the decisive evidence between two rival theories or to have decisively disproved a given theory, only when we look backward from a time when the decision has finally been made, for many different reasons, and when there is already a broad consensus on the meaning and the result of the given experiment. Contemporaries rarely deem experiments crucial or final; they often do not even agree on what the result of the experiment was. In all of those cases, when we think that an experiment was crucial and that it decisively falsified a given theory, we can see that many contemporaries actually kept believing in the old theory and did not see the experiment as decisive. They often argued that the experiment produced the unfavorable result only because it was performed incompetently.

To conclude, I believe not only that the initial question (i.e., why theories persist even when experiments do not confirm them or even disprove them) is a legitimate inquiry for the history of magic, but also that it is equally legitimate in the history of science. The answers we can give to it are no less complex in the territory where we tend to believe that experiments actually have true and testable results.

NOTES

My research was supported by two Hungarian grants, the OTKA K 101544 and the Bolyai János Postdoctoral Fellowship. I would like to thank the anonymous readers of my article and the editors of this volume for their constructive remarks.

1. For the experiments of the *Liber aggregationis*, see Isabelle Draelants, *Le liber de virtutibus herbarum lapidum et animalium* (*Liber aggregationis*) (Florence: Sismel, 2007).

2. Thérèse Charmasson, *Recherches sur une technique divinatoire: La geomancie dans l'Occident medieval* (Geneva: Librarie Droz, 1980), 63–64. See also Charmasson, "Les premiers traites latins de geomancie," *Cahiers de Civilisation Medievale* 21 (1978): 121–36.

3. For an edited version of the text, see Francis J. Carmody, ed., *The Astronomical Works of Thabit b. Qurra* (Berkeley: University of California Press, 1960), 180–94.

4. Nicolas Weill-Parot, Les "images astrologiques" au Moyen Âge et à la Renaissance: Speculations intellectuelles et pratiques magiques (XIIe–XVe siècle) (Paris: Honoré Champion, 2002), 605; and Jean-Patrice Boudet, Le "Recueil des plus célèbres astrologues" de Simon de Phares édité pour la Société de l'Histoire de France, 2 vols. (Paris: Champion, 1997–99), 2:257.

5. For the "social history of magic," see, among others, Richard Kieckhefer, Magic in the Middle Ages (Cambridge: Cambridge University Press, 1989); Kieckhefer, Forbidden Rites: A Necromancer's Manual of the Fifteenth Century (Stroud: Sutton, 1997); Jean-Patrice Boudet, Entre science et "nigromance": Astrologie, divination et magie dans l'Occident médiéval (XIIe–XVe siècle) (Paris: Publications de la Sorbonne, 2006); and Benedek Láng, Unlocked Books: Manuscripts of Learned Magic in the Medieval Libraries of Central Europe (University Park: Pennsylvania State University Press, 2008).

6. My earlier attempt to answer this question can be found in my monograph Unlocked Books, 270–72. As the present article is a further elaboration on the same question, I have occasionally incorporated ideas from that monograph.

7. Karl Popper, Conjectures and Refutations: The Growth of Scientific Knowledge (London: Routledge & Kegan Paul, 1963), 37.

8. Ibid.

9. Imre Lakatos, "Falsification and the Methodology of Scientific Research Programmes," in Criticism and the Growth of Knowledge, ed. Imre Lakatos and Alan Musgrave (Cambridge: Cambridge University Press, 1970), 91–196.

10. Larry Laudan, "The Demise of the Demarcation Problem," in Physics, Philosophy, and Psychoanalysis: Essays in Honor of Adolf Grünbaum, ed. R. S. Cohen and Larry Laudan (Dordrecht: D. Reidel, 1983), 111–27.

11. Pierre Duhem, La théorie physique, son objet et sa structure (Paris: Chevalier & Rivière, 1906); see the English translation of the second, 1914 edition, The Aim and Structure of Physical Theory (Princeton: Princeton University Press, 1954).

12. On Whiggism, anti-Whiggism, and anti-anti-Whiggism, see Helge S. Kragh, An Introduction to the Historiography of Science (Cambridge: Cambridge University Press, 1989), 93–94; and Thomas Nickles, "Philosophy of Science and History of Science," and Stephen G. Brush, "Scientists as Historians," both in "Constructing Knowledge in the History of Science," ed. Arnold Thackray, special issue, Osiris, 2nd ser., 10 (1995): 139–63 and 214–31, respectively.

13. Lynn Thorndike, A History of Magic and Experimental Science, vol. 4 (New York: Macmillan, 1934), 612. To be fair, we should also quote Thorndike's final paragraph from the same chapter: "Frankly, it is not for this contribution towards modernity that we most prize these writings of two remote centuries which we have been at some pains to decipher and to set forth. We have taken them as we have found them and we esteem them for what they are in their totality, their fourteenth and their fifteenth century complexio—a chapter in the history of human thought. Read it and smile or read it and weep, as you please. We would not credit it with the least particle of modern science that does not belong to it, nor would we deprive it of any of that magic which constitutes in no small measure its peculiar charm. Perhaps it would be well to read it and think of what the future historian may say of the mentality and scholasticism of the present era and with what sympathy or antipathy he would be justified in regarding us" (615).

14. Karin Figala, "Newtons rationale System der Alchemie," Chemie in Unserer Zeit 12 (1978): 101–10.

15. Frances Yates, "The Hermetic Tradition in Renaissance Science," in Art, Science, and History in the Renaissance, ed. Charles S. Singleton (Baltimore: Johns Hopkins University Press, 1968), 255–74; Floris Cohen, The Scientific Revolution: A Historiographical Inquiry (Chicago: University of Chicago Press, 1994), 286–96; Wouter Hanegraaff, "Beyond the Yates Paradigm: The Study of Western Esotericism Between Counterculture and New Complexity," Aries: Journal for the Study of Western Esotericism 1, no. 1 (2001): 5–37; and Randall Styers,

Making Magic: Religion, Magic, and Science in the Modern World (New York: Oxford University Press, 2004), 152–63.

16. Thomas Kuhn, "The History of Science" *International Encyclopedia of the Social Sciences*, vol. 14, ed. David L. Sills and Robert K. Merton (New York: Macmillan, 1968), 76.

17. Stuart Clark, "One-Tier History," *Magic, Ritual, and Witchcraft* 5, no. 1 (2010): 84–91 (emphasis in original).

18. See, for example, Nickles, "Philosophy of Science"; and Brush, "Scientists as Historians."

19. Kragh, *Historiography of Science*, 104.

20. Edward Bever, *The Realities of Witchcraft and Popular Magic in Early Modern Europe: Culture, Cognition, and Everyday Life* (Basingstoke: Palgrave Macmillan, 2008), xiv. In fact, the objective of Bever's project is to answer three interrelated questions: "First, to what extent did people really engage in and experience the things contained in the beliefs? Second, to what extent did their activities have real effects, and their perceptions reflect objective events? Third, to the extent that their perceptions did not reflect external reality, what were the actual sources and nature of these subjective experiences?" Ibid.

21. With the last qualifications, I hope to avoid some problematic issues related to the use of "reality" discussed in the fascinating debate about Bever's monograph in *Magic, Ritual, and Witchcraft* 5, no. 1 (2010): 81–121.

22. Compare the central question of Jonathan Z. Smith's "I Am a Parrot," *History of Religions* 11, no. 4 (1972): 391–413, particularly 393: "How should the historian of religion interpret a religious statement which is apparently contrary to fact?"

23. Frank M. Turner, "Rainfall, Plagues, and the Prince of Wales: A Chapter in the Conflict of Religion and Science," *Journal of British Studies* 13 (1974): 46–95, particularly 64, quoted in Thomas F. Gieryn, "Boundary-Work and the Demarcation of Science from Non-Science: Strains and Interests in Professional Ideologies of Scientists," *American Sociological Review* 48 (1983): 781–95.

24. Similar experiments on the efficacy of forms of "distant healing" (prayer, mental healing, therapeutic touch, or spiritual healing) have been conducted recently. See John Astin et al., "The Efficacy of 'Distant Healing': A Systematic Review of Randomized Trials," *Annals of Internal Medicine* 132 (2000): 908–10. I thank Edward Bever for calling my attention to this article.

25. See Láng, *Unlocked Books*, chap. 2.

26. On the modern history of the word *experience*, see Peter Dear, *Discipline and Experience: The Mathematical Way in the Scientific Revolution* (Chicago: University of Chicago Press, 1995), particularly 11–25.

27. For the fifteenth-century chancellor of the University of Paris, Jean Gerson, "*experientia docuit*" the existence of demons. See Gerson, *Opera omnia*, "Trilogium," 21, propositio: "Oppositum posuerunt qui negaverunt daemones esse . . . fuerunt etiam experientiae multae in oppositum." On Gerson's use of "experiments" and "experience," see Benedek Láng, "Experience in the Anti-Astrological Arguments of Jean Gerson," in *Expertus sum: L'expérience par les sens dans la philosophie naturelle médiévale, Actes du colloque international de Pont-à-Mousson, 5–7 février 2009*, ed. Thomas Bénatouil and Isabelle Draelants (Florence: Edizioni del Galluzzo—Sismel, 2010), 309–21.

28. I borrow this characterization from Isabelle Draelants's paper "The *Liber aggregationis (Experimenta/Secreta)*: Another Link Between Albert the Great and Arnoldus Saxo?," given at the Warburg Institute, May 1, 2002.

29. Daryn Lehoux, "Tropes, Facts, and Empiricism," *Perspectives on Science* 11 (2003): 326–44.

30. Such medieval and early modern objects are shown in great number in Liselotte Hansmann and Lenz Kriss-Rettenbeck, eds., *Amulett und Talisman: Erscheinungsform und Geschichte* (Munich: Verlag Georg D. W. Callwey, 1966). For textual amulets, see Don C.

Skemer, *Binding Words: Textual Amulets in the Middle Ages* (University Park: Pennsylvania State University Press, 2006).

31. For the stories, see Charles Burnett, "Thābit ibn Qurra the Harrānian on Talismans and the Spirits of the Planets," *La Corónica* 36 (2007): 13–40; Boudet, *"Recueil des plus célèbres astrologues,"* 2:257; and Weill-Parot, *"Images astrologiques" au Moyen Âge*, 897–900.

32. The issue of replicability is not without problems in the modern "hard sciences" either. See the discussion in specific articles in the journal *Nature* highlighting failures in the reproducibility of laboratory research results, accessed May 5, 2016, http://www.nature.com/nature/focus/reproducibility/index.html.

33. Charles Burnett, "Remarques paléographiques et philologiques sur les noms d'anges et d'esprits dans les traités de magie traduits de l'arabe en Latin," *Mélanges de l'École Française de Rome* 114 (2002): 657–68.

34. Láng, *Unlocked Books*, 83–94.

35. Láng, "Anti-Astrological Arguments of Jean Gerson."

36. Quoted in James MacLachlan, "A Test of an 'Imaginary' Experiment of Galileo's," *Isis* 64 (1973): 375.

37. Alexandre Koyré, *Metaphysics and Measurement: Essays in Scientific Revolution* (Cambridge: Harvard University Press, 1968), 84, quoted in ibid., 376.

38. Ibid.

39. Dear, *Discipline and Experience*, 144–47.

40. See, for example, Harry Collins and Trevor Pinch, eds., *The Golem: What You Should Know About Science* (Cambridge: Cambridge University Press, 1998). See also Kragh, *Historiography of Science*, chap. 14.

4

WITCHES AS LIARS:
WITCHCRAFT AND CIVILIZATION IN THE EARLY
AMERICAN REPUBLIC

Adam Jortner

Andrew Oehler had been a carpenter in Switzerland, a vagabond in New Orleans, a soldier in Napoleonic France, and a balloonist in Havana, but he outdid himself in 1806 in Mexico City. Invited by the governor to present an evening's entertainment, he dressed a suite of rooms in black, drew down thunder and lightning, and "converse[d] with a departed spirit"—all via sleight of hand, as he explained in his mawkish autobiography, *The Life, Adventures, and Unparalleled Sufferings of Andrew Oehler*. For his trouble, the authorities threw Oehler into prison for witchcraft and trafficking with demons. His hosts, Oehler wrote, "could not but believe I must be assisted by supernatural agency," given that Mexicans were "Ignorant of philosophy and the powers of nature" and believed "these appearances to be real and substantial facts" that they looked upon "with a mixture of jealousy and admiration, as though it had been something supernatural." An enlightened Spanish marquis secured Oehler's release. With remorse, the governor offered Oehler Mexican citizenship, but Oehler hesitated to "take the oath of allegiance to the superstitious laws, and I suppose religion too, of the country." He returned to the United States, where he was promptly robbed and forced to flee naked across an open swamp.[1]

Oehler's book has him not only imprisoned in Mexico but accused of murder in Frankfort, shipwrecked off the coast of China, battling lions on a tropical island, and commanding a legion of rebellious slaves alongside Toussaint L'Overture in Haiti. Sadly, if Oehler's "governor" of Mexico was in fact the Spanish viceroy, his description of the man bears no resemblance to any of the men who held the office in 1807 or 1808, when Oehler claims the incident occurred. Moreover, Oehler's description of his stage magic repeats almost verbatim the account of a more successful and better-known magician—the phantasmagorist Robertson (Étienne Gaspard-Robert), who *did* perform in

Mexico City, in 1798, and was *not* thrown in prison. Oehler's unparalleled sufferings were fictional.[2]

Oehler went to some trouble to catalogue the events and fads of a nineteenth-
century world at war: Bonaparte, Egypt, ballooning, the Haitian revolution. But
the *Sufferings* perhaps came closest to describing the Jeffersonian world when
Oehler alluded to the interaction between superstition and politics. In 1812, a
year after Oehler's autobiography was published, the newly minted congress-
man from South Carolina, John C. Calhoun, debated the venerable John Randolph of Virginia on the question of whether the recent New Madrid earthquakes
portended peace or war. Randolph informed his colleague that the quakes
proved "we are on the brink of some dreadful scourge—some great desolation—
some awful visitation from that Power whom, I am afraid, we have as yet, in our
national capacity, taken no means to conciliate." Calhoun's response was swift
and bitter: "I did hope that the age of superstition was past, and that no attempt
would be made to influence the measures of Government, which ought to be
founded in wisdom and policy, by the vague, I may say superstitious, feelings of
any man, whatever may be the physical appearances which give rise to them. . . .
It would mark a fearful retrograde in civilization; it would prove a dreadful
declension toward barbarism."[3]

Taken together, Calhoun and Oehler outlined an interpretation of witchcraft and magic that striated the world of the American Republic in the early
nineteenth century. There was a coherent, well-articulated body of thought on
witchcraft in the early American Republic, running through sermons, tracts,
lectures, plays, novels, speeches, advertisements, and manuals for stage magic.
Even if this interpretation rarely came in the form of a fully articulated theory,
it nevertheless aided the creation of the social and political structures of the
Jeffersonian and Jacksonian United States. It was perhaps less an ideology or a
system of thought than a discourse on magic—which in turn was connected
to the evolving revolutionary assumptions about nature, senses, liberty, the
nation, God. This theory of magic joined religious and intellectual problems of
epistemology to the social and political anxieties arising from the terrifying
implications of democratization.

Neither Calhoun nor Oehler fully explained their anti-magic logic, but they
did not need to: one does not explain what one expects an audience to understand. Some general features, however, are worth noting. Both the magician
and the politician believed that magic and the supernatural were entirely false
and that magic (*not* faith) was the antithesis of reason. And since reason was
the basis of free government, magic and the supernatural could have no place
in the decisions of the Republic (thus Calhoun's complaint and Oehler's refusal
to remain in Mexico). Finally, and perhaps most significantly, both Oehler and

Calhoun employed their arguments about witchcraft as part of a larger program of invective and ridicule. The charge of belief in the supernatural was not
simply a mild corrective; it was an assault on the moral and intellectual fiber of
one's opponent. Calhoun and Oehler did not believe, and they did not expect
any reasonable republican to believe, in magic, divination, or the supernatural
activities of higher beings in the earthly realm. Belief in magic, witches, or any
kind of supernatural interference in worldly affairs belonged to foreigners and
slaves, Catholics and tyrants; to believe in such things would tear the nation
from the sacred place of liberty down through the stages of civilized development to a state of monarchy or theocracy.[4]

Nor was such language mere rhetoric; the supernatural had a rude habit of
intruding on the democratic process. In 1787, while the delegates to the Constitutional Convention gathered, a mob on the streets of Philadelphia lynched a
woman on suspicion of witchcraft.[5] In 1809, Maryland's Jeffersonian governor
saw his career terminated in part owing to his participation in a court case that
had accepted the testimony of a ghost.[6] An 1838 Election Day riot against the
Mormons began when a local tough accused them of believing in supernatural
rituals such as "healing the sick by laying on of hands, speaking in tongues,
and casting out devils."[7] Violence against Shakers, Mormons, and Native
Americans was frequently justified by the claims that their leaders were magicians and imposters, gathering credulous citizens under their banners to
overthrow the duly elected authorities. In 1807, the American frontier official
Frederick Bates worried about the growing power of a witch-hunting Shawnee
"impostor" named Tenskwatawa, whom Bates derisively called "His Divinity-
ship" and whose "Apotheosis" was intended to make him the ruler "from Dan
to Beersheba, from the Lakes to the Missouri."[8]

Thus inquiry into the nature of magic and witchcraft was not incidental to
the politics of the early Republic; such inquiry was essential to the Jeffersonian
and Jacksonian confrontation with the problems of freedom and tyranny,
savagery and civilization. As Owen Davies has pointed out concerning Britain,
questions about witchcraft, magic, curses, and the supernatural lingered long
after Anglophone governments decriminalized witchcraft. Witch hunts
declined, but concerns about witchcraft and magic continued—perhaps in a
form more appropriate to democracy.[9] Indeed, American states issued new
laws against those who *claimed* to practice magic, as for example in New
Hampshire, where "*pretended* knowledge of magic, palmistry, conjuration,
&c." was a crime. Similar laws existed in Connecticut, Massachusetts, and
Maryland, while in New York such a crime could bring sixty days of hard
labor.[10] After all, as the Congregationalist divine Joseph Lathrop explained,
"Hearkening to diviners tends, not only to destroy religion, but to dissolve our

mutual confidence and subvert our social security. . . . On social, therefore, as well as on religious principles, these diviners ought to be prosecuted rather than encouraged—to be punished rather than patronized."[11] This, in a nutshell, was the early Republic's witchcraft problem.

The historical study of witchcraft and magic is in large measure the study of *ideas about* witchcraft and their social, political, and religious ramifications. (Undergraduates in witchcraft courses are often saddened to hear this.)[12] Stuart Clark writes that the focus of the historian should not be the "referential truth or falsity" of beliefs in the supernatural, "other than as, themselves, subjects of debate" in a particular time and place.[13] Virtually all civilizations have had notions about magical powers, even cultures in which a broad consensus prevailed that such powers were always, or nearly always, false. Despite the relative lack of witch trials in the early American Republic, there was still a witchcraft problem.[14] Early American debates over witchcraft denied the power of supernatural forces, attributing reports of such powers to the natural world or to epistemological error. In the early American Republic, the answer to the question of what witches could do was straightforward: nothing. Witches were imaginary, *maleficium* illusory.[15]

That was the trouble. Witches had no magical powers, yet people acted as though they did. If there was no longer a "shared assumption at all levels of society that powers existed beyond everyday physical powers," as Diarmaid MacCulloch describes the world of the Reformation, the very fact that this belief was no longer *shared* troubled the minds of some in the early Republic. If people still believed in magic and witches, the argument went, then they were mistaken. If they were mistaken, they could be tricked into acting against their own self-interest. If people acted against their own self-interest, the polity was doomed.[16]

The evil of witches therefore came from the harm they inflicted through belief; the power of delusion was no vanishing nightmare under a republican order. "There is power in a popular delusion and general excitement of the passions of a community to pervert the best of characters," wrote Charles Upham in his history of the Salem witchcraft trials; it would "turn the hearts even of good men to violence."[17] William Pinchbeck wanted "to oppose the idea of supernatural agency in any production of man," at least after his own money-making hoaxes were finished. Pinchbeck wrote a book explaining "how dangerous such a belief [in the supernatural] is to society, how destructive to the improvement of the human capacity, and how totally ruinous to the common interests of mankind." To Pinchbeck's mind, each of his astute readers, on learning of the threat of superstition, would seek to "reclaim the obstinate believers in ghosts."[18] Upham had a similar civic purpose three decades later. His *Lectures on Witchcraft* assumed that a citizen who understood how fears of witchcraft had subjugated reason in 1692 would inevitably "do what he may to enlighten, rectify, and control public sentiment . . . to accelerate the decay of superstition, to prevent an unrestrained exercise of imagination."[19]

The historiography of witches and witchcraft provides numerous studies of the ways in which societies perceive "the other" or "otherness." While the explanatory power of these terms is easily overstated, the idea of witches as a society's "other" can be useful if employed in conjunction with other methods of analysis. By epitomizing abnormality, witches as "others" establish parameters for acceptable behavior. This definitional process is often thought by historians to operate at a broadly social or psychic plane, crafting personal affectations and taboos, but it could also function in concrete ways. Stuart Clark has explained how the particular conception of witches as others in early modern Europe lent credence to developing theories of divine right and absolutist monarchies. By ridding the countryside of witches—and by proving resistant to their magic—monarchs showed themselves and their reign to be of God. As Clark writes, "successful dispossession validated the authority in whose name it was made, thus making [political] propaganda not a corruption of valid exorcism but one of its necessary presuppositions." The "wild disorders" of demoniacs were therefore in some senses political.[20]

Citizens of the American commonwealth, however, were more likely to hear a warning against the way in which superstitious fears would alter election outcomes, as seen in this bit of early republican doggerel:

How often I have seen fanatic zeal,
Where superstition rules the public weal
Call a town meeting, and request a vote;
To send for a young candidate in haste,
To have him come forthwith and peddle out
Brimstone, and fire, and supernatural war.[21]

American concerns about superstition and the public mind mirrored developments across the Atlantic. Though scholars disagree on when, how, and to what extent European witchcraft beliefs dissipated, it seems clear that belief in and fear of witchcraft had a significantly reduced public and legal role by the eighteenth century. Enlightenment philosophes and writers took the opportunity to kick them when they were down. Sometimes alongside and sometimes in the wake of the legal end of witch trials, Enlightenment writers condemned witchcraft and witch beliefs as relics of medieval barbarism that they sought to sweep away. Voltaire called witchcraft the "errors of ancient charlatans who judged without reasoning, and who, being deceived, deceived others." Ignorance bred slavish control, which, Voltaire complained, had facilitated the dominance of the Catholic Church. In Scotland, David Hume sighed that in former days "men utterly lost sight of reason" when they enforced witchcraft laws "founded altogether upon ignorance and terror." Enlightenment thinkers did not themselves end the witch trials, but they did seize upon the stories of witchcraft—both in former days and in their own time—as efforts by conniving politicians and crafty churchmen to exercise control over ignorant masses. Such a campaign fit quite well, of course, with the broader efforts of certain Enlightenment thinkers to limit the powers of the church generally.[22]

Thus, when John Greenleaf Whittier informed his readers of "that stern duty which the true man owes to his generation, to expose error" of "Superstition [which] in one form or another still has such a hold on the common mind," he was not engaging in an exclusively American project.[23] Nevertheless, Americans often believed they had embarked on a unique quest; Upham's 1831 *Lectures on Witchcraft* claimed that "the doctrines of demonology have been completely overthrown and exterminated in *our* villages," but "in many places the auspicious event remains to take place." He followed this assertion with cautionary tales of nineteenth-century witch lynchings in Great Britain.[24] Frederick Quitman's 1810 treatise circled the globe to document dirty barbarian magical practices: the Chinese "offer sacrifices to Satan," Jews followed a divine name found "in a bunghole," Muslims wore talismans. American writers often assured Americans of their country's precocious rationality compared to other nations but warned readers not to be complacent: although "the inhabitants of the United States of America are often styled in public print, the most enlightened nation on earth," Quitman wrote, "magic of the coarsest kind has not entirely discontinued among us." Thus the campaign against magic would have to continue.[25]

One theater of that campaign was the incipient American literary establishment. Fiction—especially popular fiction—both creates and reflects the culture in which it is produced. Philip Gould and Gretchen Adams have described how early national writers used Salem as a metaphor, as for example in the Unitarian-Congregationalist debate, or as a way for secessionist-minded southerners to tar northern education.[26] Yet the rhetoric and explanations of magic were not merely a metaphor. They not only explained politics; they explained and defined *magic* to the first generations of U.S. citizens. While these writings did not represent any uniform notion "commonly held" by those in the early Republic, they did represent *a* conception of magic. Popular literature and plays do not reveal to historians *precisely* what people thought about witchcraft, but they do reveal thoughts about witchcraft. As James Sharpe writes about *Macbeth*, "even in plays where witchcraft and magic were not central themes, the language of the occult, of astrology, even of alchemy is frequently to be found. This is not to say that playwrights or their audiences were obsessed with magic," but rather "that their audience would be familiar with such issues and at least some of the discourse surrounding them," particularly when "the play-wrights of the period were for the most part professionals, aiming to meet current tastes and reflect rather than lead opinion."[27]

Theater's importance had not diminished in the years between the estab-lishment of Shakespeare's Globe and Joseph Jefferson's Astor Place. Theater expanded in the early Republic; demand for plays was so high that in 1793 a well-organized public outcry in Massachusetts forced revocation of the state's traditional ban on theaters.[28] The increased wealth of the colonies made theat-rical performances a luxury good that more and more people could afford, and this shift made the stage an important site of American self-definition.[29] The newly independent audiences clamored for American plays, and theater man-agers and playwrights took up the challenge.

What, then, did the American theater of the early Republic assume its audi-ences would understand about magic? When the subject came up, playwrights expected their American audiences to understand that belief in magic, encour-aged by charlatans and enforced by the mob, handed power to tyrants. *The Tragedy of Superstition* features a nameless Puritan village (standing in for Salem) in thrall to its minister, Ravensworth. When the public clamors for witch trials, Ravensworth obliges, despite the warning that

> If reason in a mind like yours . . . can bow down
> Before the popular breath, what shall protect
> From the all-with'ring blasts of superstition
> The unthinking crowd, in whom credulity,
> Is ever the first born of ignorance?

Nothing, of course, can save the crowd from itself, since

> . . . such folly,
> When it infects the crowd, is dangerous.
> Already we've had proof what dreadful acts
> Their madness may commit, and each new day
> The frenzy spreads.[30]

In 1797, audiences in Philadelphia and Baltimore were treated to the adventures of Sir Credulous Testy in *The Comet*; the dashing Belmont tricks the aptly named Credulous in order to marry the old man's ward, the lovely Emily. Belmont and Lady Candour team up to use an "electrical jar" and phosphorus to stage a faux Armageddon for Credulous, and "while his senses are bewilder'd ... he will imagine a thousand horrours, and may perhaps give his consent to your union." The tricksters succeed, and Emily is liberated from her superstitious guardian, "whose preposterous ignorance, joined to his extreme tyranny, render[ed] the pangs of separation from Belmont doubly poignant."[31] A similar ending resolved the 1820 production of *The Magician and the Holy Alliance*, poking fun at contemporary New England's sea serpent sightings; at the play's climax, "A Huge Black Snake supposed to be the grand papa of the '*Sea Serpent*' lately seen in the east" swallows the nefarious magician Katterfelto, and the audience is told that "in the end, we always see ... TRUTH triumphs over hypocrisy."[32]

The theater featured more than plays. Traveling exhibitions made similar claims. As we have seen, William Pinchbeck made a career of displaying astounding marvels and then made a second career of exposing them. He toured the early United States with the famed "Pig of Knowledge," which could respond to certain questions by picking correct answers out of a hat. (There were reports of several "Pigs of Knowledge" and at least one "Goat of Knowledge.")[33] Perhaps distressed that several observers thought the pig bewitched, Pinchbeck turned in the 1800s to exposing miraculous contraptions, the most famous of which was the "Acoustic Temple" displayed in Boston in 1804—the point of which, one broadside declared, was to make citizens "Attend, and never after give credit to the improbable tales of Witchcraft and Supernatural Agency!"[34]

The nonfiction of the early Republic sounded alarms similar to the warnings of its fictional counterparts. The stories of witchcraft and ghosts in the early Republic went to great lengths to assure readers that such things did not exist and that anyone who thought otherwise was foolish at best and dangerous at worst. In his volume on magic, Quitman detailed his battle with a stone-throwing spirit; he simply corralled the children he felt were responsible, and the spirit ceased. The people, however, "took the shortest and easiest way, and attributed it to witchcraft," he wrote. "In this persuasion, they sent to a famous conjuror from the west side of the river; but the demons equally superstitious, and fearing the magical staff of the conjuror, departed before his arrival."[35] A year after the witch lynching near the Constitutional Convention, Philadelphia's Temple Patrick Society published its debates on the reality of witchcraft;

the argument in the negative exclaimed that a "magic picture or a magic lantern . . . could yet deceive thousands, and in the hands of adepts, might be managed . . . to revive the faith and superior power of magicians and witches at this day." That in turn would result in "priests and priestcraft," with all the revolutionary associations of Roman Catholicism and priest-craft with falsehood and tyranny.[36] A collection of ghost stories appeared with the revealing (if lengthy) title *Ghost Stories Collected with a Particular View to Counteract the Vulgar Belief in Ghosts and Apparitions and to Promote a Rational Estimate of the Nature or Phenomena Commonly Considered as Supernatural.* The introduction to this collection assured readers that in ancient days, "The vulgar were afraid of spirits, and wiser heads left them under the influence of that apprehension, which they sometimes employed for good, at others for sinister purposes."[37]

History, in fact, was full of charlatans. One of the great benefits of early republican analyses of magicians was how readily they explained historical as well as contemporary tyrannies. King Saul, for example, had been misled by the phantasmagoria of the Witch of Endor. "She was probably possessed of some secret knowledge of natural properties," Charles Upham explained, and "had perhaps the peculiar powers of a ventriloquist, and by successful imposture, had acquired an uncommon degree of notoriety and the entire confidence of the public."[38] Upham, Lathrop, and Quitman all offered exegeses of 1 Samuel 28 and found in the passage the evidence of the witch's theatrical tricks. The theologians disagreed as to the details, but they all followed Lathrop's general line regarding the tendency of supernatural claims to "dissolve our mutual confidence and subvert our social security."

Then as now, however, the preeminent example of American witchcraft was Salem, Massachusetts, and in the early Republic Salem offered a morality tale of credulity run wild. The witchcraft trials had long served as a warning to the colonials; immediately after the proceedings closed, Cotton Mather and John Hale wrote books declaring that the devil had been in Salem (though the two men disagreed on Satan's tactics). Robert Calef thought the devil had stirred up Puritan imagination to create a delusion, and then "Witchcraft became a Principal Ecclesiastical Engine (as also that of Heresie was) to root up all that stood in their way."[39] Eighteenth-century histories leaned toward Calef, but they found the fault less in the devil than in a political leadership that succumbed to clerical demands.[40] These works indicted the courts and the laws of the land for their failure to protect the innocent. Thomas Hutchinson, in his 1767 account, had no doubt that some of the women who confessed had "persuaded themselves they were witches," but he felt that on the whole the crisis was prompted by "a scene of fraud and imposture, began [*sic*] by young girls . . . continued by adult persons, who were afraid of being accused themselves."[41] The problem was not the accusations but the shoddy law of the court of oyer and terminer, the use of decades-old accusations, and the acceptance of spectral evidence.[42]

Beginning with William Bentley's 1799 "History of Salem," however, the fault no longer lay with the judges who listened to the people but with the people themselves. "Witchcraft," Bentley wrote, "soon proved itself to be an evil to be corrected in the public opinion, and not in a court of justice." The "terror of the imagination was so great" that people confessed, especially under threat to their life, and "confessions blinded the judges." But the blame, in Bentley's view, still went to "the public clamours" that "urged [the judges] on, and the novelty of the calamity deprived them of all ability to investigate its true causes, till nineteen innocent persons were victims of the public credulity."[43] So the story of Salem became the story of a superstitious public overrunning the established law of the community. Hannah Adams's 1806 *Abridgement of the History of New-England: For the Use of Young Persons* lamented the execution of nineteen people, but "even this circumstance was insufficient to open the eyes of the people," who presumably could have stopped the trials had they wanted to. Yet "the prevailing credulity of the age" prevented them.[44]

Charles Upham's 1831 *Lectures on Witchcraft* was the early Republic's most extensive scholarly treatment of the trials; at the same time, Upham stitched together many of the elements of the early republican critique of witchcraft.[45] Upham began with the falseness of witchcraft: "it is, at present, the universal opinion that the whole of this witchcraft transaction was a delusion, having no foundation whatever but in the imaginations and passions." Imagination triumphed over reason, courts credited the accusations, and the result was predictable: "whenever a community gives way to its passions . . . and casts off the restraints of reason, there is a delusion that can hardly be described in any other phrase."[46]

For Upham, this state of affairs created the opening for an unscrupulous and conniving politician to seize control of the state; Upham cast Cotton Mather in this role. Mather's plan had been to incite a witchcraft panic "in order that he might increase his own influence over an infatuated people, by being regarded by them as mighty to cast out and vanquish evil spirits." Mather "combined an almost incredible amount of vanity and credulity, with a high degree of cunning and policy; an inordinate love of temporal power and distinction, with every outward manifestation of piety and Christian humility; and a proneness to fanaticism and superstition with amazing acquisitions of knowledge." The people of Salem, their imagination run wild, became captives of Mather's controlling interest. Upham clarified the allusion to the developing party politics of his own day, writing that Mather, "like other ambitious and grasping politicians . . . was eager to have the support of all parties at the same time." Nor was politics the only danger: "the clergy were also instrumental in promoting the proceedings. Nay, it must be acknowledged that they took the lead in the whole transaction." Where credulity ruled the public, priest-craft and politicians thrived.[47]

In this way, Upham constructed an argument not only about Salem but also about the United States in the Jacksonian era. Credulity, enticed by superstition, opened the door to slavishness and tyranny. This formulation of magical powers was compatible with the Federalist-Whig tendencies of several of its main proponents—Upham, Morse, Whittier, and Bentley. Upham warned against "the excesses of popular feeling . . . a power which thus seizes all that it can reach . . . sweeps them round and round like the Maelstroom [sic]."[48] Quitman insisted that "those, who are appointed guardians and teachers of the people" had a duty "to deliver those that were entrusted to my care, from the shameful yoke of superstition, and to help them to the enjoyment of rational liberty."[49] Francis Wayland wrote that when the people's "decisions become the dictates of passion and venality, rather than of reason and of right . . . that moment are our liberties at an end."[50]

Thus exposing magic was in an important sense a republican activity.[51] Indeed, early exposés of magic in the early Republic—those of Pinchbeck and famed showman P. T. Barnum, most prominently—claimed to be working in the public interest by exposing the subterfuge behind stage magic. But there was also a broad stock-in-trade in books and pamphlets explaining tricks that could be done at home by amateur performers—and these instruction manuals came with a heavy dose of warning and opprobrium. *The Art of Conjuring Made Easy* taught its readers how "to make a room seem all on fire," but insisted that practitioners "have a care there be no women with child in the room, for *you yourself would be frightened, if you did not know the trick*."[52] *Parlour Magic* of 1838 explained that magic tricks should be attempted only to edify the public; "the principal objects of the following little Work" were to show how "to furnish the ingenious youth with the means of relieving the tediousness of a long winter's or wet summer's evening—to enable him to provide for a party of juvenile friends, *instructive as well as recreative entertainment*."[53] The anonymous author of *Ventriloquism Explained* (1834) hoped that "by calling the attention of youth to the subject, to diffuse some information respecting jugglery [i.e., sorcery] among those, who, while too much enlightened to practice it, have not been sufficiently enlightened, in many instances, to avoid being deceived."[54]

Professional stage magicians also advertised their shows as educational and as a source of improvement; in one case, the "Amazing Ranni" beckoned spectators to attend—for their own civic good, of course,

> INGENUITIES which he means to lay open to his audience, so that they will be able to exhibit the same for their own amusement, and what had too long passed in the world for *Magic, Necromancy,* or some other Occult Science, but which is in reality no more than the effect of a certain agility in the practice, which, when properly examined, may prove a useful lesson to the unexperienced, by warning them of the dangers to which they might be exposed thro' the arts of unprincipled men who would apply such means to corrupt their morals, warp the understanding, & in the end lay snares for their property.[55]

Unlike earlier magic guides, which tended to be a hodgepodge of general household advice, early national magic marketed itself as a republican venture. Magic shows, magicians insisted, offered the best education about magic and liberty.[56]

The American republican case against magic fashioned itself as wisdom versus ignorance, but there was more to it than that. Ideas usually make claims to intrinsic merit or "better logic" (whatever that might mean), but their appeal and success, or lack thereof, are often tied to larger cultural shifts and values.[57] The republican case against witchcraft was no different. There were in its tenets and judgments numerous notions that fit well with the broad Atlantic Anglophone culture of the eighteenth century, and especially with the postrevolutionary ethos of the developing American state.

The particular cultural values enshrined in this anti-magic thesis were also those of the developing natural philosophical societies. Natural philosophy of the eighteenth century became associated with gentility, refinement, and masculinity. The practice of natural philosophy prided itself on its rationality, but it also described and promoted itself as a civilized, male way of thinking. That promotion also depended on associating other ways of thinking with nonpersons in republican society: women, children, and "savages," that is, the disenfranchised of American democracy. Alongside, and possibly even stronger than, any academic argument came the denunciation of belief in witchcraft and superstition as vulgar, the province of lower classes, primitive peoples, and women. Bentley knew where to lay the blame when he explained how the people of Salem lost their heads; they spent too much time listening to people who were not white men: "Children, below twelve years of age, obtained a hearing before magistrates. Indians came and related their own knowledge of invisible beings. Tender females told of every fright, but not one man of reputation ventured to offer a single report."[58]

Whatever the other nuances of their position, writers who opposed witchcraft as superstition all agreed that women were particularly susceptible to superstitious beliefs, and urged men, therefore, to guard against its pernicious influences. The Temple Patrick debates explained that "if the male nature had been as subject to nervous weakness, or spasmodic affectations, as the female," then men too would have been seized as witches "in primitive times."[59] Hannah More's *Tawny Rachel* (U.S. editions 1800 and 1807) warned "young men and maidens not to have anything to say to CHEATS, IMPOSTERS, CUNNING WOMEN, FORTUNE TELLERS." More explained the reason: "God never reveals to weak and wicked women those secret designs of his providence."[60] William Lloyd Garrison's weekly newspaper the *Liberator* praised Wendell Phillips's 1838 lecture on witchcraft for the "manly and dignified ridicule" it heaped upon "that silly notion, which credits the existence of ghosts and demons."[61] David Reese exposed the "humbugs of New York" in 1838, and particularly bemoaned the influence of humbugs on women, "intoxicating the 'weak sisters and female brethren' whose intellectual imbecility renders them an easy prey to delusion."[62]

In particular, old women were often singled out as troublemakers; the crone figure shifted easily from a confederate of the devil to a teller of pernicious stories that ruined the mind. Whittier abhorred "the evil of impressing the young mind with belief, unwarranted by reason or revelation, tormenting with strange terror the sleep of childhood, and inducing . . . a strong and dangerous reaction in after life."[63] Quitman worried about old women because "their minds are weak and their imagination lively."[64] Edward Bickersteth's *Memoir of Simeon Wilhelm . . . with Some Accounts of the Superstitions of the Inhabitants of West Africa* helpfully informed readers that "the power of darkness and ignorance . . . works upon the minds of the old people," instigating superstition that is then passed to the next generation.[65] Pinchbeck, too, feared (literal) old wives' tales; the effect of stories of monsters and goblins "has been known to be so deeply implanted, and lasting, that even *manhood* itself could not erase its power."[66]

Indeed, "manhood" and masculinity were often the victims of superstition. A popular tract from 1802 titled *False Alarms* consists of a number of "false" ghost stories told by a father and uncles to a group of children, in which (as in any good Hanna-Barbera cartoon) the perpetrator is always unmasked as something either harmless or, at worst, criminal, but not supernatural. Credulity is set against masculinity in *False Alarms,* as when a servant girl falls in a swoon on seeing a white ghost in the basement. Although the apparition is revealed to be only a leg of mutton wrapped in a napkin, she is not easily dissuaded: "It was several minutes before she could be convinced of her ridiculous mistake. At first, she would insist upon it, that the phantom stared at her in the face with eyes as large as saucers." Another story tells of a brave sister who investigates and finds out the true nature behind a ghost; but the lesson in the story is for little boys, not girls, for the main character of the tale is the brother John, who is humiliated by his sister's bravery: "This had such an effect on little John, that he never more gave way to the idle imagination of ghosts and apparitions."[67]

The peoples beyond the margins of Western Europe and its colonies had the same predilection for superstition—and tyranny. Oehler followed this line when writing about his Mexican hosts, and, lest the reader miss the allusion, he also included a story about how the sight of a hot-air balloon provoked "agreeable surprise and astonishment to the ignorant and superstitious Mexicans."[68] Bickersteth, reporting from Sierra Leone, explained the religious practice of Africans as "the tyranny and cruelty of Satanic delusions . . . affectingly displayed."[69] Dramatic works invariably contrasted Indian "superstition" against European reason and religion; James Nelson Barker's famed *Indian Princess* (1808) concludes with Captain John Smith rejoicing that wild America will be at last "Free from those bonds which fraud and superstition / In barbarous ages have enchain'd her with."[70] The fabulously popular play *Metamora* told the story of Metacom's war and had Metamora (Metacom) assault virtuous maidens by crying to thinly disguised demonic gods, "the great spirit has sent me; the ghosts are awaiting for thee in the dark place of doom!"[71] Washington Irving satirized the Dutch aristocracy of old New York by connecting them to African American storytelling. Irving wrote in the voice of the unreliable Diedrich Knickerbocker, who longed for the times when "young folks would crowd around the hearth, listening with breathless attention to some old crone of a negro, who was the oracle of the family,—and who, perched like a raven in a corner of a chimney, would croak forth . . . incredible tales about New England witches—grisly ghosts—horses without heads."[72] *Ventriloquism Explained* made the same comment, but did not have comedy in mind when it warned that "colored servants are invariably addicted to telling stories of ghosts and goblins to their master's children, and often make use of *terror* as a penalty among their own children. . . . A colored nurse was once detected in his own family, in the very act of personating an evil spirit, to frighten a child."[73]

The association of witchcraft, superstition, and credulity with nonwhite peoples had obvious implications for a slaveholders' Republic in an era of expansion into lands claimed by Native Americans and Mexicans. The American warmonger William Henry Harrison, for example, repeatedly damned the recalcitrant "Shawnee Prophet" Tenskwatawa (who occupied lands Harrison intended for white settlement) as a superstitious savage with a penchant for witch hunting. Charles Colcock Jones warned of the dangers of African beliefs in American slave quarters: "Superstitions brought from Africa have not wholly been laid aside." Slaves, he wrote, "believe in second sight, in apparitions, charms, witchcraft," which in turn led to the rise of "the influence of some leader or conjuror or minister, that they dared not to disobey." Jones was almost certainly alluding to men like Nat Turner, Gabriel of Virginia, and Gullah Jack, whose religious preaching and powers inspired slave revolts.[74]

America's white commentators were hardly alone. European imperial ambitions in the nineteenth century often described their targets as benighted people afflicted with belief in witchcraft. One of the most famous descriptions of a *vaundun* ceremony in Haiti—the revolutionary rites at Bois Caïman in 1791, with the rebel Dutty Boukman presiding—was recorded in an 1811 treatise by Antoine Dalmas, who used his description of revolutionary slaves sacralizing their rebellion to buttress an argument for a Napoleonic reconquest of the island and the defeat of such an "ignorant and stupid people" and their "superstitious rituals."[75]

The bearing of these depictions of race, gender, age, and gentility on the larger republican questions of self-rule and liberty is exemplified in Irving's "Legend of Sleepy Hollow," a mainstay of American literature that is virtually without a moral unless it is considered in light of the antebellum American case against witchcraft. The plot of the tale, when seen in relation to the other faux ghost stories of the era, is not particularly original: a superstitious man is tricked into seeing a false ghost and consequently loses both his reputation and the woman he seeks to marry. The devil, so to speak, is in the details: Ichabod Crane, the principal character, has all the qualities that endanger republicanism. He is physically weak ("one might have mistaken him for the genius of famine"), gluttonous ("a huge feeder, and though lank, had the dilating powers of an Anaconda"), proud and lazy ("a kind of idle gentleman-like personage, of vastly superior taste and accomplishments to the rough country swains"). He is also a gold digger, out to marry Katrina Van Tassel for her father's money and farm. Irving pits Ichabod against Brom Bones, the "burly, roaring, roystering blade" whose strength and "hardihood" are legendary and who wears a fur cap and ruffles the feathers of society with boyish good humor—a Jacksonian to the teeth.[76]

Moreover, Ichabod has the flaw of superstition: "He was, in fact, an odd mixture of small shrewdness and simple credulity. . . . No tale was too gross or monstrous for his capacious swallow." He owns a copy of Cotton Mather and believes every word, and he spends his time with "the old Dutch wives" by the hearth, drinking in their stories and superstitions, which then terrify him on his journey home. Perhaps this gives Ichabod his "soft and foolish heart." Brom Bones, dressed as the notorious Headless Horseman, so terrifies Ichabod one night that the schoolmaster leaves Sleepy Hollow forever, his reputation ruined. When the good citizens of Sleepy Hollow examine the effects Ichabod leaves behind—"Cotton Mather's history of Witchcraft, a New England Almanack, and a book of dreams and fortune telling"—they consign the lot to the flames.[77]

The victory of Brom Bones, like the resolution of many nineteenth-century American stories about witchcraft, has elements that would have been familiar in many European countries. Dressing witchcraft beliefs as feminine, foreign, and weak was a common tactic in eighteenth- and nineteenth-century texts against supernatural beliefs. The moral of this very American tale follows the general line of other Enlightenment and post-Enlightenment writings on witchcraft: credulity, weakness, and femininity are not to be tolerated among people who are supposed to rule themselves. Those who believe in goblins get what they deserve.[78]

But "The Legend of Sleepy Hollow" also has Brom Bones wedding Katrina, and that does indeed represent something different. It is the scholar, Ichabod Crane, who believes in the witches, and the cunning Bones who humiliates him. The "Herculean" Bones, acknowledged leader of men and Jacksonian yeoman, destroys the scholar's books and marries Crane's intended fiancée. The fictionalized and idealized backcountry whites—not the scholars or educated elites—were the ones who would defend manhood and democracy against superstition and, by extension, against Indians, Africans, and Mexicans. Just as the United States had gone significantly beyond Enlightenment ideals of balanced republicanism into a broader democracy, so too its invectives against witchcraft were meant to appeal to the broader electorate that would now be entrusted with tamping down credulity and superstition in the name of rational order.

But before ending his tale, Irving provides a postscript from Diedrich Knickerbocker detailing the circumstances under which he heard the tale. It came, he writes, from "a pleasant, shabby, gentlemanly old fellow . . . one whom I strongly suspected of being poor." The story ends on an odd note: when the gentleman is challenged as to the story's veracity (by a character who may in fact be Ichabod), the old man replies, "Faith, sir . . . I don't believe half of it myself."[79]

And that is the historian's rub: many of these pieces were fictional, and even the pieces parading as fact might well have been half-imagined or invented outright. They were warning pieces that bemoaned qualities that *might* have been widely practiced by advocating principles that *might* have been widely imitated. Yet what James Sharpe has written about demonological tracts in early modern England might well apply to the early United States: "these pamphlets did not merely describe witch beliefs and witch trials; they also located them in a moral framework. . . . The later pamphlets rarely lost sight of the didactic function explicit here: their readers had to be warned against witchcraft."[80] Americans needed to be warned against witchcraft, but the war this witchcraft waged was not that of God against the devil but of white democrats versus tyrants. Not everyone in the general population might accept the idea of witches as liars, but with these publications circulating, most could be expected to be familiar with the idea.

The idea that the problem of superstition and belief in witchcraft was intimately connected with the shift to republicanism and democracy kept witchcraft in the public mind. The "witch" had become a conniver. The threat to citizen and state was not that supernatural powers were real but that they were false: they took advantage of the ignorant, they poisoned morals, and they doused the fires of natural government. So too with those who saw signs in nature beyond a mild, natural providence: they filled the public mind with falsehoods and thus set the republican ship adrift. That those threats to the nation were also defined as Indians and blacks, and the countervailing forces as masculine country farmers, was no accident in an expanding slaveholder Republic. Politics and religion were connected not only through policy but also through epistemology. Witchcraft was a problem for white republicans even though—in fact precisely because—it was *not* true.

NOTES

1. Andrew Oehler, *The Life, Adventures, and Unparalleled Sufferings of Andrew Oehler* (Trenton, N.J.: D. Fenton, 1811), 116, 132, 133, 150.

2. Charles J. Pecor, *Magician on the American Stage* (Washington, D.C.: Emerson and West, 1977), 105ff. Further evidence weighs against Oehler's truthfulness. Oehler's description of Mexico and its legal system are typical anti-Catholic fantasies. In fact, the colonial legal systems of Latin America were "highly developed and would have surprised any Anglo-American jurist of the period. Colonial peoples were aware of their privileges, and they were skilled in using the legal system to preserve them." Carlos A. Forment, *Democracy in Latin America, 1760–1900*, vol. 1 (Chicago: University of Chicago Press, 2003), 42.

3. *Debates and Proceedings of the Congress of the United States*, 12th Cong.,1st sess., May 6, 1812 (Washington, D.C.: Gales and Seaton, 1853), 1386, 1398.

4. The outlines of Oehler's tale would have possessed the same overtones in the event that his story was true. James W. Cook, *The Arts of Deception: Playing with Fraud in the Age of Barnum* (Cambridge: Harvard University Press, 2001), 175–76, unequivocally accepts Oehler's story and takes it as evidence that Americans understood magic in a more "rational" way than did Mexicans or Spaniards, that Americans were well on their way to disenchanting magic. In

fact, Oehler's work as a whole is less an effort to disenchant than to show how an ingenious white footpad (Oehler) can successfully hoodwink people of lesser intelligence (which, in Oehler's *Sufferings*, are often people with darker skin). As the real reception of Robertson in 1798 suggests, Mexicans were no less rational or rationalizing than Americans; in fact, those terms are problematic when applied to the late eighteenth and early nineteenth centuries.

5. Edmund S. Morgan, "The Witch and We, the People," *American Heritage* 34 (August–September 1983): 6–11.

6. *Authentic Account of an Appearance of a Ghost* (Baltimore, 1807). I was alerted to this episode by reading Elaine Foreman Crane, "A Ghost Story, or How an Apparition Entered National Politics," paper delivered at the joint MCEAS-OAH seminar at Fordham University, March 28, 2008.

7. John D. Lee, *Mormonism Unveiled* (1877) (Albuquerque: Fierra Blanca, 2001), 60, also cited in Reed C. Durham Jr., "The Election Day Battle in Gallatin," *BYU Studies* 13, no. 1 (1972): 36–61.

8. Frederick Bates to William Clark, July 25, 1907, in *Life and Papers of Frederick Bates*, ed. Thomas M. Marshall (St. Louis: Missouri Historical Society, 1926), 1:167–68.

9. The notion of a "decline" in supernatural beliefs finds its most prominent defense in Keith Thomas, *Religion and the Decline of Magic* (New York: Scribner, 1971). Thomas and his successors held that the rise of Protestantism and its Weberian economics assured the decline of magical thinking. With Thomas as the backdrop, a new generation of scholarship has questioned the extent and geography of that supposed decline. See Wolfgang Behringer, *Witches and Witch-Hunts: A Global History* (Cambridge: Polity Press, 2004); Owen Davies, *Magic, Witchcraft, and Culture, 1736–1951* (Manchester: Manchester University Press, 1999); Bengt Ankarloo and Stuart Clark, eds., *Witchcraft and Magic in Europe*, vol. 5, *The Eighteenth and Nineteenth Centuries* (Philadelphia: University of Pennsylvania Press, 1999); Adam Ashforth, *Madumo: A Man Bewitched* (Chicago: University of Chicago Press, 2000), and *Witchcraft, Violence, and Democracy in South Africa* (Chicago: University of Chicago Press, 2005); Peter Geschiere, *The Modernity of Witchcraft: Politics and the Occult in Postcolonial Africa*, trans. Janet Roitman (Charlottesville: University Press of Virginia, 1997); and Gábor Klaniczay, "The Decline of Witches and the Rise of Vampires," in *The Witchcraft Reader*, ed. Darren Oldridge (New York: Routledge, 2002), 387–98. On the conception of civilization, race, and barbarism in the European and Euro-American imaginations, see Patrick Griffin, *American Leviathan: Empire, Nation, and the Revolutionary Frontier* (New York: Hill and Wang, 2007); Anthony F. C. Wallace, *Jefferson and the Indians: The Tragic Fate of the First Americans* (Cambridge: Belknap Press of Harvard University Press, 1999); and Anthony Pagden, *The Fall of Natural Man: The American Indian and the Origins of Ethnography* (New York: Cambridge University Press, 1982).

10. *New Hampshire Patriot*, September 1, 1818 (emphasis added); *Public Laws of the State of Connecticut* (Hartford, 1808), 1:659; *The Town Officer . . . as Contained in the Laws of the Commonwealth of Massachusetts* (Boston, 1802), 251; *Laws of Maryland Made and Passed at a Session of the Assembly. . . .* (Annapolis, 1801), unnumbered page (13); D. Michael Quinn, *Early Mormonism and the Magic World View* (Salt Lake City: Signature Books, 1998), 27, 119; and *Laws of the State of New-York* (Albany, 1813), 1:114.

11. Joseph Lathrop, *Illustrations and Reflections on the Story of Saul's Consulting the Witch of Endor* (Springfield, Mass.: Henry Brewer, 1806), 14.

12. Robin Briggs, *Witches and Neighbors: The Social and Cultural Context of European Witchcraft* (New York: Penguin, 1996), 1–13.

13. Stuart Clark, *Thinking with Demons: The Idea of Witchcraft in Early Modern Europe* (Oxford: Oxford University Press, 1997), 8.

14. The actual *existence* of self-described "witches" is, of course, a separate question requiring a different set of historical lenses. H. C. Erik Midelfort, for example, has determined that at most *one* "witch cult" was active in Europe during the time of the early modern witch trials, while scholars such as Ronald Hutton and Chas Clifton have demonstrated how "witch-

craft" emerged as a religious system in the twentieth-century West and led to the establishment of modern witchcraft covens. See H. C. Erik Midelfort, "Were There Really Witches?,"
in *Transition and Revolution: Problems and Issues of European Renaissance and Reformation History,* ed. Robert Kingdon (Minneapolis: Burgess, 1974), 189–205; Davies, *Magic,
Witchcraft, and Culture*; Ronald Hutton, *The Triumph of the Moon: A History of Modern
Pagan Witchcraft* (Oxford: Oxford University Press, 1999); and Chas Clifton, *Her Hidden
Children: The Rise of Wicca and Paganism in America* (Lanham, Md.: AltaMira Press,
2006). The extent and nature of witchcraft *practice* among the diverse peoples of the early
American Republic is a separate question, mostly dealt with piecemeal in a variety of texts.
See, for example, Alan Taylor, "The Early Republic's Supernatural Economy: Treasure Seek-
ing in the Northeast, 1780–1830," *American Quarterly* 38, no. 1 (1986): 6–34; Craig James
Hazen, *The Village Enlightenment in America* (Urbana: University of Illinois Press, 2000);
Jeffrey E. Anderson, *Conjure in African American Society* (Baton Rouge: Louisiana State
University Press, 2005); Quinn, *Early Mormonism*; John L. Brooke, *The Refiner's Fire: The
Making of Mormon Cosmology, 1644–1844* (Cambridge: Cambridge University Press, 1994);
Alfred A. Cave, "The Failure of the Shawnee Prophet's Witch Hunt," *Ethnohistory* 42 (1995):
445–75; and Matthew Dennis, *Seneca Possessed* (Philadelphia: University of Pennsylvania
Press, 2010).

15. As Davies points out, this conception of witchcraft as imaginary was one of several
beliefs at the end of the nineteenth century. Davies's study of witchcraft beliefs in modern
Britain provides numerous examples of popular reactions to witchcraft in England in the
eighteenth and nineteenth centuries and further warns that reducing witchcraft beliefs to a
single "popular" and a single "elite" viewpoint is not tenable. My comments on "anti-
witchcraft" are therefore intended as a broad description of a repeated argument found in
multiple cultural contexts in the early United States, not as the sole or even the (exclusively)
elite point of view. See Davies, *Magic, Witchcraft, and Culture,* 1–29, 79–100, and 120–24.
Davies's point embellishes Roger Chartier, *The Cultural Uses of Print in Early Modern France*
(Princeton: Princeton University Press, 1987).

16. Diarmaid MacCulloch, *The Reformation: A History* (New York: Penguin, 2003), 564.

17. Charles Upham, *Lectures on Witchcraft Comprising a History of the Delusion at Salem
in 1692* (Boston: Carter, Hendee, and Babcock, 1832), 90.

18. William Pinchbeck, *The Expositor, or Many Mysteries Unraveled* (Boston: Printed for
the author, 1805), 5; and Pinchbeck, *Witchcraft, or The Art of Fortune-Telling Unveiled* (Boston:
Printed for the author, 1805), 12.

19. Upham, *Lectures on Witchcraft,* vi–vii.

20. Clark, *Thinking with Demons,* 579, 580. See also Hartmut Lehmann, "The Persecution
of Witches as Restoration of Order: The Case of Germany, 1590s–1650s," *Central European
History* 21 (1988): 107–21.

21. A Connecticut Brick-Layer [Thomas Anderson], *Superstition Detected* (Philadelphia:
Printed for the reader, 1831), 9. The "Author's Nephew" reprinted the text of the play/poem in
the 1830s from the original "at the end of the last century."

22. Roy Porter, "Witchcraft and Magic in Enlightenment, Romantic, and Liberal Thought,"
in Ankarloo and Clark, *Witchcraft and Magic,* 5:220–21, 235–36; Hume quoted in Michael Wasser, "The Mechanical World-View and the Decline of Witch Beliefs in Scotland," in *Witchcraft
and Belief in Early Modern Scotland,* ed. Julian Goodacre, Lauren Martin, and Joyce Miller
(New York: Palgrave Macmillan, 2008), 206–26; and Davies, *Magic, Witchcraft, and Culture,*
18–39. As Wasser and others have pointed out, the decline of witchcraft beliefs does not easily
correlate with the end of prosecutions, but the fact that Hume and Voltaire could publish their
criticisms of witch beliefs and witchcraft law without much legal fanfare does point to a significant reduction in both the legal and cultural status of witchcraft.

23. John Greenleaf Whittier, *Supernaturalism* (1847) (Baltimore: Clearfield, 1997), vii,
ix, 13.

24. Upham, *Lectures on Witchcraft,* 227.

25. Frederick Quitman, *A Treatise on Magic, or The Intercourse Between Spirits and Men* (Albany, N.Y.: Balance Press, 1810), 64, 26.

26. See Philip Gould, "New England Witch-Hunting and the Politics of Reason in the Early Republic," *New England Quarterly* 68, no. 1 (1995): 58–82; and Gretchen A. Adams, *The Specter of Salem: Remembering the Witch Trials in Nineteenth-Century America* (Chicago: University of Chicago Press, 2008).

27. James Sharpe, *Instruments of Darkness: Witchcraft in Early Modern England* (Philadelphia: University of Pennsylvania Press, 1996), 42.

28. Vernon Stauffer, *The Bavarian Illuminati in America* (1908) (Mineola, N.Y.: Dover, 2006), 14–22.

29. See Joseph R. Roach, *Cities of the Dead: Circum-Atlantic Performance* (New York: Columbia University Press, 1996); and Jason Shaffer, *Performing Patriotism: National Identity in the Colonial and Revolutionary American Theater* (Philadelphia: University of Pennsylvania Press, 2007). The idea of "performative ethos," in which all public actions are deemed to be so informed by literary and dramatic works that they become something performed rather than actual, can easily be taken too far. Indeed, the notion that political actions are "performed" suggests that they are substitutes for "real" action, which echoes the social-control hypothesis made famous by Whitney R. Cross in *The Burned-Over District: The Social and Intellectual History of Enthusiastic Religion in Western New York, 1800–1850* (Ithaca: Cornell University Press, 1950), and criticized by Lois W. Banner, "Religious Benevolence as Social Control: A Critique of an Interpretation," *Journal of American History* 60 (June 1973): 23–41, before being resurrected by Paul E. Johnson, in *A Shopkeeper's Millennium: Society and Revivals in Rochester, New York, 1815–1837* (New York: Hill and Wang, 1978), and his successors. However, the robust state of theater in the early Republic, its widespread appeal, and its prominent themes of liberty and Americanization all make theater a vital part of political culture in the age of Jefferson and Jackson.

30. James Nelson Barker, *The Tragedy of Superstition* (Philadelphia: A. R. Poole, 1826) 44, 46.

31. William Milns, *The Comet, or He Would Be an Astronomer* (Baltimore: J. Robinson, 1817), 19. The play was performed first in 1797; there were British, American, five-act, and two-act versions. The play was published in 1817 in two acts. George Oberkirsh Seilhamer, *History of the American Theatre*, vol. 3 (New York: Haskell House, 1969), 388.

32. Tobias S. Alltruth [Reynaldo de Moscheto], *The Magician and the Holy Alliance* (Philadelphia, 1820), 24.

33. See Jennifer Mason, *Civilized Creatures: Urban Animals, Sentimental Culture, and American Literature, 1850–1900* (Baltimore: Johns Hopkins University Press, 2005), 72; and Peter Benes, *New England's Creatures, 1400–1900* (Boston: Boston University Press, 1995), 157.

34. Leigh Eric Schmidt, *Hearing Things: Religion, Illusion, and the American Enlightenment* (Cambridge: Harvard University Press, 2000), 78–80. Schmidt's history of hearing in the early United States is a recent variation on Weber's disenchantment thesis, with the slight exception that Schmidt views the triumph of reason with wan regret. In his discussion of Pinchbeck, Schmidt correctly identifies a political concern in the attack on oracles, but his triumphalist account assumes that the "reeducation" of the senses was a successful endeavor rather than an intellectual and cultural struggle. Indeed, far from hearing "loss," Upham wrote in 1867 that "the principal difference in the methods by which communications were believed to be made between mortal and spiritual beings, at the time of the witchcraft delusion and now, is this. Then it was chiefly by the medium of the eye, but at present by the ear." Charles Upham, *Salem Witchcraft* (1867) (Mineola, N.Y.: Dover, 2000), 605.

35. Quitman, *Treatise on Magic*, iv.

36. William Young, *A debate proposed in the Temple Patrick Society . . . whether witches, wizards, magicians, sorcerers, &c. had supernatural powers* (Philadelphia: Young, 1788), 18, 22.

37. *Ghost Stories Collected with a Particular View to Counteract the Vulgar Belief in Ghosts.* . . . (London: Ackermann, 1823), xvi (a U.S. edition was published in 1846).

38. Upham, *Lectures on Witchcraft*, 147.

39. Robert Calef, *More Wonders of the Invisible World* (1700), in George Lincoln Burr, ed., *Narratives of the New England Witchcraft Cases* (1914) (New York: Dover, 2002), 304.

40. Again, Gould cites the histories of Salem from 1790 to 1830 as an expression of the political and social anxieties of the early Republic. Gretchen Adams traces this political lineage back at least to 1738. I agree with both of them, but I argue that the important shift is seen in where these political accounts lay the blame, and that this rhetoric was not *merely* metaphor—the use of Salem witchcraft as a means to explain something that was not witchcraft—but an actual fear of lying witches or magicians subverting democracy, as the laws of New York, Massachusetts, and other states suggest. Writers on witchcraft, I contend, are sometimes concerned with witches.

41. Thomas Hutchinson, *History of the Colony and Province of Massachusetts-Bay*, ed. Lawrence Shaw Mayo (Cambridge: Harvard University Press, 1936), 2:19, 44. Note Bernard Rosenthal's comment about "girls"; they were in fact mostly grown women. Rosenthal, *Salem Story: Reading the Witch Trials of 1692* (New York: Cambridge University Press, 1993).

42. Hutchinson, *Province of Massachusetts-Bay*, 2:44.

43. William Bentley, "History of Salem," *Collections of the Massachusetts Historical Society*, first ser., vol. 6 (New York: Johnson Reprint, 1968), 212–77 (quotations at 268–70).

44. Hannah Adams, *An Abridgement of the History of New-England: For the Use of Young Persons* (Boston: Homans and West, 1805), 82, 83.

45. Upham is more famous for his later work on the trials, *Salem Witchcraft* (1867), from which Paul Boyer and Stephen Nissenbaum drew their map of Salem in *Salem Possessed: The Social Origins of Witchcraft* (Cambridge: Harvard University Press, 1974). Most of what is in his *Lectures on Witchcraft* can be found in *Salem Witchcraft*, but the reverse is not true; in the 1867 version, Upham added an extensive section on the social and economic conditions of Salem village, an aside on hallucinatory experience, and an extensive supplement on those who objected to the trials. The 1831 version is much more narrowly focused on the problem of superstition, credulity, and order. See Upham, *Salem Witchcraft*, 1–214, 317–22, 617–82.

46. Upham, *Lectures on Witchcraft*, 57, 278.

47. Ibid., 114, 107, 103, 110, 89.

48. Ibid., 276.

49. Quitman, *Treatise on Magic*, iii.

50. Quoted in Gould, "New England Witch-Hunting," 64.

51. For related arguments, see Cook, *Arts of Deception*, 177–80.

52. *The Art of Conjuring Made Easy* (New York: Borradaile, 1822), 5 (emphasis added).

53. *Parlour Magic* (Philadelphia: H. Perkins, 1838), v (emphasis in original).

54. *Ventriloquism Explained, and Juggler's Tricks, or Legerdemain Exposed, with Remarks on Vulgar Superstitions* (Amherst, Mass.: J. S. and C. Adams, 1834), 40.

55. *European Ventriloquist's Exhibition* (Portsmouth, N.H.: Whidden, 1808), 4.

56. It should also be noted that magicians' claims to promote the public interest and republican uprightness were not disinterested, as they may have helped generate revenue for both books and performances.

57. Owen Chadwick, *The Secularization of the European Mind in the Nineteenth Century* (New York: Cambridge University Press, 1990), 10.

58. Bentley, "History of Salem," 268.

59. Young, *Debate proposed in the Temple Patrick Society*, 9. Men were, of course, seized and executed as witches in earlier times.

60. Quoted in Davies, *Magic, Witchcraft, and Culture*, 159.

61. A Hearer, letter to the editor, *Liberator*, March 9, 1838, 1.

62. David Reese, *Humbugs of New-York: Being a Remonstrance Against Popular Delusion; Whether in Science, Philosophy, or Religion* (New York: J. S. Taylor, 1838), vi.

63. Whittier, *Supernaturalism*, viii.

64. Quitman, *Treatise on Magic*, 54.

65. Edward Bickersteth, *Memoir of Simeon Wilhelm . . . with Some Accounts of the Super-stitions of the Inhabitants of West Africa* (New Haven: S. Converse, 1819), 90.

66. Pinchbeck, *Witchcraft*, 14 (emphasis added).

67. R. Johnson, *False Alarms* (Philadelphia: Benjamin and Jacob Johnson, 1802), 10–11, 17.

68. *Sufferings of Andrew Oehler*, 123.

69. Bickersteth, *Memoir of Simeon Wilhelm*, 87.

70. J. N. Baker, *The Indian Princess, or La Belle Sauvage*, in Montrose J. Moses, ed., *Representative Plays, by American Dramatists* (New York: E. P. Dutton, 1925), 1:73.

71. John Augustus Stone, *Metamora, or The Last of the Wampanoags*, in Barrett H. Clark, ed., *Favorite American Plays of the Nineteenth Century* (Princeton: Princeton University Press, 1943), 33.

72. Washington Irving, *A History of New York* (1809), in *Washington Irving: History, Tales, and Sketches*, ed. James W. Tuttleton (New York: Penguin, 1983), 479.

73. *Ventriloquism Explained*, 14–15.

74. Charles Colcock Jones, *The Religious Instruction of the Negroes* (Savannah, Ga.: Charles Purse, 1842), 127–28. For Harrison and the Shawnee Prophet, see Adam Jortner, *The Gods of Prophetstown: The Battle of Tippecanoe and the Holy War for the American Frontier* (New York: Oxford University Press, 2011). On slave religion, rebellion, and white reactions thereto, see Albert Raboteau, *Slave Religion: The "Invisible Institution" in the Antebellum South* (New York: Oxford University Press, 1978), 147, 163; and Yvonne P. Chireau, *Black Magic: Religion and the African American Conjuring Tradition* (Berkeley: University of California Press, 2003), 60–67.

75. Laurent Dubois, "The Citizen's Trance: The Haitian Revolution and the Motor of History," in *Magic and Modernity: Interfaces of Revelation and Concealment*, ed. Birgit Meyer and Peter Pels (Stanford: Stanford University Press, 2003), 103–28 (Dalmas quoted at 110). Dubois well summarizes the historiographical debates since 1988 on whether Dalmas in fact invented the episode as part of his invective against African self-government; what is clear, however, is that Dalmas's description (whether related, invented, or embellished) formed part of an intellectual case against "witchcraft" as the province of "lesser" races (even when those races completed a revolution more thorough than either the American or French variants.)

76. Irving, "The Legend of Sleepy Hollow," in *Washington Irving: History, Tales, and Sketches*, 1061–63, 1069.

77. Ibid., 1062–66, 1085.

78. The connection between the rise of Enlightenment ideals and a masculine power structure has been discussed in Lorraine Daston and Katharine Park, *Wonders and the Order of Nature, 1150–1750* (New York: Zone Books, 1998); and Brian Eslea, *Witch Hunting, Magic, and the New Philosophy: An Introduction to Debates of the Scientific Revolution, 1450–1750* (Brighton, UK: Harvester Press, 1980).

79. Irving, "Legend of Sleepy Hollow," 1088.

80. Sharpe, *Instruments of Darkness*, 100.

Part 2 | MAGIC IN MODERNITY

5

LOAGAETH, Q CONSIBRA A CAOSG:

THE CONTESTED ARENA OF MODERN ENOCHIAN ANGEL MAGIC

Egil Asprem

In the early 1580s, the Elizabethan natural philosopher John Dee (1527–1608 or 1609) commenced on a program, simultaneously religious, philosophical, and scientific, to contact angels through a "showstone"—a practice better known as crystal gazing.[1] With the aid of various scryers, most significantly Edward Kelly (1555–1597), Dee conversed with the archangels Michael and Gabriel and with a number of idiosyncratic angelic beings by such names as Ave, Madimi, and Nalvage. Dee kept studious records of these "actions" or "colloquiums," filling hundreds of folio pages with information about the reformation of the world, the end of days, cosmology, angelic hierarchies, the language of Adam, and a number of intricate magical systems based on letter squares, sigils, and the invocation of secret names of God.[2]

In this chapter I am concerned with how the last two aspects in particular—the language of Adam and the magical systems for contacting angels and demons—have given rise to the contested field of modern Enochian angel magic, through processes of religious creativity, reinterpretations, corruption of sources, and other historical permutations.[3] Dee's diaries have been the source of inspiration for modern, self-identifying ritual magicians, and the creative reception of their content continues to evolve today. Owing to this creative reception, equating "Enochian magic" with the magical system(s) of John Dee would be grossly anachronistic: very few modern magicians actually follow the details of any of the magical systems set forth in the original sources. The first part of this chapter sets up a cross-historical comparison that helps us see the gradual reconfiguration of Enochian magic and the different historical contexts that shaped it. Such a comparison requires us first to assess the original context of Dee's Elizabethan angel magic. Tracing the genealogy of Enochian magic in rough lines allows us to assess, in the second part of this chapter, the current status of this particular set of ritual magical theory and practice as a disputed field of religious discourse. I argue that a careful study of the way in which individual, self-defined magicians position themselves both toward other Enochian magicians and toward authorized discourses such as science, psychology, and religion affords important correctives to recent discussions on the dis- and re-enchantment of modern culture.

The Sources of Enochian Magic

John Dee's magical material can be divided and classified in several different ways.[4] To begin with, a line should be drawn between the angel conversations themselves—the way in which Dee and Kelly worked to get in touch with angels—and the arcane magical material "received" *through* these conversations. In this sense, the first level of "Dee's magic" is a type of catoptromantic crystal gazing aimed at communion with the angels and revelations of higher knowledge concerning natural philosophy, the apocalypse, and God's salvific project. The second level, by contrast, comprises a number of magical systems, grimoirelike in form, that appeared in the course of the angel diaries.

This "received" material can be subdivided into five components, based on a distinction made by Dee himself. While Dee recorded every session diligently and chronologically, describing the dialogues with various angels, including their commands, answers, and revelations, he also produced five distinct "received books" detailing the different parts of the magical system.[5] Briefly summarizing the contents of these books gives a concise overview of the multi-faceted system of Elizabethan angel magic that would later, in a variety of different combinations and interpretations, fall under the heading of Enochian magic.

The first book is commonly referred to as *Liber Logaeth* (or *Loagaeth*) (the Book of the Speech of God).[6] The book contains the outcome of the first transmission of the alleged Adamic language.[7] It takes the form of ninety-five tables filled with letters and forty-nine "calls" or prayers prefacing the tables.[8] The prayers are supposedly in the Adamic tongue and were not translated (with the exception of a few individual words). Also included toward the end of the manuscript is the twenty-one-letter alphabet that goes with this ostensibly divine language. Although the intended use of the tables is somewhat unclear, the angels did insinuate to Dee that "when the time is right," it would be used to initiate the apocalyptic "redefinition of the natural world."[9] No other instructions about its function or use are extant, except obscure hints that the mysteries of the tables will be revealed by God only at God's chosen moment.

The second revealed book bears the title *De heptarchia mystica* and is a compendious collection of the essential information received by Dee and Kelly before they left England for the continent in 1583.[10] The content of this book forms a magical system that enables the magician to call upon the "heptarchical Kings and Princes" who were thought to rule the seven days of the week.[11] The book includes names of these "good heptarchical Angels," their various seals and sigils, the nature of their offices (imparting arcane knowledge or teaching alchemy, for example), and supplications to call them forth.

The third revealed book is the *48 Claves angelicae* (Forty-Eight Angelic Keys).[12] These are nineteen short verses written in a second divine, "angelic" language.[13] This time, the angels provided English translations. While the first eighteen verses are freestanding invocations of unclear function, the nineteenth is dedicated to the so-called thirty Aires, a set of entities that are explained more systematically in the *fourth* revealed book, *Liber scientiae, auxilii, et victoriae terrestris* (Book of Terrestrial Science, Support, and Victory).[14]

The thirty Aires appear to be spirits, spiritual realms, or principles located in various parts of the air surrounding the earth. Each of the Aires controls a small number of spirits (ninety-one in all), which rule lesser spirits, all of which in the end make up a vast hierarchy of angelic creatures. Each of the ninety-one spirits corresponds to a country or geographical region in the world as it looked through European Renaissance eyes (actually, as it had looked already for Ptolemy), and a mystical name is given to each of the regions. For instance, we learn that Egypt is Occodon, Syria Pascomb, and Mesopotamia Valgars, that these regions are ruled by the angels Zarzilg, Zinggen, and Alpudus, and are controlled by the Aire called LIL.[15] The twelve tribes of ancient Israel are also listed, with directions apparently pointing out where each has disappeared. The intention of this system seems to be that by "calling" the right Aires with the nineteenth "key" of the *Claves angelicae*, the magician can gain authority over the geographical entities and presumably the power to control great geopolitical events (thus indicated by the title of the book, "Terrestrial Victory"). This was a form of magic most desirable for Dee, an occasional counselor to the imperial Elizabethan throne. Deborah Harkness suggests that another intention had millennialist implications: to localize the twelve lost tribes and bring them back.[16] According to various prophecies, the tribes should return to Israel at the end of times; Dee may have envisioned a role for himself in that project.

The fifth and last revealed book is known as *Tabula bonorum angelorum* (The Table of Good Angels).[17] Here, we find another collection of prayers or invocations, this time related to a specific fourfold magical square or table made up by four lesser "watchtowers." From the four "watchtower" squares, connected to form the "Great Table" by inserting what is referred to as "the black cross" between them (a cross scribbled black by Dee, containing more secret names of God), are extracted numerous angels, "Seniors" (purportedly the six that stand before the throne of God in Revelation), kings, secret names of God, and even demons, all ordered in an elaborate hierarchy.

The methods of extracting the names and the function of each entity were described by the angel Ave, who declared the Great Table to contain:

1. All human knowledge.
2. Out of it springeth Physick.
3. *The knowledge of the elemental Creatures, amongst you.* . . .
4. *The knowledge, finding and use of Metals.*
   The vertues of *them.*
   The congelations, and vertues of *Stones.*
5. *The Conjoining and knitting together of Natures. The destruction of Nature, and of things that may perish.*
6. *Moving from place to place, [as into this Country, or that Country at pleasure.]*
7. *The knowledge of all crafts Mechanical.*
8. Transmutatio formalis, sed non essentialis.[18]

This resembles the panoply of promised effects we know from the early modern grimoire traditions, which usually ranged from uncovering hidden treasure or harming enemies to gaining hidden knowledge and supernatural transportation from one place to another.[19] The *Tabula bonorum angelorum* is Dee's systematic ordering of all the material relating to the Great Table. In addition to the table itself, this text includes lists of angels and divine names, indexed with their specific powers and attributions, and also different prayers or invocations to contact and control the entities in hierarchical order, from the highest secret twelve names of God to the lowest serving angels. Also included are the names of demons and wicked spirits who can perform the negative of what their corresponding angels do. For example, if an angel of "physick" (i.e., medicine) can heal wounds, the corresponding "cacodaemon" can cause them.

Based on these books, we can speak of *four key components* making up the foundations of Dee's "angelically received" magic:

(1) The heptarchic system (*De heptarchia mystica*);
(2) The angelic/Adamic language, later referred to as "Enochian" (from *Liber Loagaeth,* but especially *48 Claves angelicae*);
(3) The Aires, or (in later conventions) "Aethyrs" (*Liber scientiae, auxilii, et victoriae terrestris,* together with *Claves angelicae*); and
(4) The magic of the "Great Table" or "Four Watchtowers" (*Tabula bonorum angelorum*).

These four types interact, overlap, and mix with one another to some extent. For example, the angelic language is a key component in the system of the Aires, as shown above. In addition, the ninety-one spirits belonging to the Aires are linked to the Great Table by certain sigils that apply to its letter squares. Nevertheless, the four classes do stand out with a significant number of exclusive features: the cryptic apocalyptic statements surrounding the *Liber Loagaeth*; the heptarchic system with its encyclopedic, grimoire-style list of spirits, sigils, and the hours and days of calling them forth; the geopolitical and millennialist systems of the Aires; and the almost universally applicable system for evocation of angels and "cacodaemons" tabulated in the Great Table.

The Reception: Transmissions, Condemnations, and Reinterpretations

The various magical, mystical, and esoteric endeavors described above fitted within John Dee's broad vision of natural philosophy—a vision formed before mathematics became the sole key to reading the book of nature, before the triumph of the mechanistic philosophy, an era in which knowledge systems such as alchemy and kabbalah seemed to hold great promise.[20] These cultural conditions were nevertheless soon to change, leaving the reception of Dee's work with rather different foundations. The magical manuscripts, some published already in the mid-seventeenth century by Meric Casaubon, others surfacing later and finding their way into collections such as the Ashmolean and the Sloane, would provide a basis for a great deal of obscure magical and esoteric speculation, most of which was far removed from the original program of their author.

Consider the following episodes, spanning centuries of historical changes.

One hundred years after Dee, in the 1670s and 1680s, a group of three or four magicians assembled around a scryer called Rorbon, producing more than a thousand manuscript pages of notes from their sessions.[21] Here, Dee's strange angels come to life again, answering questions for the magicians. Sometimes the angels continue discussing astrological symbolism, alchemy, and kabbalah, but mostly they were forced to satisfy the magicians' mundane desire for things like buried treasure. Around the same time, a grimoire was created that dealt with the summoning of angels, and particularly the perennial problem of making sure that nothing demonic intruded in place of the angels.[22] Through the course of the manual, attributed to one "Dr. Rudd," Dee's angels appear again, but this magician did not trust the Elizabethan doctor's lofty perspective. The author was rather convinced—probably after having read Casaubon's recently published edition of the angel diaries—that Dee's angels had been demonic creatures in disguise. In the preface to his edition of the angel diaries, *A True and Faithful Relation*, Casaubon had argued that the angels were really wicked spirits, luring Dee away from piety. Seeing that Casaubon was now the only likely source for learning about the angel conversations, this demonized view had an impact even on the magicians trying to resuscitate Dee's magic. However, with the angels inverted into demons, "Dr. Rudd" took appropriate magical measures: in his manual, the originally angelic system has been embedded in a framework aimed to coerce wicked spirits into obedience.

We jump another century and a half, and yet new uses of Dee's magical system have appeared. There was a considerable revival of crystallomancy in Britain during the early Victorian period, spreading largely in Masonic circles. Some inspiration was taken from the Dee material, which was by that time available in the British Museum.[23] The central figure was Frederick Hockley (1808–1885), who, together with others such as Francis George Irwin (1828–1892) and Kenneth Mackenzie (1833–1886), was a founding father of Victorian occultist ritual magic. Hockley is known to have used a "speculatrix" (normally a young virgin girl) as a scryer in his conversation with various entities through a crystal (particularly one called "the Crowned Angel"), and he possessed copies not only of Dee's diary pieces but also of the Rudd material mentioned above.[24] Mackenzie is said to have taken a speculatrix to the British Museum in order to use Dee's original "showstone." According to Mackenzie, the scryer had seen the city of Prague unfolding in the stone, apparently enabling flashbacks of its previous owner's adventures on the continent.[25]

Some decades later, elements of Dee's magical diaries became integral parts of an elaborate new system of ceremonial magic focusing on themes of self-development, theurgy, and Rosicrucian-style adepthood, in the Hermetic Order of the Golden Dawn. Particularly owing to the creative innovations of Samuel Liddell "MacGregor" Mathers, by the close of the nineteenth century the order taught an occult synthesis in which what was now called "Enochian" magic figured as the spearhead of magical aptitude, the most sublime system that "Hermetic," "Rosicrucian," high magic had to offer.[26] In the process, the meaning of the system was entirely reworked. In the Golden Dawn synthesis (*pace* the many varied functions of the intervening centuries), Enochian magic was primarily about gaining mastery over the four elements and the quintessential "spirit."[27] Furthermore, emphasis was put on one of the two Adamic languages Dee and Kelly received (the *Claves*), now exclusively referred to as the angelic or Enochian language. Enochian was cast in the role of the most potent magical script of the Western "Esoteric tradition," phrases of which could be used for powerful invocations, while individual letters were placed in elaborate correspondence tables and used to unlock regions of the "astral spheres."[28]

All of these early varieties of Enochiana were based on relatively poor and limited access to the original sources. "Dr. Rudd" and the group surrounding Rorbon were part of a revival of interest following Casaubon's condemnation of Dee's magical work in *True and Faithful Relation*. Casaubon's edition of the angel diaries, however, did *not* include the five "received books," which explained in detail the different parts of the magical system. Instead, the magicians reading Casaubon extracted whatever they found interesting from the parts of the "raw" journals that had been published there. A similar situation obtained for the later magicians: while Hockley, Mackenzie, and the founders of the Golden Dawn *could* have seen some of the original sources in the British Museum, it appears that they were more taken by the accounts in Casaubon's *True and Faithful Relation* and by some of the manuscripts deriving from the aforementioned seventeenth-century revival. In the Golden Dawn synthesis, for example, we find incorporated only the parts that were available in Casaubon, particularly the system of the Great Table. It was only in the late twentieth century that the original sources became generally known among occultists. Simultaneously, magicians were gradually coming to realize that there were numerous gaps, discrepancies, and innovations in the received tradition.

Despite the fact that the Golden Dawn was rather short-lived as an organization, it remained vastly influential on the ritual magic practiced in the West—particularly the Anglophone West—throughout the twentieth and into the early twenty-first century. The Golden Dawn was responsible for producing a coherent system of Enochian magic, although this system is demonstrably more Victorian than Elizabethan. Meanwhile, though, the reinterpretations and creative shifts did not stop.

Throughout the twentieth century, new permutations of the system were created. Thus Aleister Crowley invoked the thirty-one Enochian "Aethyrs" in the desert of Algeria in the winter of 1909, using a variety of old-fashioned catoptromancy (i.e., seeing visions in a polished surface, but now justified by Victorian occultist theories of the astral plane, with a dash of Kantian transcendental idealism thrown in), sexual transgression, and *goetic* ritual, producing a set of revealed words and visions that became holy texts in his new religion of Thelema.[29] In the late 1960s, Anton LaVey, the founder of the Church of Satan and modern religious Satanism, inverted the references of the Enochian invocations of the *Claves* to talk about Satan and hell, employing these invocations in satanic ritual while simultaneously rethinking the question of magical efficacy in terms of purely pragmatic considerations and psychological and emotional effects.[30] New Age interpretations began to appear in the 1980s, combining Golden Dawn Enochiana with some of Crowley's interpretations, while adding some elements of transpersonal psychology and "human potential" thinking.[31]

Finally, starting in the late 1970s, other magicians argued for a return to the sources in order to find an "authentic" Elizabethan way of doing magic. In the mid-1990s, advocates of all of these various approaches congregated on the Internet to argue over the proper place and interpretation of angels, demons, and ritual.[32] There is, in short, a cacophony of practices, theories, interpretations, and discourses building on Dee's material. Before continuing with a closer reading of these late modern approaches to angel magic, we should look briefly at a more general question: how do we make sense of the presence of ritual magic in the late modern world?

The Problem of Modern Magic: Four Interpretive Models

The survival of ritual magic in modern culture has often been construed as a problem, particularly in light of narratives of secularization and disenchantment. In light of the received view of how Western culture has changed since the Reformation, the persistence of magic appears as something that scholars need to explain. How could it be that, while literacy was increasing, science progressing, and the authority of organized religion declining, occultism and ritual magic were flourishing in the late nineteenth century? As the agency of supernatural beings was being extirpated from the established worldview taught in schools and universities, why did educated people begin again to arm themselves with swords, wands, cups, and pentacles, to burn incense, and to summon angels and demons from magical circles?

That occultism and ritual magic blossomed in the nineteenth century and continued throughout the twentieth and into the twenty-first is, as we have seen, a well-established empirical fact.[33] When it comes to historical interpretations, several models have been proposed to account for magic's failure to disappear.[34] All of these models relate in some form or another to the secularization paradigm, whether embracing, rejecting, or contesting specific hypotheses of secularization, rationalization, or disenchantment.[35] For present purposes, let us differentiate between four basic approaches to this problem: (1) the opposition model; (2) the accommodation model; (3) the re-enchantment model; and (4) the discursive model. I will briefly present the first three before making a case for the fourth. In the rest of the chapter, I will substantiate my claim by using the post-nineteenth-century development of Enochian angel magic as a case study.

(1) Opposition

The opposition model includes approaches that cast the rise of occultism and magic in the middle of the modern period as part of an unfolding dialectic of reason and unreason. This model informs James Webb's two classic volumes, *The Occult Underground* (1974) and *The Occult Establishment* (1976), with the key point expressed in the opening statement of the former: "After the Age of Reason came the Age of the Irrational."[36] Webb's analysis centers on the concept of "rejected knowledge," meaning all pieces of knowledge that, with the onset of the Enlightenment, were pushed out of the Western episteme.[37] This "underground" knowledge became a repository of resources for those who resented aspects of modern life and wanted to stage a countermovement against the idolatry of reason. In this view, "the occult" in modern culture is always entangled in a discourse of opposition, friction, and conflict with mainstream or establishment views. The apparent difference between rational, secular culture and the world of the occult reflects two poles of a very real dialectic.

(2) Accommodation: Disenchantment and Psychologization

The accommodation model includes interpretations of modern occultism and magic arguing that we are witnessing a *transformation* of magic in which magic itself has been reworked to better accommodate a "disenchanted" modern worldview. "Disenchantment" (*Entzauberung*) is one of the buzzwords in sociohistorical analyses of religious change, originating with Max Weber and used to argue a rather broad range of positions.[38] In this context, it entails a focus on how modern magicians resolve questions about the reality and efficacy of magic, particularly vis-à-vis modern scientific pictures of the world, by producing disenchanted theories of magic itself.

A prime representative of this perspective has been Wouter J. Hanegraaff, who argues that, instead of outright conflict, modern magic exhibits a remarkable ability to accommodate a Weberian "disenchanted" view of the world. Renaissance systems of magic rested on genuine belief in a magical dimension of a-causal "correspondences," an invisible mediating *spiritus* (the *anima mundi*), and the very real existence of demons and spiritual intelligences of various kinds. By contrast, post-Enlightenment occultist interpretations involve an ontological shift that deemphasizes the entities and correspondences as "real and actual," presenting them instead as merely conventional and pragmatically useful symbols.[39] Modern magic is thus reworked to harmonize with a disenchanted worldview, a process Hanegraaff sees as a general "secularization of esotericism."[40]

One of the ways in which modern magicians come to terms with a disenchanted worldview, according to Hanegraaff, is by *psychologizing* magic itself. In a move away from more "realistic" interpretations, angels and demons tend to be viewed as "parts of the self," and magical practices are seen as (analogous to) psychological techniques for raising one's consciousness or attaining the "higher self." This psychological focus serves the purpose of resolving a possible cognitive dissonance: a magical worldview may be saved from the "iron cage" of disenchanted modernity by relocating "mysterious and incalculable forces" to the realm of the psyche. As Hanegraaff puts it, "the dissipation of mystery in this world is compensated for by a separate magical world of the reified imagination, where the everyday rules of science and rationality do not apply."[41] In this sense, psychologization becomes more like metaphysical escapism than anything else.[42]

(3) Re-enchantment

A third framework for understanding the rise of modern magic may be called the re-enchantment model. It proceeds generally by attributing a different kind of relevance to modern practitioners' use of the nomenclature of science and psychology, focusing on the way in which their belief systems as a whole may represent modern forms of enchantment. To a certain extent, the difference is one of emphasis, but there is also an element of adjusting the interpretation in light of a broader range of, and perhaps a deeper engagement with, empirical data. Thus, for example, a background reference for Hanegraaff's point about the relocation of mystery to the psyche is Tanya Luhrmann's observation that contemporary (that is, 1980s) ritual magicians tend to operate with a "separate-but-connected" magical world—commonly the "astral plane"—accessible and manipulable through various ritual techniques. However, as Christopher Partridge has shown, Hanegraaff needs to subtly twist Luhrmann's point about the separate magical world of modern magicians to make it fit the idea that magicians seek to balance a disenchanted worldview with a magical one.[43] By emphasizing the separation and downplaying the connectedness of this postulated magical plane, the *enchanted* idea, still very much present in modern magic, that ritual has effects *in this world* is deemphasized. The two worlds are not so neatly separated as the psychologization models suggests: "regardless of the updated metaphors, explanations, and interpretations, occultists, like most religious believers, have a single magical worldview. And one only has to read the works of contemporary magicians . . . to realize that the world they inhabit is enchanted."[44] In Partridge's view, the new religious formations of late modernity are not really "secularized religion" but represent instead the emergence of a new and socially significant religious "occulture," which increasingly challenges the secularism that, admittedly, dominates some of the major truth institutions (e.g., academia, the courts).[45]

(4) Discourse

An alternative approach, adopted in this chapter, is to take a step back from grand generalizations about the direction of modern religious, secular, or magical life and look in detail at what self-styled ritual magicians actually say and do.[46] This does not mean that we must surrender to a purely descriptive mode of scholarship; instead, informed by discursive approaches to the study of religion more broadly, we may theorize about magic in modern times in terms of constructions of identity that spring from active negotiation with various cultural "others" (positive as well as negative, internal as well as external).[47] Rather than focus on the survival or resurgence of magic as a "phenomenon" with certain characteristics (no matter how "fluid"), we can look at how the spokespersons for magic navigate discursively between various cultural systems (science, religion, philosophy, art, popular culture), employing various strategies to legitimize their practices and invest them with meaning.

Adopting an approach along these lines, disenchantment, psychologization, re-enchantment, and opposition to "mainstream" or "establishment" culture may all be viewed as strategic maneuvers available to proponents and practitioners of magic. This point was recently argued by Jesper Aagaard Petersen, who noted that "the heavy reliance on substantives and -isms [in theorizing about modern esoteric currents] occludes the fact that secularized esotericism is a strategic way of adapting to modernity *for social actors*." In short, we may view "secularized esotericism as a *strategic* process" through which stakeholders seek to win legitimacy by translating esoteric concepts into secular terms. Likewise, re-enchantment (or "esotericization of the secular," in Petersen's terms) exists as a counterstrategy for translating secular concepts (typically taken from the pool of scientific knowledge) into esoteric language.[48]

In this perspective, the whole field of modern ritual magic, including the subfield of Enochian angel magic discussed in the following pages, appears first and foremost as a *contested field of discourse*. Broadly speaking, it is contested in two different senses, one external, the other internal. Externally, Enochiana is contested in that it stakes out a range of positions within the broad discourse on "magic" in the West, which has largely been formed by Christian theology, Enlightenment rationalism, the encounter with foreign cultures, and the striving of the anthropological sciences to understand and explain those cultures.[49] In light of this Western discourse on magic, Enochiana is contested because it proposes the term "magic" as a positive self-denominator (as opposed to its long-standing use in identifying and delegitimizing various "others") and generally attempts to argue for the efficacy of its practice (as opposed to views of magical practice as stemming from fallacious or wishful thinking, misapplied logic, or an erroneous theory of causes). In short, the external contest is over the legitimacy of magic as such, vis-à-vis a generally secular, "disenchanted" mainstream culture.

While most "insiders" agree that the practice of magic is effective, meaningful, and valuable, the number of positions on *why, how, to what extent,* and *by which means*—questions that arise from external friction—create frictions internally as well. Here, the notion of strategic action by social actors becomes important in order to see what is going on: while one proponent may argue that magic works because it taps into well-understood psychological mechanisms, another may prefer to talk about "higher selves," Jungian archetypes, or the charisma of new Thelemic gods. Still others may claim that angels and demons are really "out there," as in the grimoires of olden days, and insist on taking sources seriously and literally. All of these responses can perform strategic functions within a discursive space. Internally, they beget new problems that require yet more new strategies in the struggle to define who has the right to speak authoritatively about Enochiana and what criteria should be used to determine "authenticity." In the next section, I will give a closer analysis of the external and internal strategies we find in connection with Enochian magic, focusing particularly on the latter.

Arguing with Angels: Enochian Magic as a Contested Field of Discourse

Elsewhere, I have proposed to see the external and internal dimensions of Enochian discourse as, respectively, a "struggle for legitimacy" (i.e., of magic in general vis-à-vis the values, beliefs, and practices of mainstream culture) and a discourse-internal "authenticity problem."[50] The struggle for legitimacy we have already touched upon; it is what the disenchantment and re-enchantment models have fought over. It is also out of this perceived tension that strategies for translating magical concepts into, for example, psychological or scientific language emerged. This struggle has given rise to the strategies that Olav Hammer has described for modern esoteric systems in general, especially what he calls "scientism," or "the active positioning of one's own claims in relation to the manifestations of any academic scientific discipline."[51] The two other strategies Hammer discusses, the appeal to "tradition" and the appeal to narratives of personal experience, are of more interest to the internal debates—namely, the fights between insiders over who gets to define the nature of Enochiana and what should count as criteria for authenticity. What follows will focus on these internal debates. First, however, we need to know a little bit more about the specific, historically contingent characteristics that applied to the Enochian discourse at the dawn of the twentieth century and that have continued to direct its development into the present century.

The Authenticity Problem in Modern Enochian Magic

The authenticity problem has its roots in the fall of the Hermetic Order of the Golden Dawn during the first decade of the twentieth century.[52] The Golden Dawn had provided a sophisticated and elaborate synthesis and a highly persuasive way of working with ritual magic. Enochian magic had an integral place within this broad synthesis; indeed, the teaching material circulated in the order gave no real hint at how such magic could possibly be dislodged from the rest of the order's teachings.[53] When the Golden Dawn was fragmented by schism, the canonized teachings were gradually "unlocked," and ex-members of various persuasions started to critically reassess its many sources and to evaluate its claim to a perennial Rosicrucian tradition.

Magicians soon became conscious of the discrepancy between Golden Dawn Enochian magic and the original Dee/Kelly material. Aleister Crowley seems to have been the first to confront the issue; he researched the sources in preparation for his experiments in 1909 with "the Aethyrs" (of *Liber scientiae*), a part of the Enochian system not fully covered by the Golden Dawn teachings. It seemed to Crowley that there was much more to be learned than the leaders of the Golden Dawn had let on. Later, in America, Paul Foster Case used a similar strategy to argue a rather different point. He had been the head of a Golden Dawn faction's temple in New York until he was excommunicated in 1922 by the leader Moina Mathers (née Bergson—the sister of Henri, and the wife of MacGregor Mathers) in Paris. After his excommunication, and probably after learning about the origin of the Enochian system in the crystal-gazing experiments of Dee and Kelly (a fact long obscured by the Golden Dawn's mythmaking), Case went on to argue that the Enochian system should be extirpated from the synthesis altogether. This objective was carried out in Case's own occult group, the Builders of the Adytum.

Case's motivation for this purge was his conviction that Enochiana probably arose from corrupted "black magic" and had nothing to do with "true" Rosicrucianism, which for him was the real measure of authenticity for the Golden

Dawn tradition. In a letter to the young Israel Regardie in 1933, Case expressed it this way: "I submit that 'orthodoxy' simply means 'correct teaching' and that the burden of my criticism is that MacGregor [Mathers] (and nobody else) introduced alien elements into the stream which seems to have come to us through Mackenzie, Levi and their contemporaries. In eliminating the Enochian elements, we in America have lost nothing of practical effectiveness."[54]

By contrasting the examples of Crowley and Case, we soon arrive at the core of the authenticity problem that drove much of the Enochian discourse in the twentieth century. The discrepancy between the Enochian magic of the Golden Dawn, eclectically combined with kabbalistic and elemental magic, and the original system of Dee and Kelly poses a problem of authenticity for magicians who have been taught to consider Enochian magic the highest, most potent form of magic. Where can authenticity reside after the crumbling of the Golden Dawn synthesis—the veritable "master-narrative" of modern ritual magic?[55]

Thinking in terms of ideal-typical discursive strategies, we may isolate three ways in which spokespersons in the Enochian field could handle this problem:

(1) *Purism:* Going back to the sources to correct the errors made by the eager Golden Dawn occultists. In this approach, appeals to scholarship play an important role in establishing and defending authenticity and in attacking opponents.

(2) *Perennialism:* Holding the Golden Dawn's narrative to be true in some way, typically by claiming that Enochiana was not the product of Dee and Kelly but predated them and was "restored" to its pristine state by the Golden Dawn. Here, scholarship, in the ordinary sense of the word at least, is less important for authenticity. The strategy rests instead on appeals to tradition, myth, or "verification" through various exotic techniques like clairvoyance, astral scrying, and communion with "secret chiefs."

(3) *Pragmatism* or *progressivism:* Following a pragmatic approach in which the test of truth is whether magicians get useful results from the various systems. Progressivism seems to be an appropriate alternative label in that it is often implied that the system can be altered and improved by the magician without an accompanying loss of authenticity.

These claims and strategies are found throughout the twentieth-century sources. "Purism," "perennialism," and "pragmatism/progressivism" thus constitute the three ideal discursive strategies used by post–Golden Dawn Enochian magicians to resolve the authenticity problem sketched above and to argue the legitimacy of their own particular positions.[56] With these distinctions in mind, it is time to consider some cases in which we may see these various strategies at work, starting with the perennialism characteristic of the Golden Dawn's approach.

Perennialist Authenticity

The vision of the Order of the Golden Dawn had rested for the most part on claims to tradition and lineage. Such claims were particularly connected to the standard narratives of Rosicrucianism: that a hidden society of illuminated brothers (and sisters, in the case of the Golden Dawn) had been working in secret through the ages, doing good for the world while protecting a profound, initiated knowledge. For the Golden Dawn, knowledge of Enochian magic was a part of this secret initiation: various parts were taken from the Great Table and only gradually revealed to the aspirant as he or she ascended through the initiatory degrees. After finally reaching the status of "adeptus minor" and being taken into the so-called inner order, the aspirant was confronted with the tomb of Christian Rosenkreutz and given the full picture.

During the ceremony, the candidate was told that the mysteries of the rose and the cross have existed since the dawn of time but were gathered together by Christian Rosenkreutz and brought to a small society in Europe in the late Middle Ages. Much of the primordial wisdom was then translated and written down by some of Rosenkreutz's "monastic brethren." Among the writings left to this society, the candidate was told, was "some of the Magical Language" from "the Elemental Tablets" (that is, Dee's four watchtowers, which the Golden Dawn attributed to the elements). A dictionary of the language was even said to have existed at the time. That the angelic language would form a part of Rosenkreutz's secrets was only to be expected, since "the True Order of the Rose Cross descendeth into the depths, and ascendeth into the heights— even unto the Throne of God Himself, and includeth even Archangels, Angels and Spirits."[57] The inner order of the Golden Dawn was not a terrestrial institution at all; it was a truly cosmic and spiritual order, with God as the highest "secret chief."

Against this background, it is perhaps not surprising that we find perennialist responses used among twentieth-century magicians who continued not only to practice but also to defend the Golden Dawn synthesis. I have already cited the correspondence between Paul Foster Case and Israel Regardie in which Case made a combined purist and perennialist point to argue that the Golden Dawn should be cleansed of Enochian magic. The purist challenge was that the angelic language and the magic of the Great Table could be traced back to John Dee and Edward Kelly, quite *contrary to* the primordial origins claimed in the order's adeptus minor ceremony. The perennial status of the Golden Dawn teachings was not in question, but the Enochian material was not considered an authentic part of it because it could be attributed to Dee and Kelly. Regardie took a rather different path from Case initially, choosing to join one of the successor orders of the Golden Dawn, the Stella Matutina. When he decided to publish the rituals and doctrines of the Golden Dawn toward the end of the 1930s, it was partially in order to disseminate the practice of magic. Here, we find some intriguing perennialist responses defending the authenticity of Enochian magic against the purist challenge.

One response was to have "clairvoyants" look into the secret history of the angelic system.[58] Golden Dawn's clairvoyants claimed that Dee and Kelly had gained access to the Enochian system only when they were in central Europe, through contact with alleged Rosicrucian centers in Germany, Austria, and Bohemia. Of course, this claim conflicts with the detailed accounts given by Dee and Kelly themselves, and thus would not convince purists with a decent knowledge of the sources. The truly scholarly-minded might also protest that there is no evidence of Rosicrucianism before the seventeenth century. In the emic historiography of the Golden Dawn, however, the claims of the *Fama fraternitatis* are taken at face value, and the foundation of Rosicrucianism is placed with the legendary Christian Rosenkreutz in the fifteenth century. The claim made by still other clairvoyants referenced by Regardie—that Enochian magic is part of a system originally practiced in Atlantis—is no more convincing to the academic historian.

Another strategy was to emphasize one of the allegedly most mysterious features of the system, the Enochian language. For example, it was claimed that it was a genuine "natural language," and evidence was marshaled to show that it predated Dee and Kelly. An example of this approach is found in an undated lecture written by J. W. Brodie-Innes. His speech reached aspirants who had recently been introduced to one of the perplexing Enochian letter squares in their initiation ritual. Brodie-Innes explained that the letters on the tablet had been transliterated from another script, "one of the most ancient symbols in the world." The reference is clearly to the Enochian alphabet. Brodie-Innes revealed that the language in question was "a great curiosity merely from the linguistic point of view" because it was a real language with real syntax and grammar, but one that had not been spoken "by mortal man," so far as anyone knew. Brodie-Innes went on to suggest that it was a primordial but "hidden" language, never known in its *entirety* in historical times: "We find traces of it on rock-cut pillars and on temples, apparently as old as the world. We find traces of it in the sacred mysteries of some of the oldest religions in the world, but we find no trace of it ever having been used as a living language, and we hold the tradition that it is the Angelic secret language." The language had been used by the angels since creation, while drops of it were made known to humanity through history. Brodie-Innes continued with an example: "The high priest of Jupiter in the earliest days of Rome was called Flamen *Dialis,* and you will find that the most learned are utterly ignorant as to whence came the word *Dialis.* They will tell you that it is ancient Etruscan, but beyond that they can tell you nothing. It is not the genitive of any known nominative. On that Tablet (Earth) you will see that the second of the Three Holy Secret Names of God is *Dial.*"

Regardie elaborated on this line of argumentation when he claimed to have found an Enochian word resembling a Sanskrit word of similar meaning. Linking the Sanskrit connection with linguistic theories of a proto-Indo-European language, Regardie was able to corroborate one of the more imaginative speculations made by the Golden Dawn's clairvoyants. If there was a language "which lies behind Sanskrit," then "according to the philosophy of the Ancient Wisdom," it had to be "that of Atlantis." On the basis of one single word's similarity to a Sanskrit term, Regardie argued that "the Enochian or Angelical language bears several strong points of resemblance to" the assumed Atlantean language.

Pragmatic and Progressive Arguments

The pragmatic response that Enochiana, whatever it is and wherever it comes from, need only prove itself by the fact that it *works,* is found in a number of authors, from Crowley to present-day magicians active in occult discussion forums online. This approach is often connected with other strategies, including as a reinforcement of perennialism. At other times, it is used to open up the system and legitimize creative innovations. Crowley illustrates the first tendency when, after trying out a mild version of the "primordial language" argument about the Enochian language, he asserts that "however this may be, it *works.* Even the beginner finds that 'things happen' when he uses it: and this is an advantage—or disadvantage!—shared by no other type of language. The rest need skill. This needs prudence!"[59]

The clearest example of a use of the pragmatic-progressive strategy is found in Anton LaVey's attempts to make an unlikely match between Enochiana and his new Satanist religion. For someone who styled himself as the black pope of an overtly anti-Christian religion, it is of course difficult to accept the claimed angelic provenance of Enochian magic and language. Yet steeped in the esoteric discourse of 1960s California, where the Golden Dawn's and Crowley's take on occultism could not be ignored, LaVey found it desirable to claim this most cherished piece of esoterica for Satanism. Negotiating these two conflicting interests, LaVey asserted that the angels "are only 'angels' because occultists to this day have lain ill with metaphysical constipation."[60]

In satanic ritual, the Enochian language was to be employed mainly for its perceived *psychological* benefits. It was thought to be a particularly evocative language, and the phonetic qualities were to be emphasized: "the importance should be placed upon the rhythmic and sequential delivery of the words, rather than a scholarly attempt to pronounce them properly."[61] Nevertheless, the mysterious aura surrounding the language's provenance was still worth remembering: "The magical language used in Satanic ritual is Enochian. Enochian is a language which is thought to be older than Sanskrit, with a sound grammatical and syntactical basis. . . . In Enochian the meaning of the words, combined with the quality of the words, unite to create a pattern of sound which can cause tremendous reaction in the atmosphere. The barbaric tonal qualities of this language give it a truly magical effect which cannot be described."[62] Although LaVey echoes Brodie-Innes, Regardie, and Crowley on the genuineness of the language, it is worth noting that his main focus is on sound. Enochian is to be employed chiefly because of the "truly magical *effect*" that its tonal qualities are said to possess. The emphasis is on the pragmatic effect rather than the scholarly "authenticity," metaphysical correspondence, or divine origin of the language.

Shortly after LaVey published *The Satanic Bible*, which contained the Enochian *Claves* with "satanized" references, a brief conflict broke out with Regardie and the Golden Dawn–oriented Enochianites, a dispute that underscores the difference between perennialism and pragmatic progressivism. Regardie decried *The Satanic Bible* as a "debased volume" that presented a "perverted edition" of Enochian. His attack referred specifically to the satanic revisions of the translated calls and "several other pieces of similar stupidity."[63] Regardie's attack was countered in an article by Michael Aquino published in the Church of Satan's newsletter, *Cloven Hoof*. Aquino's argument combined the purist emphasis on source material with a pragmatic plea for innovation; by documenting how the Golden Dawn and Crowley receptions of Enochian (which Regardie defended against the "perverted" satanic version) were *themselves* reinterpretations and decontextualized innovations of the original sixteenth-century work of Dee and Kelly, Aquino attacked the very premises of Regardie's argument. From a scholarly point of view, Aquino was entirely right: Regardie did not present a sound historical argument but was rather defending a particular (modern) esoteric position against the new dissenting Satanism. But in addition to deconstructing Regardie in this way, Aquino's final point was progressive: the members of the Church of Satan had found that LaVey's new versions of the calls were simply much more *effective* than the old ones. A copy of Aquino's article was sent to Regardie, who, in Aquino's words, "probably found it as palatable" as LaVey had found Regardie's attack.[64]

The Purist Turn

Although purism as a strategy was present already in Crowley's day, it was only in the late 1970s that it became a dominant trend. Indeed, there was something of a "purist turn" in occultist discourse on Enochiana around this time, sparked by a number of core publications that made the historical origin of the system—and its discrepancy from the Golden Dawn synthesis—impossible to ignore. In 1974, Stephen Skinner published a facsimile edition of Casaubon's *True and Faithful Relation*.[65] Then, in 1976 and 1978, two dictionaries of the Enochian language appeared: Leo Vinci's *Gmicalzoma* and Donald C. Laycock's *Complete Enochian Dictionary*. The first recapitulated the etymological fantasies of Brodie-Innes and Regardie. Laycock, by contrast, a trained linguist, supplied his dictionary with a solid introduction analyzing various linguistic features of the language, even debunking the claim that Enochian could be anything like a genuine "natural language."[66] With these tools available, more attention was directed toward the original sources in the 1980s.

The clearest example of a consistent purist is Robert Turner, who in the late 1970s became the head of the Order of the Cubic Stone, based in the English Midlands. Throughout the 1970s, this order had been known for its very practical approach to magic with a Golden Dawn orientation.[67] Under Turner's leadership, two things occurred. Enochian magic became the main focus of the group, and this magic was explored in a fairly academic way. As one ex-student put it, "the sole focus hinged upon what could be reconstructed from the Dee material."[68]

Based on his own diligent research on original manuscripts at the British Library and the Bodleian in Oxford, Turner published two books that have become classics of the purist turn of Enochiana, *The Heptarchia Mystica of John Dee* (1983) and *Elizabethan Magic* (1989). *The Heptarchia Mystica* was the first publication of the heptarchic system ever to appear in print. In its introduction, Turner expresses his bafflement over the neglect of the heptarchic system; it was really "the only true example of a complete magical system to be found in the Dee papers," yet modern occultists had neglected it completely.[69] Instead, they had constructed grand syntheses out of various incomplete systems.

Despite the emphasis on scholarly method, Turner's motivations were clearly practical. At the end of the introduction to *Heptarchia Mystica*, Turner declared, "A Midlands based occult group have recently reconstructed the Holy Table, wax discs and other necessary equipment and shortly hope to perform the Heptarchical rite, publishing their findings in due course. Whether or not the spirits will welcome this invasion of their four hundred year repose remains uncertain."[70] If Turner is the clearest representative of the purist current, he is by no means the only one.[71] Another important book from this era is Geoffrey James's *Enochian Evocation of Dr. John Dee* (1984), which attempted to "present the essential core of Dee's evocation system arranged in a fashion similar to other renaissance evocation texts."[72] This was the first book to publish material from the entire set of Dee's received books, while "filling in the gaps" by paying attention to the Renaissance magical theories with which Dee and Kelly would have been familiar.

What Does Contemporary Enochian Magic Tell Us About Dis-/Re-enchanted Modernity?

We have been tracking two aspects of the modern transformation of magic in this chapter. First, a cross-historical comparison demonstrated how a specific set of magical procedures first envisioned in the Elizabethan period was rediscovered, adapted, and modified through consecutive iterations to the present day. Second, the modern reception of these magical texts is characterized by a discursive complexity and tension that make for an intriguing but problematic test case for generalizations about the disenchantment or the re-enchantment of modern culture.

Two observations based on the first of these themes can be used to say something interesting about the second. First, in the processes of reinterpretation and transmission of Enochian magic, it is precisely the gaps, errors, and distortions of the sources that have provided room for creative reconstructions and the production of new meanings. Second, literature intended to *condemn* the practice (i.e., Casaubon's edition) ended up *transmitting* it and providing further tools for creative reinterpretation of the material. Indeed, condemnation may even have increased its salience for would-be occultists. These simple observations have a more general import: while we may speak of broad sociohistorical transformation processes like "secularization," "disenchantment," and the rejection of "heretical" knowledge,[73] these processes tell us little about what individual actors *do* under such conditions on the ground.[74] To adopt the language of the sociologist Karel Dobbelaere, we must distinguish between social processes on the macro level (society as a whole) and on the intermediate meso level (of institutions and forms of organization), on the one hand, and the actions, meanings, beliefs, and articulated opinions of individuals on the micro level, on the other.[75] While the "rejection" of magic by the authorized discourses of "the Establishment" does *constrain* the space of plausibility (or the episteme, in Foucauldian terms), it does not *determine* the adoption of specific positions within that space. We should expect to see a variety of positions expressed on the ground. However, these positions are constrained not merely by *external* factors but by internal ones as well, stemming from the particular genealogy of the field in question. This is the generic point in the case of Enochiana's problem with authenticity. Owing to its specific lines of transmission, the gaps and distortions of the material, and the layers of novel interpretation and system-building efforts, a structured set of strategies for authenticity have emerged among modern spokespersons.

In concluding this chapter, I wish to draw attention to how these two factors—an external epistemic pressure and an internal crisis of authenticity—together determine the positions that individual stakeholders take on the *metaphysical* questions involved: in what sense are the angels and the demons "real," and why does magic work? This is precisely the sort of question on which the disenchantment/re-enchantment debate has focused, and it has not been difficult for either side to cherry-pick individual examples of modern magicians that seem to confirm that magic has been disenchanted and psychologized, or, conversely, that it still teems with mysterious and incalculable powers. A discursive view of strategic action helps us account for the diversity of positions that are empirically attestable on the ground.

The issue of whether, or in what sense, the magical entities are "real" may figuratively be seen as occupying a space between the question of legitimacy, imposed from the outside, and the internal question of authenticity. While external cultural systems such as mainstream religion and science place constraints on the metaphysical interpretation of magic, the internal choice of strategies concerning authenticity will likewise steer the magician in specific directions. Thus the plausibility or implausibility of specific metaphysical visions is negotiated between these two dimensions.

"Disenchanted" tendencies typically make a match with pragmatic approaches to authenticity. We saw this most clearly with Anton LaVey, who argued that the semantic content of the word "angel" was the result of "metaphysical constipation." Instead, as we saw, LaVey favored a theory of the efficacy of magic that traded on psychology and emotional arousal: "rituals" as such were seen as "intellectual decompression chambers" in which stimuli (such as the Enochian calls) worked to distract the intellect and channel emotional energy.[76]

The clearest examples of the opposite view, which we may term *realism* about magical entities, are found among some of the purists. For example, Geoffrey James's *Enochian Evocation* spends several pages in an attempt to discard the criticisms and suspicions about the divinity of the Enochian language raised by Laycock. James searches the Dee material for passages that can be considered, in his words, "evidence for the presence of the supernatural." As mentioned earlier, Laycock had remarked that the Enochian language exhibited features that did not make sense phonetically. James takes this point, used to delegitimize the authenticity of the Enochian language, and inverts it completely by relating it to a worldview in which angels are real: "The Angelical language . . . exhibits characteristics that would seem to indicate that it was designed to be a non-spoken language. As Da Vinci had pointed out nearly 100 years before the keys were dictated, spirits would be unable to make audible sounds on their own, due to the lack of vocal chords with which to vibrate air."[77] James does not allow for psychologized or purely pragmatic approaches to the question of occult entities; rather, he supposes a realistic understanding of the angels. This seems to be a preferred tendency in the purist approach to Enochian—perhaps to be expected, as these authors attempt to get as close to their Renaissance forebears as possible, making them the proper authorities on magical efficacy.

While underlining the point that strategies are always chosen by social actors, are always up for negotiation, and are never fixed in one direction, we should also note with some interest that Geoffrey James changed his strategy later in his career. In the introduction to the second edition of his book, in 1998, James wrote that "Enochian angels are unlikely to be 'real' in the sense of being composed out of atoms, particle waves, or quantifiable material." By this time, he opted instead for something like a psychologizing strategy, which nevertheless retained the "enchanted" valuation of the entities: "I believe that angels may represent aspects of the human consciousness that all of us share. In that way, they exist in [the] collective unconscious, which is, in some ways at least, more 'real' than the physical world."[78] This statement, moreover, reminds us that "psychologization" cannot be taken to mean one fixed thing: there is a great discrepancy between what James does with a psychologizing perspective here and what LaVey did.

A final example illustrates the contested nature of these questions in contemporary Enochian ritual magic. With the expansion of the Internet in the mid-1990s, Enochian discourse migrated to e-lists and online discussion forums, which increased the level of open debate and confrontation over central issues. In this venue, all of the competing strategies mesh together and try their strengths through argumentation. We find a mélange of Crowleyites,

Golden Dawn practitioners, Satanists, purist scholar-magicians, and pragmatic experimentalists. Among these various factions, the question of authenticity has been much discussed, as has the question of the reality of spiritual entities. In closing, I will quote from an instructive discussion between one of the Enochian-L e-list's heroes, Benjamin Rowe, and a newcomer curious about the reality of angels.

The newcomer, signing himself variously as "Tim" and "V. H.," asked Rowe whether he believed that Enochian had in fact been delivered by angels and whether he considered understanding the motivations of these supposed angelic beings a necessary step to understanding Enochian. Rowe's response reveals an attitude that seems quite pervasive among the more eloquent segments of the contemporary occultural milieu. First, Rowe noted his own long-standing practice of putting "the word 'angels' in quotes, to show that I was using it as a convenience rather than as a statement of belief about the nature of the phenomena observed. I haven't the faintest idea as to the 'real' nature of the source of these recorded words."[79] Rowe's starting point, in other words, is a kind of noncommittal agnosticism. It is, however, a *strategic* agnosticism, a way to be noncommittal while still holding that "something's going on." "Agnostic" magicians' evaluations seldom end there, and Rowe is no exception.[80] After bracketing the reality question, Rowe proceeds to claim that the evidence of Dee's diaries provides a picture of independent, sapient beings: "In the absence of strong evidence to the contrary . . . it is simplest to deal with the material in the terms in which it presents itself, and to see where that leads." Rowe uses an amusing analogy to argue his point:

> The evidence I have for the existence of these "angels" as separate beings is of *exactly* the same sort as I have for the existence of "V. H." [i.e., the person he is responding to]. In some ways the evidence in their favor is a bit stronger; the angels I contact using the Calls frequently surprise me, while "Tim" is fairly predictable. Perhaps "Tim" is just a clever AI program running on a MacIntosh somewhere in the bowels of Apple Corp; or perhaps "Tim" is a bit of online theater, maintained over the years by a group of scriptwriters. ;-) Still, most of the time it is simpler to act as if Tim is an intelligent, individual being. The same for these "angels."[81]

This argument combines a pragmatic emphasis on experience with an affirmation of the angels' reality. Aided by an inference to the best explanation, the magician moves from noncommittal agnosticism to defending a worldview in which angels and demons are as real as anything else we assume in our daily lives on the basis of common sense.

What does all of this tell us about the survival of learned magic in the modern age? In line with the discursive approach that has been adopted in this chapter, the reason for magic's survival may be found not so much in any single descriptive trait, but rather in the cultural flexibility that results from the creativity of individual magicians vying for cultural legitimacy and authenticity among subcultural peers. This flexibility, then, is not so much a trait of "magic" itself but is grounded rather in strategic concerns and in a general religious creativity—the ability of human beings to improvise and create new meanings on the basis of the cultural ingredients present in their environment.

NOTES

The title of this article is Enochian, and translates roughly, I hope, as "Speech of God, or The Works of Men on Earth." With due apology to Adam and the angels.

1. A voluminous literature dealing with Dee in general and his angel-scrying activities in particular has emerged over the past half century. Some central works, in order of appearance, include Peter French, *John Dee: The World of an Elizabethan Magus* (London: Routledge & Kegan Paul, 1972); Frances Yates, *The Occult Philosophy in the Elizabethan Age* (London: Routledge & Kegan Paul, 1979); Christopher Whitby, *John Dee's Actions with Spirits*, 2 vols. (New York: Garland, 1988); Nicholas Clulee, *John Dee's Natural Philosophy* (London: Routledge, 1988); Deborah Harkness, *John Dee's Conversations with Angels: Cabala, Alchemy, and the End of Nature* (Cambridge: Cambridge University Press, 1999); Håkan Håkansson, *Seeing the Word: John Dee and Renaissance Occultism* (Lund: Lunds Universitets Forlag, 2001); György E. Szonyi, *John Dee's Occultism: Magical Exaltation Through Powerful Signs* (Albany: State University of New York Press, 2004); and Stephen Clucas, ed., *John Dee: Interdisciplinary Studies in English Renaissance Thought* (Dordrecht: Springer, 2006).

2. The surviving parts of these spirit diaries are preserved in the Cotton and Sloane collections of the British Library. See Cotton Appendix XLVI (detailing the angel conversations from May 28, 1583, to May 23, 1587, plus March 20 to September 7, 1607); Sloane MS 3188 (the diary for December 22, 1581–May 23, 1583); Sloane MS 3189 (the "received book" *Liber Loagaeth*); and Sloane MS 3191 (including the four "received books," *48 Claves angelicae; Liber scientiae, auxilii, et victoriae terrestris; De heptarchia mystica*; and *Tabula bonorum angelorum*). For published versions, see Meric Casaubon, ed., *A True and Faithful Relation of What passed for many Yeers Between Dr. John Dee and some Spirits* (London, 1659); Whitby, *John Dee's Actions with Spirits*; and *John Dee's Five Books of Mystery: Original Sourcebook of Enochian Magic*, ed. Joseph Peterson (York Beach, Maine: Red Wheel/Weiser, 2003). See also my discussion of the "received books" below.

3. For previous attempts to trace this development, see Marco Pasi and Philippe Rabaté, "Langue angélique, langue magique, l'énochien," *Politica Hermetica* 13 (1999): 94–123; and Egil Asprem, *Arguing with Angels: Enochian Magic and Modern Occulture* (Albany: State University of New York Press, 2012).

4. Compare György E. Szonyi's attempt at a classification of the contents of the angel diaries in "Paracelsus, Scrying, and the *Lingua Adamica*," in Clucas, *John Dee: Interdisciplinary Studies*, 216–18. It should be noted that Szonyi focuses more on the course of the conversations as a whole, rather than working toward a dissection of the "magical" components as such.

5. The "raw" diary entries are preserved in Sloane MS 3188 and Cotton Appendix XLVI in the British Library. The latter formed the basis for Meric Casaubon's 1659 *True and Faithful*

Relation, which, in addition to being the first publication of Dee's magical work, had a sizable influence on the direction of later Enochiana.

6. Preserved in Sloane MS 3189. "Logaeth" seems to be a misspelling stemming from Casaubon's edition of the manuscripts now in the Cotton Appendix; fol. 15b shows Dee spelling it "Loagaeth," which is the form that will be adopted here.

7. For the diary entries of these conversations, see *Dee's Five Books of Mystery*, 257–59.

8. See Sloane MS 3189. This book is written in Kelly's handwriting. See also Harkness, *Dee's Conversations with Angels*, 41.

9. Harkness, *Dee's Conversations with Angels*, 41.

10. Ibid. The manuscript is now in Sloane MS 3191, fols. 32–51.

11. See especially ibid., fols. 45b–51a.

12. Ibid., fols. 1a–14b.

13. Linguistic analyses of the two sets of language—as far as possible based on such limited material—shows that the two languages have very different phonetic and syntactic structures. The linguist Donald C. Laycock suggests that the first, untranslated language was produced by glossolalia, while the second bears all the characteristics of a standard constructed language: its syntax is identical to English syntax, and many of the words bear similarities to words known in early modern European languages, while others appear to be constructed randomly from strings of letters (i.e., without considering the distribution of vocals and consonants, as any naturally evolved language would have done). See Donald C. Laycock, "Enochian: Angelic Language or Mortal Folly?," in *The Complete Enochian Dictionary*, ed. Donald C. Laycock (Boston: Weiser Books, 1994), 19–64.

14. Sloane MS 3191, fols. 14a–31b.

15. Ibid., fol. 16a.

16. Harkness, *Dee's Conversations with Angels*, 187–92.

17. Sloane MS 3191, fols. 52b–80b.

18. Ibid., fol. 179 (emphasis in original).

19. Cf. Owen Davies, *Grimoires: A History of Magic Books* (Oxford: Oxford University Press, 2009).

20. See especially Harkness, *Dee's Conversations with Angels*; and compare Clulee, *John Dee's Natural Philosophy*.

21. These diaries are preserved in Sloane MSS 3624–28. See Harkness, *Dee's Conversations with Angels*, 222–23.

22. Now in Harley MS 6482, British Library. The grimoire was published by Adam McLean, ed., *A Treatise on Angel Magic* (1989) (York Beach, Maine: Weiser Books, 2006). For a detailed discussion of provenance and analysis of the contents, see Egil Asprem, "False, Lying Spirits and Angels of Light: Ambiguous Mediation in Dr Rudd's Seventeenth-Century Treatise on Angel Magic," *Magic, Ritual, and Witchcraft* 3, no. 1 (2008): 54–80; and Asprem, *Arguing with Angels*, chap. 2.

23. See Joscelyn Godwin, *The Theosophical Enlightenment* (Albany: State University of New York Press, 1994), chap. 9.

24. Robert Gilbert, "Secret Writing: The Magical Manuscripts of Frederick Hockley," in *Rosicrucian Seer: Magical Writings of Frederick Hockley*, ed. Robert Gilbert and John Hamill (Wellingborough, UK: Aquarian Press, 1986), 32; see also the "crystal manuscripts" partially reproduced in this text at 109–28.

25. Godwin, *Theosophical Enlightenment*, 185.

26. For the Order of the Golden Dawn, see especially Ellic Howe, *Magicians of the Golden Dawn: A Documentary History of a Magical Order, 1887–1923* (York Beach, Maine: Samuel Weiser, 1978); Mary Greer, *Women of the Golden Dawn: Rebels and Priestesses* (Rochester, Vt.: Park Street Press, 1995); and Alex Owen, *The Place of Enchantment: British Occultism and the Culture of the Modern* (Chicago: University of Chicago Press, 2004). For concise overviews of the Golden Dawn's history, teachings, structure, and impact, see Robert A. Gilbert, "The Hermetic Order of the Golden Dawn," in *Dictionary of Gnosis and Western Esotericism*, ed.

Wouter J. Hanegraaff, in collaboration with Antoine Faivre, Roelof van den Broek, and Jean-Pierre Brach (Leiden: Koninklijke Brill, 2005), 544–50.

27. Asprem, *Arguing with Angels*, chap. 3.

28. As detailed in the manuscript reproduced in Darcy Küntz, ed., *The Enochian Experiments of the Golden Dawn: The Enochian Alphabet Clairvoyantly Examined* (Sequim, Wash.: Holmes Publishing, 1996).

29. See, e.g., Owen, *Place of Enchantment*, 186–220; and see Asprem, *Arguing with Angels*, chap. 5. For published primary sources, see Aleister Crowley, Victor B. Neuburg, and Mary Desti, *The Vision and the Voice, with Commentary and Other Papers*, ed. William Breeze (York Beach, Maine: Weiser Books, 1998).

30. Asprem, *Arguing with Angels*, chap. 6. See Anton Szandor LaVey, *The Satanic Bible* (New York: Avon Books, 1969), 159–272. For modern religious Satanism, see especially the essays in Jesper Aagaard Petersen, ed., *Contemporary Religious Satanism: A Critical Anthology* (Burlington, Vt.: Ashgate, 2009).

31. This tendency is especially clear in the works of Gerald and Betty Schueler. See, for example, Gerald Schueler, *Enochian Physics: The Structure of the Magical Universe* (St. Paul, Minn.: Llewellyn, 1988); Gerald Schueler and Betty Schueler, *Enochian Yoga: Uniting Humanity and Divinity* (St. Paul, Minn.: Llewellyn, 1995); Gerald Schueler and Betty Schueler, *Advanced Guide to Enochian Magick: A Complete Manual of Enochian Magick* (St. Paul, Minn.: Llewellyn, 1995); and Gerald Schueler and Betty Schueler, *The Angels' Message to Humanity: Ascension to Divine Union-Powerful Enochian Magick* (St. Paul, Minn.: Llewellyn, 1996) (2002 edition with a foreword by Donald Tyson).

32. For details, see Asprem, *Arguing with Angels*, chaps. 7 and 8.

33. See, e.g., Godwin, *Theosophical Enlightenment*; Owen, *Place of Enchantment*; James Webb, *The Occult Underground* (London: Open Court, 1974); and Asprem, *Arguing with Angels*. For Victorian ritual magic specifically, see Christopher McIntosh, *Eliphas Lévi and the French Occult Revival* (New York: Samuel Weiser, 1974); Howe, *Magicians of the Golden Dawn*; Jocelyn Godwin, Christian Chanel, and John Patrick Deveney, eds., *The Hermetic Brotherhood of Luxor: Initiatic and Historical Documents of an Order of Practical Occultism* (York Beach, Maine: Samuel Weiser, 1995); Greer, *Women of the Golden Dawn*; and Francis King, *Ritual Magic in England: 1887 to the Present Day* (London: Neville Spearman, 1970).

34. *Pace* Keith Thomas, *Religion and the Decline of Magic* (New York: Scribner, 1971).

35. I am broadly following Steve Bruce's argument that "the secularization thesis" ought to be replaced by a broader secularization *paradigm*, in which different and sometimes conflicting theories of religious decline and/or change are formed. See Steve Bruce, *God Is Dead: Secularization in the West* (Oxford: Blackwell, 2002).

36. Webb, *Occult Underground*, 5; significantly, this book was originally titled *The Flight from Reason*.

37. Ibid., 191–92; and see also Michael Barkun, *A Culture of Conspiracy* (Berkeley: University of California Press, 2003), 23–24. Interestingly, Colin Campbell's highly influential model of the "cultic milieu," which makes a similar point regarding rejected knowledge, was formulated around the same time, seemingly independently from Webb. Colin Campbell, "The Cult, the Cultic Milieu, and Secularization," *Sociological Yearbook of Religion in Britain* 5 (1972): 119–36.

38. For a critical review, see Egil Asprem, *The Problem of Disenchantment: Scientific Naturalism and Esoteric Discourse, 1900–1939* (Leiden: Brill, 2014), 17–49.

39. Wouter J. Hanegraaff, "How Magic Survived the Disenchantment of the World," *Religion* 33 (2003): 361–64, 366–67.

40. E.g., Wouter J. Hanegraaff, *New Age Religion and Western Culture: Esotericism in the Mirror of Secular Thought* (Albany: State University of New York Press, 1998), 520–21.

41. Hanegraaff, "How Magic Survived," 366ff (quotation at 370).

42. The "psychologization thesis" of modern magic has been the subject of a debate over the past decade. The key contributions to date are Asprem, "Magic Naturalized? Negotiating

Science and Occult Experience in Aleister Crowley's Scientific Illuminism," *Aries: Journal for the Study of Western Esotericism* 8, no. 2 (2008): 139–65; Marco Pasi, "Varieties of Magical Experience: Aleister Crowley's Views on Occult Practice," *Magic, Ritual, and Witchcraft* 6, no. 2 (2011): 123–62; Christopher A. Plaisance, "Israel Regardie and the Psychologization of Esoteric Discourse," *Correspondences: Online Journal for the Academic Study of Western Esotericism* 3 (2015): 5–54.

43. Christopher Partridge, *The Re-Enchantment of the West*, vol. 1 (London: T&T Clark International, 2004), 40–41. See Tanya M. Luhrmann, *Persuasions of the Witch's Craft: Ritual Magic in Contemporary England* (Cambridge: Harvard University Press, 1991).

44. Partridge, *Re-Enchantment of the West*, 1:41.

45. Ibid., 1:38–46. But see also Asprem, *Problem of Disenchantment*.

46. Since the present chapter was first written, in 2010, I have developed this actor-oriented perspective in a different direction by joining the discursive approach to insights borrowed from the cognitive science of religion and reframing the discussion of disenchantment in view of a "problem history" (*Problemgeschichte*). While these shifts have implications for the topic of this chapter, I have decided to leave the text more or less in its original form. See, however, Asprem, *Problem of Disenchantment*.

47. See, for example, Kocku von Stuckrad, "Reflections on the Limits of Reflection: An Invitation to the Discursive Study of Religion," *Method and Theory in the Study of Religion* 22 (2010): 156–69. Another important background reference for the approach adopted here is Olav Hammer's rhetorical analysis of modern esoteric currents, in Hammer, *Claiming Knowledge: Strategies of Epistemology from Theosophy to the New Age* (Leiden: Brill, 2001).

48. Jesper Aagaard Petersen, "'We Demand Bedrock Knowledge': Modern Satanism Between Secularized Esotericism and 'Esotericized' Secularism," in *Handbook of Religion and the Authority of Science*, ed. Olav Hammer and James R. Lewis (Leiden: Brill, 2010), 4.

49. See, for example, Randall Styers, *Making Magic: Religion, Magic, and Science in the Modern World* (New York: Oxford University Press, 2004); and Marco Pasi, "Magic," in *The Brill Dictionary of Religion*, ed. Kocku von Stuckrad (Leiden: Brill, 2005), 3:1134–40.

50. See Asprem, *Arguing with Angels*, chap. 3.

51. Hammer, *Claiming Knowledge*, 206.

52. This event and the people involved have been discussed thoroughly in previous research. See, for example, Howe, *Magicians of the Golden Dawn*; and Gilbert, "Order of the Golden Dawn." For the aftermath and formation of new branches across the world, see King, *Ritual Magic in England*; and Francis King, *Modern Ritual Magic: The Rise of Western Occultism* (New York: Avery Publishing, 1989).

53. The only possible exception is the lesser-known instruction manual *Book "H,"* which detailed the summoning of angels and demons after the recipe of one of the many systems received by Dee and Kelly. Significantly, this instruction was edited out of the Golden Dawn corpus published by Israel Regardie in the 1930s—precisely because it did not seem to fit the focus of the order's other teachings.

54. Paul Foster Case ["Perseverantia"] to Regardie, January 15, 1933, available in the online archives of the Fraternity of Inner Light, at http://www.lvx.org/files/QuickSiteImages/letter1.pdf. It should be noted that Case's historical analysis was incorrect. The Enochian material was present already in the so-called cipher manuscript upon which the Order of the Golden Dawn had been founded, predating Mathers's involvement. The cipher manuscript was probably compiled by Mackenzie, one of Case's "Rosicrucian" heroes.

55. To paraphrase Jean-François Lyotard, *The Postmodern Condition: A Report on Knowledge* (Manchester: Manchester University Press, 1979), xxv.

56. "Perennialism" corresponds here roughly to Hammer's "appeal to tradition," while pragmatism/progressivism bears similarities to the appeal to experience.

57. "Ceremony of the Grade of Adeptus Minor," in Israel Regardie, ed., *The Golden Dawn: The Original Account of the Teachings, Rites, and Ceremonies of the Hermetic Order of the Golden Dawn* (1937–40) (St. Paul, Minn.: Llewellyn, 1989), 231.

58. Unfortunately, Regardie does not reveal who these clairvoyants were or when the experiments took place. It appears likely, however, that it was in the Stella Matutina period. The information and quotations in this and the following two paragraphs are from Regardie, *Golden Dawn*, 626–29. The lecture by Brodie-Innes mentioned below is reproduced in part at pp. 627–28.

59. Ibid., 628–29.

60. LaVey, *Satanic Bible*, 155.

61. LaVey, "Enochian Pronunciation Guide," *Cloven Hoof*, May 1970, available online at http://www.churchofsatan.com/Pages/EnochianGuide.html.

62. Ibid. See also LaVey, "Satanism," appendix no. 1, in Michael Aquino, *The Church of Satan*, 5th ed. (San Francisco: Michael Aquino, 2002), 442.

63. Quoted in Aquino, *Church of Satan*, 65.

64. Ibid., 66. Aquino later split from the church to found his own group, the Temple of Set.

65. Stephen Skinner, ed., *John Dee's Action with Spirits* (London: Askin Publishers, 1974).

66. See Pasi and Rabaté, "Langue angélique, langue magique," 119; Leo Vinci, *Gmical-zoma! An Enochian Dictionary* (London: Regency Press, 1976), 12; and Laycock, "Angelic Language or Mortal Folly?"

67. See, for example, King, *Ritual Magic in England*, 187.

68. Steven Ashe, e-mail to the author, March 2, 2008.

69. *The Heptarchia Mystica of John Dee*, ed. Robert Turner (Edinburgh: Magnum Opus Hermetic Sourceworks, 1983), xxii.

70. Ibid., 12.

71. For a full discussion, see Asprem, *Arguing with Angels*, chap. 7.

72. Geoffrey James, *The Enochian Evocation of Dr. John Dee* (Gillette, N.J.: Heptangle Books, 1984), 194.

73. See Wouter Hanegraaff, *Esotericism and the Academy: Rejected Knowledge in Western Culture* (Cambridge: Cambridge University Press, 2012).

74. See also Asprem, *Problem of Disenchantment*.

75. Karel Dobbelaere, "Assessing Secularisation Theory," in *New Approaches to the Study of Religion*, ed. Peter Antes, Armin Geertz, and Randi Warne (Berlin: De Gruyter, 2004), 2:229–53.

76. LaVey, *Satanic Bible*, 119.

77. James, *Enochian Evocation*, xxiv, xxii.

78. Geoffrey James, *The Enochian Magick of Dr. John Dee: The Most Powerful System of Magick in Its Original Unexpurgated Form* (St. Paul, Minn.: Llewellyn, 1998), xii.

79. Benjamin Rowe, "Are the Angels Real?," *Enochian-L Archives* (1996–2001), accessed April 27, 2008, http://www.hollyfeld.org/heaven/Email/enochian-1, November 1996.

80. Neither is this strategy uncommon: I also noticed and discussed it in my qualitative research on ritual magicians in Norway. See Egil Asprem, "Thelema og ritualmagi: Med magi som livsholdning i moderne vestlig esoterisme," *Chaos* 46 (2006): 113–37.

81. Rowe, "Are the Angels Real?," November 15, 1996.

6

BABALON LAUNCHING:

JACK PARSONS, ROCKETRY, AND THE "METHOD OF SCIENCE"

Erik Davis

Is it difficult, between matter and spirit?

—*Liber 49, The Book of Babalon*

Jack Parsons, who was born in Southern California in 1914, racked up a good number of conventional successes in his short life. A self-taught chemist and rocket enthusiast, Parsons co-founded the Jet Propulsion Laboratory as well as a successful aerospace company, while making breakthroughs in solid fuel technology that helped launch America's space program.[1] Yet, as he pursued his scientific work, Parsons also threw himself into intense occult practice. He became an exuberant follower of Aleister Crowley's "magickal" religion of Thelema and a hedonistic libertarian whose polyamorous and psychedelic mores foreshadowed the sexual, esoteric, and Dionysian counterculture to come.[2] The conjunction of significant aerospace innovation and intense occult activity, together with Parsons's early demise in a home laboratory explosion at the age of thirty-seven, lends his story a strikingly mythic character. Indeed, if the story of Jack Parsons did not exist, it would need to be invented. But if it were invented—that is, if his life were presented as the fiction it in so many ways resembles—it would be hard to believe, even as fiction. The narrative would seem contrived, at once too pulp and too poetic, and too finely keyed to the central theme that inspires this chapter: the modern relationship between technology and the occult, between rationality and the ecstatic, between what Crowley himself called, in the motto for the A∴A∴—the esoteric teaching order he created in 1907 to propagate the philosophy and practice of Thelema—the "method of science" and the "aim of religion."

Understood as a specifically modern current of discourse, practice, and more or less explicit religiosity, "the occult" casts its enchanting shadows against the implacable backdrop of rationalism and the process that Max Weber famously described as the disenchantment of the world. In "Science as a Vocation," a speech delivered in Munich toward the close of World War I, Weber made clear that this disenchantment—*Entzauberung*—is rooted in thousands of years of cultural development and cannot be tied solely to the rise of modern science and its pursuit of "rational experiment." Disenchantment has less to do with the accuracy or social prevalence of naturalistic accounts of the world than with the dominance of an internal—one might even say a "spiritual"—attitude of rationalization, an attitude rooted partly in transformations of Protestant sensibility but manifested in the secular notion that "one can, in principle, master all things by calculation." As such, even though the actual objects, forces, tools, and processes encountered in the modern world remain mysterious to most of its subjects, the ideology of rationalism banishes magical spirits and otherworldly forces from our accounts of and interactions with such mysteries. Along similar lines, Weber believed that technical and instrumental processes and motives were necessarily riven from the world of meanings provided by religion, arguing that "the tension between the value-spheres of 'science' and the sphere of 'the holy' is unbridgeable."[3]

The career of Jack Parsons—who passionately embraced both science and the occult—suggests that the space between Weber's two value spheres may not be quite as unbridgeable as Weber asserted. However, some close readers of Weber discern more ambiguity in his writings than the passage quoted above suggests.[4] Indeed, "Science as a Vocation" includes Weber's own perceptive insights into those modes of rationalism that are sometimes employed by modernity's apparently irrationalist refuseniks. In support of his claim that science provides no answers to questions about ultimate values, Weber describes the romantic and mystical rejection of rationalization announced by the youth of his day, who sought redemption from the artificial abstractions and "specifically irreligious power" of science:

> Living in union with the divine . . . is one of the fundamental watchwords one hears among German youth, whose feelings are attuned to religion or who crave religious experiences. They crave not only religious experience but experience as such. The only thing that is strange is the method that is now followed: the spheres of the irrational, the only spheres that intellectualism has not yet touched, are now raised into consciousness and put under its lens. For in practice this is where the modern intellectualist form of romantic irrationalism leads.[5]

Here, Weber eerily prophesies many of the alternative streams of spirituality to come, what we might term—with the esoteric and bohemian milieu of Jack

Parsons and his circle in mind—"countercultural spirituality." A key element of this countercultural spirituality is the link between religious subjectivity and "experience as such," a somewhat paradoxical commingling of mystical aspirations and hedonistic excess into a single cult of experience intentionally directed against a disenchanted workaday existence and toward a recovery of what Weber calls, with a mixture of nostalgia and irony, "the blood-and-the-sap of true life."[6]

As a disciple of the sorts of personal commitments to scientific rationality that his essay describes, Weber himself remained essentially unmoved by the claims of countercultural spirituality, whose hunger for exotic religious traditions and psychic experiences he dismissed, in rather "scientific" tones, as "plain humbug or self-deception."[7] Nonetheless, as Peter Pels points out, Weber's own account of science includes and even stresses irrational affects or intensities. Weber describes the "strange intoxication" of and "passion" for precise intellectual labor that he believes is required of someone who authentically chooses science as a vocation, a dedication whose character he elsewhere compares to the "ghost of dead religious beliefs."[8] In addition, he describes the "intuitions" that lead to scientific advancement; resembling creative leaps of art, they have "nothing to do with any cold calculation."[9] This Dionysian dimension of science will reverberate through our consideration of Parsons, and it suggests at least one bridge that links the spheres of science and religion. But such a bridge runs both ways, as Weber himself recognized in his canny acknowledgment (quoted above) of the rationality at play within the romantic mysticism of his day, a rationality that takes the form of various "methods" by which the irrational is brought to consciousness. As we will see, this precise conjunction of technical procedures with mystical or unconscious domains of experience characterizes the occult current that Parsons embraced and that led Tanya M. Luhrmann to describe modern magic, in a perhaps unconscious echo of Weber, as "the romantic rationalist's religion."[10]

Many strains of Weber's "modern intellectualist form of romantic irrationalism" exist, but there is something uniquely dynamic and revealing about modern magic. As Randall Styers has shown, magic has long been treated as a moving target that both reinscribes and subverts modernity's self-representations, making magic "a foil for modernity."[11] But what sort of foil? In Jonathan Z. Smith's view, magic sometimes appears in classic anthropological accounts as a double negation or as "doubly dual." Magic may be characterized in opposition to religion or to science (which are themselves opposed), but this characterization does not, by way of that contrast, come any closer to establishing an identity or positive relation between magic and the remaining term of the opposition; contrasting magic to religion, say, does not thereby square magic with science. Even in

those comparisons between magic and science or religion that stress the continuity of the terms, magic still plays an essentially negative role—as a "shadow reality" that reflects the more substantive characteristics of religion or science "in a
distorting fun-house mirror."[12]

This flickering antinomy is also reproduced in the tension between the two
main accounts of traditional magic proffered by classic anthropologists (and
trotted out perennially in discussions like this one). The "intellectualist" views
of Tylor and Frazer cast magic as a protoscience of calculated instrumental
control that depends upon a semideterministic theory of animist forces, but
whose underlying "analogic consciousness" undermines the rational application of associations, thereby rendering magic "the bastard sister of science."[13]
On the other hand, the "symbolic" account of magic, ultimately derived from
Durkheim's conception of the social function of religion, instead looks at
magical practices and behaviors as an expressive, cultural communication
whose meaning and effects should be judged in terms of symbolic or dramatic
significance rather than in the causal terms of protoscientific efficacy and
instrumental control. Stanley Tambiah, who contributed to the symbolic
approach through recourse to J. L. Austin's notion of performative speech,
offers this account of magic's Janus face: "On the one hand, [magic] seems to
imitate the logic of technical/technological action that seeks to transform
nature or the world of natural things and manifestations. On the other hand,
its structure is also transparently rhetorical and performative (in that it consists of acts to create effects on human actors according to accepted social
conventions)."[14] Whether this split is considered an artifact of our interpreta-
tive categories or not, the important point here is the persistence of the antinomy itself. Once again, magic *flickers*, a shadowy ambivalence defined against
and through the more substantial conflict between religion and science, con-
testable terms that nonetheless achieve some measure of coherence precisely
through the fluctuations of magic's "doubly dual" contrast. For these and other
reasons, Smith thinks that *magic* has outlived its usefulness as a term within
the study of religion, which already possesses sharper, more analytically exact
words to describe the various domains and practices covered by its umbrella.
Yet there may be something paradoxically useful about the term's instability,
particularly in discussions of magic in modernity. Rather than a reified category that co-founds a set of oppositions, magic might perhaps more productively
be understood as a boundary condition, a phantasmic phenomenon that, for us
moderns anyway, cannot help but flicker between symbol and technique, religion and science, desire and device.

For the purposes of this chapter, we will therefore make a distinction
between *the occult* as a "holy" value sphere and *magic* as a more ambiguous and

mobile set of practices and attitudes that fluctuate between religion and science. This difference is particularly important given Crowley's explicit desire to present Thelema as a revealed religion that involves, but is not strictly identified with, the practice of magic. Thelema's aim, again, is "religion," but though its method is "science," that science is better understood as a naturalist revision of magical method, one that is itself partly based on the classical sociological accounts of magic. Crowley, who, as Marco Pasi has noted, attended Trinity College when Frazer taught there, loved *The Golden Bough,* and Parsons frequently recommended the book to newcomers interested in the ways of wizardry. Both Crowley and Parsons were influenced by Frazer's account of magic as a protoscience, an influence whose intoxicating fruit introduced a striking irony into modern magical discourse. Although *The Golden Bough* was intended to marshal evidence of the intellectual errors of benighted primitives in the superior light of modern science, Frazer's evolutionary account inadvertently provided dissatisfied moderns with material that enabled them to imaginatively contest the dominance of Frazer's rationalist and evolutionary account of science—an account that, in Parsons's case, also arguably frames his own technological practice. This is only one of the productive paradoxes that characterize Jack Parsons's peculiar life, and even with the distortions of condensed biography in mind, we must now sketch the bare outlines of that life before we explore the interaction of magic and science within one midcentury Californian milieu.

Pulp Parsifal

John Whiteside Parsons was born in Pasadena, a genteel community of arts and science tucked beneath the San Gabriel Mountains, from which flows the seasonal stream that carves out the Arroyo Seco canyon that borders the city to the west.[15] Parsons's mother divorced his father shortly after his birth, and the boy was raised in privilege by his mother and grandparents, although the family later fell on hard times. As a youth, Parsons was a pampered, dreamy sort, lost in books and without many friends. At the age of thirteen, he attempted to conjure up the devil and balked in terror at the apparent success of his efforts. He also became interested in chemistry and, especially, rocketry, which at the time was largely the province of boys and amateur enthusiasts who, like Parsons, consumed science-fiction pulp magazines like Hugo Gernsback's *Amazing Stories.* Given his struggles in school and the many spelling errors in his texts, some have concluded that Parsons was dyslexic; in any case, his formal education did not go very far beyond high school.[16] Nonetheless, his knowledge of chemistry took off, along with many of the black-powder model rockets he built with his pal Ed Forman, with whom he adopted the motto *Ad astra per aspera*—through hardships to the stars.

In 1935, after marrying his first wife, Helen, Parsons invited Forman to accompany him to a lecture at nearby Caltech that concluded with speculations about "stratospheric passenger carriers." Through contacts made at the gathering, Parsons and Forman met Frank Malina, a Caltech student who worked for GALCIT, an aerodynamics laboratory run by the legendary Hungarian professor Theodore von Kármán. Excited by the encounter, Malina was able to convince von Kármán to let the three young men, two of them unschooled amateurs, form a team to study rocket propulsion under the auspices of GALCIT. Setting up in the Arroyo Seco, just above Devil's Gate Dam, the team began experimenting with stationary rockets. Eventually, they were allowed to perform their experiments on the Caltech campus itself, although a few wayward tests forced the group—now labeled the "suicide squad"—to return to the arroyo.[17] For years, the squad worked without financial support, Parsons and Forman picking up extra work at explosives firms; in the way of Southern Californians, Parsons and Malina also co-wrote a screenplay they hoped to sell to Hollywood. In 1939, Caltech was granted $1,000 to continue the research; later that year, von Kármán submitted a successful proposal to found a research station in the arroyo that would eventually grow into the Jet Propulsion Laboratory. Leaving the dream of stratospheric sounding rockets behind, the team began to focus on constructing rocket motors for military planes, devices that they called JATOs (for jet-assisted takeoffs). (To distance the project from the adolescent associations of "rocket," von Kármán and Malina had started using the term "jet" instead.)[18] As the chemist and explosives expert, Parsons experimented with both liquid and solid fuels. In August 1941, the GALCIT crew attached JATOs to a test airplane, enabling the craft to achieve rapid takeoff on rocket power alone.

Unfortunately, the solid fuel used for the JATOs was quite unstable. But in the summer of 1942, Parsons made a breakthrough in the science of solid fuel, creating a material called GALCIT-53, the subsequent development of which would lead directly to the Minuteman and Polaris missiles of the postwar era.[19] One tale suggests that Parsons's leap—which by all accounts was a classic eureka moment—was inspired by his historical knowledge of Greek fire, a flaming viscous weapon of unknown composition used most famously by the Byzantine Empire. Other stories invoke the humbler inspiration of roofers laying down tar.[20] With the success of GALCIT-53, Parsons and Forman decided to form a company that would manufacture JATOs; along with von Kármán, Malina, and a few others, the men founded the Aerojet Engineering Corporation, which became one of the world's largest manufacturers of rockets.[21] In 1958, von Kármán declared Parsons, whom he described as "a delightful screwball," the third-most important person in the development of the American space program.[22]

While Parsons was refining GALCIT-53, he and Helen moved into an ornate redwood mansion in Hollywood once owned by Arthur Fleming, Caltech's greatest benefactor. Parsons converted the building into a rooming house and placed ads in the local paper specifying that "only bohemians, artists, musicians, atheists, anarchists, or other exotic types need apply."[23] The building also became the new home of the Agapé Lodge No. 2, the only functioning lodge of the Ordo Templi Orientis at the time. A quasi-masonic order founded by German esotericists in the early twentieth century, the OTO had been reconstructed by Aleister Crowley in the 1910s to become, along with the A∴A∴, the principal institutional vehicle of Crowley's religion of Thelema. Parsons had first visited the Agapé Lodge in 1938 after coming across a copy of Crowley's early work *Konx om Pax* on the shelves of a Pasadena used-car dealer he knew. Parsons avidly consumed Crowley's writings and took to the lodge's weekly performances of the Gnostic Mass. The head of the lodge, Wilfred Smith, became a good friend of Parsons's and his magical mentor. Parsons also corresponded with Crowley himself, who was dependent on the lodge for the meager income that sustained him until his death in 1947. Jack and Helen were initiated into the lodge in 1941, Jack adopting a motto in atrocious Latin—*Thelema Optentum Procedero Amoris Nuptiae*—that formed the acronym TOPAN, i.e., *to Pan*.[24]

"The Parsonage," as Parsons's mansion came to be called, was briefly "an adult playground saturated with philosophical hopes and pungent romanticism," according to one of Parsons's biographers.[25] Shortly after Parsons and his circle moved in, the police showed up upon receiving reports of a nude pregnant woman jumping over an open fire in the backyard. Many in the Agapé Lodge and the Parsonage were committed to free love; though the sexual magic—solo, hetero, and homo—enshrined in the higher grades of the OTO might have been a factor, this partner swapping may also simply reflect the erotic realities of midcentury Los Angeles bohemia linked to both esotericism and political radicalism.[26] When the couple moved into the Parsonage, Helen was already sleeping with Smith, while Parsons had taken up with Helen's younger half sister, Sara, who went by the name Betty. Parsons became the most charismatic man in the lodge. Given his wit, good looks, and money, it is unsurprising that the senior disciple Jane Wolfe unofficially declared Parsons "the real successor of Therion"—i.e., of Crowley himself.[27] For his part, Crowley was disappointed in Smith's hedonism and lackluster recruiting and saw

Parsons as the dynamic leader that Thelema required. In 1943, Parsons became head of the lodge.

Like many occultists, Parsons avidly consumed science fiction and fantasy literature. In the early 1940s, he attended meetings of the Los Angeles Science Fiction Society, where he befriended Robert Heinlein and met the young Ray Bradbury. In 1945, he also encountered a voluble redheaded sci-fi writer named L. Ron Hubbard, whom Parsons described to Crowley as "the most Thelemic person I have ever met."[28] Hubbard moved into the Parsonage and soon took up with Betty. The affair wounded Parsons, but it did not stop him from recruiting Hubbard to play a key role in what would become one of the most storied occult rites in American history: the Babalon Working.[29] Using the Enochian system of calls received by John Dee at the close of the sixteenth century, and with Hubbard playing the role of Dee's scryer, Edward Kelly, the two men embarked on a series of intense workings that incorporated, at various points, the OTO's "VIII° rite of masturbation," Prokofiev's Violin Concerto no. 2, and a number of moderately impressive paranormal phenomena. The first part of the ritual, designed to evoke an "elemental," or nature spirit, resulted, to Parsons's mind anyway, in the relatively synchronistic appearance at the Parsonage of the striking Marjorie Cameron, his next—and last—great love and sex magic partner.[30] The latter parts of the working were intended to invoke Babalon herself, the holy whore of Thelemic mythology. Though Parsons sometimes suggested that Babalon was an apocalyptic force of transformation that would express itself through existing human beings, he seemed to have generally believed that a literal incarnation would take place. Such a thing did not, apparently, come to pass, although the Babalon Working did lead Parsons, echoing his spiritual father, to produce his own revealed text. In February 1946, alone and positioned next to the two power lines whose crossing framed his favorite power spot in the Mojave Desert, Parsons invoked Babalon, who appeared before him and commanded him to write down *Liber 49*—a bold and, it must be said, unsuccessful attempt to add a fourth chapter to *The Book of the Law*, the core scripture of Crowley's religion, channeled through Crowley's wife, Rose, in a Cairo hotel room in 1904.[31]

In late 1944, the General Tire and Rubber Company acquired Aerojet, and Parsons was out of a job. In George Pendle's account, both Parsons and Forman were pressured to sell their shares on the eve of the acquisition, partly because Parsons was deemed an inappropriate shareholder thanks to his eccentricity and constant womanizing.[32] Parsons subsequently poured the bulk of his life's savings into a new company formed with Hubbard, who proceeded to take off with both Betty and the funds. Pursuing the couple to Florida, Parsons discovered that the pair had sailed away on a newly purchased yacht.

A few hours later, Parsons invoked the martial spirit Bartzabel in a hotel room; "coincidentally," as J. Gordon Melton has it, a terrible squall forced Hubbard to return to shore.[33] Disgusted with Parsons's foolishness and his increasingly wayward occult workings, Crowley grew disenchanted, and by the end of 1946 Parsons had sold the Parsonage and resigned as head of the lodge. In 1948, owing to his involvement with the "love cult" as well as with a Communist group whose meetings he briefly attended, the FBI revoked Parsons's security clearance. It was restored for a time, but by January 1952, Parsons was permanently barred from the burgeoning military-industrial complex and earned his keep making explosive effects for Hollywood movies. The intensity of Parsons's postlodge magical work waxed and waned, and though he wrote a few powerful and prophetic essays on both the occult and the politics of freedom, his final letters both reflect and describe a worrying oscillation between what he called "manic hysteria and depressing melancholy."[34] In June 1952, on the eve of a move to Mexico, Parsons was working in his home laboratory when, according to most accounts, he accidentally dropped a highly explosive chemical and blew himself up. Hideously maimed, Parsons remained conscious for an hour or so before passing away at the age of thirty-seven. Twenty years later, the International Astronomical Union named an astronomical feature after him: a crater on the dark side of the moon.

This astonishing story has been told and retold many times both inside and outside occult circles, with Kenneth Grant's *Magical Revival* (1972) standing as the first published account beyond Agapé Lodge records.[35] The tale was also brought to light by writers seeking to expose the wayward origins of the Church of Scientology, though for its part the CoS insists that Hubbard was sent in by the government to "break up a black magic group."[36] Mike Davis could not resist including a brief and garbled account in *City of Quartz*, so marvelous an allegory did it provide for the emergence of Southern California's "postwar science-based economy."[37] Richard Metzger called Parsons the "James Dean of occultism"—a charismatic figure, in both a Weberian and a Hollywood sense, whose story resonates with the mythic yarns in the pulp "scientific romances" he consumed.[38] Tellers of the tale, including those who are critical of Parsons, also cannot help but point out the apparently synchronistic elements of the story, the way in which "the facts" themselves seem to resonate on a level of fiction and symbol. Readers familiar with the life of John Dee, for example, remark on the curious echoes between Parsons's relationship with Hubbard and Dee's with his scryer, Edward Kelly, who is often represented in the literature as a charlatan and whose angelic messages—especially those received from the same Seventh Aire that Parsons and Hubbard explored in the Babalon Working—convinced Dee that the two men should swap wives.[39] On another track, and in light of the circumstances of Parsons's death, writers from Grant forward have noted the recurrent image of fire in *Liber 49* and *The Book of Babalon*, Parsons's unpublished but widely circulated account of the Babalon Working; in one ritual commandment, spoken through Hubbard to Parsons, Babalon declares that "thou shalt become living flame."[40] Even the material that Parsons accidentally dropped in the lab—fulminate of mercury—strikes an esoteric chord that would not resound had Parsons dropped nitroglycerin.

These seductive serendipities and symbolic reverberations recall Jeffrey Kripal's argument that occult and paranormal phenomena are, "like the act of interpretive writing itself, primarily semiotic or textual processes." In other words, they act in some ways like texts, and in particular like *fantastic* texts—a genre of writing that Kripal links with the uncertainty induced by the "inability to decide what is real and what is fictional within a text (or a life)." Moreover, the productive uncertainty of the paranormal text is contagious. Engaging the occult hermeneutically, we find ourselves "reading the paranormal writing us."[41] One might say that writing about the life of Jack Parsons means, in part, to be written by the expressive and symbolic "magic" that marks that life—replicating, at least for the sake of the story, some of what E. P. Thompson characterized as the "psychic compulsion" inherent in occult material.[42]

But what sort of tale is this? In terms of pulp genre, Parsons's "real life story" is not just an occult fantasy—it is a *science* fantasy. In other words, whatever historical significance we may draw from Parsons's role in the transmission of Thelema into countercultural California, the charismatic force of the man's story equally involves the explosive technology of American rocketry. It is impossible to know whether Parsons "actually" crossed the Abyss and deserved to declare himself, as he did late in his career, a Magister Templi, one of the supreme grades of the A∴A∴. But he unquestionably co-founded the Jet Propulsion Laboratory, held U.S. patents no. 2,563,265, and 2,783,138 (among others), and invented the method of casting rocket fuel used to produce the solid fuel boosters for the space shuttle.[43] Parsons compels because his story takes place at a crossroads: the *conjunctio* of the irrational and the rational, of hedonistic mysticism and high technology, of ascent as spiritual ecstasy and as rocket thrust. In Weber's terms, Parsons seems to have recognized and incarnated a dedicated "vocational" attitude toward both science and the romantic irrationalism of "the holy." In straddling the spheres—and sometimes knocking them together—he provides an unusually clear view of the flicker of modern magic as it leaps between the poles of science and the supernatural, naturalism and religion.

The rest of this chapter will look at how Parsons negotiated the relationship between his occult and his scientific work, an ongoing and perhaps inevitably contradictory negotiation made more interesting by the clear distinctions Parsons himself drew. Martin Starr, in his exhaustive biography of Wilfred Smith and the Agapé Lodge, asserts that Parsons's technical career did "not intersect with his occult life," and that Parsons actively sought to keep the "hemispheres of his life" apart.[44] Malina, who was skeptical about the occult but tolerant of Parsons's interests, also wrote that his GALCIT partner operated in "two domains." In their discussions about rocket design, "there was no input from what you would say alchemy or magic. In other words he functioned in compartments."[45] The compartmentalization that Malina describes is not uncommon among scientists with religious commitments, but Parsons was too dynamic and erratic a person to keep his commitments so static. Science and the sacred may have remained conceptually separated hemispheres in Parsons's mind, but in practice they leaked into each other—desires crossed boundaries, images and representations resonated, method snuck into magic and symbol into science. Stanley Tambiah, echoing Bronislaw Malinowski, has argued for the need to pay close attention to those cultural situations in which "a person can in a certain context behave mystically, and then switch in another context to a practical empirical everyday frame of mind." In such situations, the interpretive goal is not only to understand these different contexts but to appreciate the transitional or boundary conditions "in which code switching occurs."[46] The intellectual pluralism that allowed Parsons to keep the value spheres of science and the occult apart only intensifies the interest and illumination of their points of contact and resonance. Indeed, at the close of this chapter I suggest that magic, even as it feeds the marginal milieu of occult religiosity and countercultural spirituality, also makes its home in modernity *as this very code switching itself*—a pragmatic, relativistic, and in some ways naturalist fluctuation between science and the holy.

The Method of Science

In a brief autobiographical text written toward the end of his life, Parsons describes his adolescent interest in chemistry and science as a "counterbalance" to his coming magical awakening. His knowledge of rocketry and explosives paved a practical route to prestige and financial success, but it also became the matrix that provided the "scientific method" necessary, he says, for magical attainment.[47] Here, on the one hand, the worldly achievements linked with Parsons's technical prowess are contrasted with the less tangible rewards of magical experience. But science also provides a "method"—and not, please note, a theory—that affords a productive passage between the worlds and a technique for mystical success. While there are a number of points where the code switching between occult religion and science occur in Parsons's life, this notion of "method" is the most significant. It is not, certainly, original to him; many modern accounts in both occult and, as we have seen, anthropological literature speak of magic as a sort of applied "science" linked to protocols and material processes. The most important emic account, certainly to Parsons, belongs to Crowley, who at times provided a deeply pragmatic, experimental, and naturalistic account of "magick." As noted, Crowley also enshrined the scientific method in the motto for the A∴A∴, the Thelemic mystery school he founded before remaking the Ordo Templi Orientis (to which Parsons also belonged): "The Method of Science, the Aim of Religion."

Since Crowley's understanding of "the method of science" was so significant to Parsons, we must spend some time with it here. To begin, we should turn to Olav Hammer's *Claiming Knowledge*, in which the author identifies three central strategies employed by modern esoteric movements in their quest for legitimization: tradition, experience, and science. The category of tradition does not help much with the self-conscious innovations of Thelema; experience, through which groups and individuals ground their claims in the direct personal experience of spiritual realities, will be discussed later (although in a different register from that of Hammer, who stresses the unitive and mystical dimension of esoteric experience). The important strategy here is science—more precisely, the attempts to legitimize occult theories through some adaptation of scientific discourse. Beginning with Theosophy and its "esoteric science," Hammer shows how various groups use science as both a foil and a base of support, at once a source of naturalistic confirmation of belief and a more ambivalent indication that the holistic integration of religion and science has yet to arrive or can be achieved through the development of the esoteric current in question. Hammer proclaims that the esoteric position "bases the precise details of its scientism, its critique, and its picture of a spiritualized or 're-enchanted' science on a form of parasitism on the mainstream science of its age."[48] In other words, the *body of doctrines* associated with science forms the positive basis of esoteric comparison. Blavatsky, for example, hitched various cosmic vibrations—the Fifth Element, the Akasha, the *anima mundi*, etc.—to the now discredited concept of the interstellar luminiferous ether.[49] Esoteric groups today often turn to the sort of quantum physics found in Fritjof Capra's *Tao of Physics* or the 2004 documentary *What the Bleep Do We Know?* Besides the significant distortions and inevitable anachronism involved in this strategy, the appropriation of dominant theories, often leaning heavily on analogy, largely ignores what Hammer and others argue is the most crucial characteristic of science: its method of inquiry. Defining this method as "intersubjective, repeatable, and error-correcting," Hammer cites Carl Sagan: "the method of science, as stodgy and grumpy as it may seem, is far more important than the findings of science."[50] Although sociological studies of science, especially in the wake of Thomas Kuhn, have significantly qualified the idealized Popperian view of scientific progress (especially with respect to the concrete practice of falsification), the scientific method remains functionally open-ended and self-correcting.[51] And it is this method, Hammer states, that one "rarely if ever finds in Esoteric movement texts."[52]

So what, then, are we to make of the "method of science" that Aleister Crowley proclaims to be one of the core tactics of his "Scientific Illuminism" and that so compelled Parsons? On the surface, this method does not appear so different from the theosophical parasitism that Hammer critiques. In his *Confessions,* Crowley claims, for example, that Thelema "co-ordinates the disconnected discoveries of science, from physics to psychology."[53] This assertion of holistic integration is also implied by the terms of the motto itself—"The Method of Science, the Aim of Religion" is not terribly far from William Q. Judge's roughly contemporary claim that Theosophy was a "scientific religion and a religious science."[54] Nonetheless, there is an important difference between these claims, one of which lends the Thelemic current and many of its offshoots a different valence from the New Age line of "esoteric science" that Hammer critiques. Crowley believed that it was possible to base an experiential religion like the A∴A∴ not on theory (quantum, dharmic, or otherwise) but on "practice and methods."[55] This pragmatic methodology was, he claimed, sufficient to achieve illumination, or "spiritual experience." Such methodology, of course, does not resemble normative applications of scientific method—the absence of conventional frameworks of repeatability and the challenges of quantifying subjective impressions and subjecting them to falsification assure that it cannot. Nonetheless, Crowley's invocation of "practice and methods" represents a more reflexive, pragmatic, and potentially naturalistic attitude toward esoteric claims and evidence that those found in theosophical cosmology or the majority of its later offshoots.

In an important article on Crowley's embrace of naturalism, Egil Asprem identifies three central elements of Crowley's scientific method: "the careful use of a magical record to stress the externalization of personal experience which makes inter-subjectivity possible, the conception of rituals as scientific experiments, and the idea of testing the obtained results through inter-subjectively verifiable methods."[56] Against the argument that Crowley was simply repackaging magic for a more scientific age, Asprem argues conclusively that, however we might judge the rigor of Crowley's method, we must recognize his naturalism as sincere. Crowley's empiricism partly reflects his early exposure to Theravada Buddhism, whose dry and disenchanting operations of self-analysis were typically interpreted in his era as signs of a "rational religion." But it also stems from the practical and psychological orientation of the Hermetic Order of the Golden Dawn, the extraordinarily influential British occult group in which Crowley cut his esoteric teeth. While the Golden Dawn's interest in initiatory rituals, ancient gods, and recondite angelic tongues certainly reflects a romantic reaction to the positivist intellectual orientation of fin de siècle Britain, its pursuit of the mysteries was also, as Alex Owen argues, "entirely regulated by reason." Rejecting the passive mediumistic acceptance of incoming preternatural forces represented by spiritualism, the Golden Dawn occultists instead stressed the control of the mind and the active cultivation of will, even as they explored the intuitive, hallucinatory, uncanny, or irrational dimensions of human consciousness (or, as some were learning to call it, the subconscious). In a crucial passage, Owen clarifies the Golden Dawn's precise partnership between intuition and reason: "If we assume the mythopoeic capabilities of the hidden regions of the mind, then advanced occult practice can be understood as an extraordinary and controlled performance of the conscious 'I' in a mythos of mutual unconscious creation. By this reckoning, it is the crucial alignment of rational consciousness with the apparently irrational world of the myth-creating unconscious that produces the powerful experience of the occult 'real.'"[57] While such experiences served in part to confirm the reality of occult theories, a certain instrumental skepticism—a key element of science—played an important role in the alignment that Owen describes. One of the strongest examples that Owen provides is from Crowley, who warns astral travelers of the need to distinguish between "authentic astral phenomena and figments of personal imagination." Leaving aside the ontological implications of this distinction, what is important to note here are the terms that Crowley uses: "We must not assert the 'reality' or 'objectivity' of an Astral being on no better evidence than the subjective sensation of its independent existence. We must insist on proof."[58] As Asprem points out, what is particularly significant here is not only the invocation of scientific values (objectivity, evidence, proof) but the fact that such assessments would necessarily occur *after the fact* and would therefore reframe the raw material of visionary experience into a data set for later analysis (which also explains Crowley's insistence on keeping records). In this way, Crowley partially undermines the "subjective sensation" of authentic experience that underlies so many esoteric claims.

While the tradition of testing and identifying spirits is fundamental to the rites of exorcism and strongly informs the Renaissance angel magic so important to the Golden Dawn, Crowley is not demanding proof of divine origin but of *independent* origin—in other words, of some degree of reality beyond the individual imagination.[59] For Crowley, such proof could sometimes be found in the operations of *gematria*, kabbalistic numerological procedures that, taking advantage of the numerical equivalents of Hebrew letters, had originally been developed as an esoteric engine of scriptural exegesis. Combining *gematria* with the elaborate tables of correspondences that Crowley developed in *777*—which Asprem calls a "periodic table of magic"—Crowley was able to sift through the visual phantasmagoria of an astral trance to discover "internal evidence" for the objective content of the visionary material and the independent existence of any beings encountered. As Asprem puts it, Crowley transformed a premodern hermeneutical procedure into "a 'scientific' *formalism* which (allegedly) makes it possible to *quantitatively* assess certain visual experiences and say something about their validity."[60] Given the recondite procedures necessary to adjudicate such claims—which are certainly beyond this author—let us nonetheless insist that Crowley's deployment of *gematria* also reflects his unapologetic embrace of *quantification,* one of the defining characteristics of modern science and Weberian rationalization alike. "For the Work is to reduce all other Conceptions to these of Number," Crowley writes in *Liber Aleph,* "because thus thou wilt lay bare the very Structure of thy Mind, whose rule is Necessity rather than Prejudice." His conclusion is veritably Baconian: "Not until the universe is thus laid naked before thee canst thou truly anatomize it."[61]

Quantification hardly exhausts Crowley's method of science. The sort of evidentiary interrogations described above were paralleled (and in some significant ways contradicted) by a strong vein of Jamesian pragmatism, one that reflected a disinclination to bother much about the ontological status of astral or other magical phenomena. Crowley's most skeptical and positivist views along these lines were expressed early in his career, especially in the "Initiated Interpretation of Ceremonial Magic," which served as the introduction to the version of the *Goetia* he published in 1904, itself largely based on material prepared by Samuel MacGregor Mathers.[62] Here, the demonic spirits conjured in the "Triangle of Art" are considered to be nothing more than "portions of the human brain," different from ordinary sensory neural events only in that they are willed by the magician and "caused" by the operations of ceremonial magic. Later, after receiving *The Book of the Law* and chalking up a myriad of preternatural encounters, Crowley would abandon such materialism, but an element of it continued to feed the pragmatic and even constructivist dimension of what he later called the "skeptical Theurgy" of the A∴A∴.[63] In a famous appendix to *Magick and Theory in Practice,* for example, he noted, "In this book it is spoken of the Sephiroth, and the Paths, of Spirits and Conjurations; of Gods, Spheres, Planes, and many other things which may or may not exist. It is immaterial whether they exist or not. By doing certain things certain results follow; students are most earnestly warned against attributing reality or philosophical validity to any of them."[64] Here, Crowley specifically calls for an avoidance of ontological speculation, an avoidance that suspends reality claims and forces a subjective and self-referential process of evaluating spiritual and magical experiences. This is why I must disagree with Owen's claim that the modern occult self "did not recognize the relativism of its own self-reflexivity."[65] Here, and throughout his oeuvre, Crowley sounds a note of pragmatic relativism whose emphasis on practice ("doing certain things") can also be seen as a more nuanced and reflexive expression of the "method of science"—a method that here has less to do with objective analysis than with a commitment to an ongoing experimental and empirical process that unfolds through a provisional and constructed "paradigm" of signs, symbols, and ritual procedures. In Hammer's terms, Crowley certainly embraced the legitimizing role of direct spiritual experience—as he wrote in a founding statement of the A∴A∴: "There is only one Rock which Skepticism cannot shake; the Rock of Experience."[66] At the same time, Crowley, and Parsons after him, also appealed to an experimental and constructivist methodology in the staging and analysis of these individual "facts" of experience.

Ad Astra

Jack Parsons left us no systematic account of his understanding of the relationship between Thelema's method of science and rocketry's method of science. Perhaps such an account was never in the cards. As we will see, Parsons was involved in a variety of contradictory kinds of "code switching" between science and magical religion—sometimes rigorously policing the borders, at other times poetically and perhaps indiscriminately mixing up the spheres. Given this ambivalence, which itself reflects the methodological "flicker" of modern magic, we need to approach Parsons's magical science by taking a closer look at the scientific methodology he employed when building rockets and testing explosives. In other words, we will understand what sort of magician he was only by understanding what sort of scientist he was.

Malina characterized Parsons as "a self-trained chemist who, although he lacked the discipline of a formal higher education, had an uninhibited and fruitful imagination."[67] Elsewhere, Malina referred to Parsons and Forman as "enthusiasts." In one letter, Malina used the term "machinist," though this may have referred to Forman; in 1940, at a point of evident frustration, he compared the two men to "inventors, in the worst sense of the word."[68] Here we have a

cluster of associations—invention, imagination, amateur passion—that identify Parsons more as an "artisan of directed explosives" than as a trained
practitioner of the rationalized and institutional knowledge production associated with the modern research university. That Parsons and Forman were able
to do research under the auspices of the institution at all is a testament not only
to von Kármán's good sense but also to the emergence of the modern research
university itself. As Mike Davis notes, under the guidance of George Hale and
Robert Millikan, Caltech was establishing a new kind of partnership between
science and business, "a seamless continuum between the corporation, laboratory, and classroom."[69] As later technological developments in California have
shown with great clarity, this "emergent technostructure" has thrived in part
through its ability to capture eccentric technological innovators like Parsons.
That said, Parsons was, in the end, a bit too much for the budding military-
industrial complex. Though the reasons for Parsons's departure from Aerojet
and the later loss of his security clearance are complex, they do point to his
fundamental refusal to conform to structures of institutional authority.[70]

Given the very different institutional commitments of Parsons and Malina,
their partnership combined fundamentally different kinds of method. The two
young men did share the "dream" of rocket flight, a dream bequeathed to them
by science fiction and considered risible by many physicists and aeronautical
specialists in the 1930s.[71] But they worked toward manifesting that vision along
very different lines. Along with Forman, Parsons expressed the uninhibited
and imaginative experimentalism of the artisan, an intense (and for many
years unremunerated) level of affective commitment, and a willingness to
repeatedly perform dangerous—albeit exciting—tests. Though hardly a strait-
laced nerd, Malina had the outlook and priorities of a formal researcher; he not
only contributed his mathematical skills but also insisted on the disciplined
application of rationalized procedure. After the initial hope of building sound-
ing rockets was abandoned, the team focused on "theoretical studies" and
"elementary experiments." Rather than blast model rockets into the sky, Parsons and Forman spent most of the first few years at GALCIT testing stationary, comparatively fun-free rocket motors. In an account of the early GALCIT
program presented to a professional society, Malina attributed this approach to
von Kármán:

> He always stressed the importance of getting as clear as possible an
> understanding of the fundamental physical principles of a problem
> before initiating experiments in a purely empirical manner. . . . Parsons
> and Forman were none too pleased with an austere program that did not
> include the launching, at least, of model rockets. They could not resist the

temptation of firing some models with black powder motors during the next three years. Their attitude is symptomatic of the anxiety of pioneers of new technological developments. In order to obtain support for their dreams, they are under pressure to demonstrate them before they can be technically accomplished.[72]

Here, the "temptation" to fire off rockets is seen as a kind of performative dream that supplements the establishment of "fundamental physical principles" that might lead to actual technical achievements. While certainly having fun with their unauthorized launches, Parsons and Forman were also ritualistically engaging in technological dramas whose expressive content invoked or symbolically satisfied desires that were still as imaginative as they were technically feasible. While Malina may have been overreading the anxiety at work in their drive—sometimes an exploding projectile is just an exploding projectile—his understanding of the nonrational or symbolic dimension of their technological performances also helps illuminate the psycho-logic of magical ritual. Years later, after the founding of Aerojet, Parsons would regularly display even more overtly ritualistic behavior during test rocket launches that had already become institutionalized: he would stamp his feet and, to the unease of the engineers, loudly chant Aleister Crowley's stirring "Hymn to Pan." In both these practices, which recall Malinowski's portrayal of magic as a symbolic supplement to technological control, we see the flicker of magic as it crosses back and forth across sacred and technical registers.

In his biography of Parsons, George Pendle provides a clear account of the methodological contrast between Malina and Parsons, a contrast that in some ways replicates the conventional contrast between theory and experiment. To satisfy their research grant from the National Academy of Sciences, the GALCIT crew needed to devise an engine capable of propelling a rocket for ten seconds. No one had yet succeeded in building a rocket that sustained its propulsive force for more than five. Parsons attacked the problem experimentally, trying different mixtures of powder, using glues and other binders for consistency, and consulting with powder experts at the explosives firms that sometimes employed him. At one point, he employed a design for a multicellular fuel cell that he took from *The Crucible of Power*, a 1939 Jack Williamson science-fiction novelette. In the spring of 1940, apparently tired of hearing explosions echoing across the Caltech campus, von Kármán concocted four differential equations, telling Malina that their solutions would show whether such a motor was theoretically possible; if not, Parsons would be asked to stop testing. According to the historian of science Benjamin Zibit, these equations provided an important insight into the necessary relationship between the surface area of the burning propellant and the size of the nozzle throat that expelled the resulting gas.[73] Parsons was encouraged to continue the work, which eventually led to GALCIT-53, his breakthrough invention. With this material (or, more accurately, this method of making the material), rocket engines were eventually scaled up to the size and power necessary to penetrate the stratosphere and, ultimately, space.

In the language of the gods, however, we must say that Parsons's rocket science drew more from Pan than from Apollo. Consider how we might account for the nature of Parsons's technological breakthrough. Keeping the romantic overdetermination of the eureka moment in mind, and acknowledging whatever influence local roofers or Parsons's knowledge of ancient warfare may have played, Parsons's idea was by all accounts an essentially intuitive innovation, the sort of spontaneous insight or bolt from the blue that cannot be deterministically generated through application of method or accounted for in terms of inductive or deductive logic. Proclaiming that scientific intuition had "nothing to do with any cold calculation," Weber himself wrote that the psychological processes behind inspiration in science and art were essentially the same: "both are frenzy (in the sense of Plato's 'mania') and 'inspiration.'"[74] In James Hillman's post-Jungian archetypal language, such mania is the work of Pan, at least in his guise as the avatar of *spontaneity*: "Spontaneity means self-generating, non-predictable, non-repeatable. It does not belong within the domains of natural science as science is defined, although it does seem to be a natural phenomenon. To find laws of the spontaneous world would be a contradiction in terms. For these events are irregular, lawless."[75]

Von Kármán's equations proved that the rocket performance the GALCIT crew needed was theoretically possible, but Parsons still needed to compose—or discover, or invent—a material that would burn consistently. As in metallurgy, the mother of such materialist sciences, Parsons's research was an empirical process of trial and error that, informed by his considerable knowledge of chemistry, probed or—in Deleuze and Guattari's words—"followed" the variable potentials immanent in matter, rather than imposing a form or procedure from the outside. In such a probe, the object being pursued "is less a matter submitted to laws than . . . material traits of expression constituting affects." Parsons needed more than an explosive combination of chemical elements; in order to avoid the cracks and separations that would destabilize combustion, he also needed to alter—or deterritorialize—the solidity or consistency of the material in order to achieve new and emergent properties. It was a matter of intervening in what Deleuze and Guattari call *the machinic phylum*, an "energetic, molecular dimension" that represents "matter in movement, in flux, in variation, matter as a conveyor of singularities and traits of expression."[76]

GALCIT-53 was a novel chemical formulation whose energetic potentials were wedded to a literal "flux" of matter—the flexible, semiliquid flow of heated asphalt whose phase transition or "threshold" state allowed the material to be poured directly into the cylinders before solidifying.

Though some historians of aerospace have been chary in their accounts of Parsons's contribution to space flight, Malina always acknowledged his contribution.[77] In a historical account of the GALCIT program, Malina described Parsons's breakthrough as "radical" and the fuel itself as "a new kind of material." Though the article is reasonably formal and aimed at a technical audience, Malina also added that Parsons made his insight "no doubt after communing with his poetic spirits."[78] Malina is being wry here, but only to a degree. Although a skeptic, he did believe in the productivity of "poetry" as a mode of thought, in science as well as art.[79] He certainly recognized the role that the visionary imagination played in the pursuit of rocket science in the 1930s, when pulp magazines inspired rocket clubs, and the technical literature of space flight written by isolated pioneers like Konstantin Tsiolkovsky and Robert Goddard "was generally regarded more in the nature of science fiction."[80] Malina admired Parsons for his "uninhibited and fruitful imagination." His reference to "poetic spirits" is thus more than an allusion to Parsons's occult beliefs and their possible role in his asphalt inspiration; it is also a figure for Parsons's imaginative or intuitive "method" of experimentally probing the singular potentials of matter itself.

Parsons's subsequent scientific career shows that, despite his genius and his vocational commitments, he was never able fully to submit to the rationalized protocols that, for Weber, made modern life a grim and impersonal "struggle of the gods" in a disenchanted world.[81] But despite his romantic temperament, Parsons did not follow proponents of "New Age science" in attempting holistically to fuse the value spheres of science and the holy. Instead, Parsons affirmed the polytheistic struggle as such. As his late libertarian essay "Freedom Is a Two-Edged Sword" makes clear, Parsons rejected the rationalist ideal of a consistent theory of the world and instead embraced a sort of ontological anarchism grounded in spiritual autonomy. "However useful, spectacular, or necessary our ideas and experiments may be, they still have nothing to do with absolute truth or authority," he wrote. "Such a thing can only exist for the individual, according to his whim or fancy, or his inner perception of his own truth in being." Similarly, Parsons argued that "any system of intellectual thought, whether it be science, logic, religion, or philosophy, is based on certain fundamental ideas or axioms which are assumed, but which cannot be proven. This is the grave of all positivism."[82] Magic, by contrast, was not so much a system, in Parsons's view, as a method of navigating the polytheistic terrain, a method that anticipates the "pluralism, relativism, probabilism, and pragmatism" that have come to characterize so many contemporary spiritual practitioners and new religious movements.[83] In relativistically skirting foundational axioms, magic dances on positivism's grave.

Per Aspera

While Parsons could be said to have brought a certain occult "style" or sensibility to his rocket science, he conceptually maintained a separation between the two spheres. The influence of Parsons's science on his occult work and spiritual philosophy, however, is a more mixed affair. A number of comments in his correspondence and essays suggest that he saw magic and science as, in one biographer's words, "different sides of the same coin." For example, writing to Helen in 1943, Parsons noted that rocketry "may not be my True Will, but it's one hell of a powerful drive. With Thelema as my goal, and the stars my destination and my home, I have set my eyes on high."[84] Here, desire is split into the Thelemic will for transcendence and the Freudian drive for technological achievement—or at least atavistic excitement, the sort of thrill seeking that, we will see, Parsons pursued in his occult rituals as well. However, even as Parsons splits his desire, he fuses it together again with the romantic and polyvalent image of "the stars"—at once the literal goal of Parsons's rocket science and a scripturally significant figure for his Thelemic aspirations. "Every man and every woman is a star" is one of the best-known lines in *The Book of the Law*, an image of cosmic singularity that represents both true origins ("my home") and the final goal of spiritual transformation.[85] The image of the stars brings Parsons's twin desires into accord and thus stages the very code switching that Tambiah describes and that we will continue to track in the remainder of this chapter. While maintaining a degree of separation between science and the occult in his life and mind, Parsons nonetheless drew a thread of consistency between them, subjecting them to a practical resonance. In other words, the very space between science and the supernatural became a site—a second-order magic, if you will—where new relations were conjured: relations between ritual and experiment, spell and equation, method and madness.

Although Parsons did not keep the most meticulous magical diaries, and although much of his correspondence remains in private archives, there is, in addition to *The Book of Babalon* and his published essays, a valuable record of Parsons's correspondence to Marjorie Cameron in 1949 and 1950.[86] Though initially bemused by Parsons's occult beliefs, Cameron became a willing student, and Parsons's occult pedagogy offers insight into his understanding of

Crowley's "method of science" as well as his broader intellectual framework, which included Frazer, Joseph Campbell, and other nonoccultist scholars. In his lessons, Parsons echoed Crowley's admonition to question and analyze all the material gained through astral travel, telling Cameron that it was "necessary patiently to check and compare every source of information, eliminating all possible errors and being sure that you are not fooled or fooling yourself." Parsons called this "the application of ingenious scientific method to transcendental ends." Such a method does not attempt to "ground" transcendental claims in a scientific or quasi-scientific theory but to critically test the affective and mythopoetic phenomena of the inner planes. The grounds for establishing the criteria for not "fooling yourself" are, needless to say, somewhat obscure—one can hardly suppress the voice of Adorno, writing his "Theses Against Occultism" in nearly the same place and time: "Their procedure is to be strictly scientific: the greater the humbug, the more meticulously the experiment is prepared."[87]

Following the contradiction earlier identified in Crowley, Parsons also somewhat undermines his truth-seeking use of "ingenious scientific method" with a self-reflexive attitude of epistemological relativism: "Indeed my personal and interior experience, however hallucinated, must be at least equally valid with the things I have been taught to call 'objective' and 'real.' But these are also my truths—they are part of me—part of the equipment of my cosmic laboratory wherein I can begin an experiment in truth." Here, the rhetoric of science is at once undermined and redeployed. Inner experiences, Parsons acknowledges, may have nothing in them of science—of what, as moderns, we are taught to recognize as reality or objectivity—since they may be nothing more than hallucinations. Nonetheless, those groundless perceptions are valid enough, presumably in their purely subjective effects, to become "equipment" that can in turn be instrumentally applied to a deeper "experiment in truth." Relativism here does not lead to the abandonment of the experimental framework of instrument, operator, and object; far from undermining the veridical quest, relativism is precisely what lends the "method of science" a cosmic rather than a positivist or even strictly psychological character.

Parsons concludes the passage, "I can think of no better starting point than 'Do what thou wilt shall be the whole of the Law'—no better equipment than the magical, scientific, and psychological techniques I have inherited. But all these boil down to will, experiment, and honesty in regard to data."[88] Notice the absence of occult *theory* here. Instead, magic, science, and psychology are all integrated on the same open plane of method and practice, a plane of experience that involves a subject that *itself is tested*. Here, faintly, we get a glimpse of an "occult science" that does not attempt to offer a theoretical account of the nature of reality but instead treats experience as a kind of phenomenal flux that is tested and intensified within a contingent and relativistic framework whose conditions cannot be known so much as experimentally engaged. Though we are now at a considerable distance from a conventional Popperian understanding of scientific method, we are not so terribly far from a constructivism that understands that the equipment of the laboratory has a say in the results of the experiment. Moreover, Parsons's "experiment in truth" is, at least in principle, open-ended and even self-correcting, or at least self-intensifying, as the operator integrates honest data into further iterations of practice. We can see a self-conscious deployment here of the same process that Tanya Luhrmann identified among British magical practitioners in the 1980s. "The basic attitude was that you took nothing on faith, but you experimented with the practice, and eventually you would conclude on the basis of personal practice, that the magical ideas were probably correct."[89] Luhrmann described this process, somewhat limply, as "interpretive drift." Rather than embrace new beliefs, the new practitioner commits to practices whose penumbra of symbols and concepts begin to make sense productively as the budding magician begins to perceive reality in different modes; these initial glimmers then set the stage, in a sort of positive feedback loop of practice and perception, for new sorts of emotions and experiences that in turn make occult concepts more useful or resonant.

That said, for all his talk of patience and care in the application of "ingenious scientific method," Parsons's most thoughtful commentators describe him as an erratic, reckless, and dangerously proud magician. The parallels with his rocketry are impossible to ignore, and Parsons drew them himself. In 1949, at the height of his mystical inflation, Parsons wrote, "if I had the genius to found the jet propulsion field in the US, and found a multimillion dollar corporation and a world renowned research laboratory, then I should also be able to apply this genius in the magical field."[90] Noting that Parsons had performed rituals far in advance of his OTO grade work, Pendle claimed that, "as in his rocket work, he left theory behind in the wake of his will to experiment."[91] John Carter, who believes that Parsons was "essentially a failure" as a magician, writes that, "in his metaphysical life, the fearless Parsons showed the same methodology he used in his rocket propulsion work, a tenaciousness in testing and a thrill-seeker's lack of caution concerning what he may 'conjure.'"[92] By describing him as a thrill seeker, Carter is calling attention to Parsons's attraction to spectacular manifestations of what we might call, in light of today's growing Jedi faith, "the dark side of the force." Well before Parsons commenced the Babalon Working, members of the Agapé Lodge were already concerned with the flavor of his ritual intent. In 1945, Jane Wolfe wrote to Karl Germer, "our own Jack is enamored with witchcraft, the hounfort, voodoo. From the start he always wanted to evoke something—no matter what, I am inclined to think, as long as he got a result."[93] In 1945, Gerald Gardner had yet to found the Bricket Wood coven that ignited and reconstructed witchcraft as a positive religious identity for moderns; when Wolfe wrote her letter, "witchcraft" retained the same sort of dangerous aura among white Euro-American occultists that voodoo did. For our purposes, what is most important about Wolfe's letter is the coupling of black magic with a definitive "result."

In a letter to Cameron written five years later, Parsons provides another angle on this linkage: "The invocation of Gods (which pertains to a higher magic) is subtle and subject to individual variation and personal composition. The invocation of lesser forces is exact, and, since love does not usually enter in so much, in one sense far more dangerous. In the higher work you are actually wooing the god—it is an act of art. In the lower you are compelling, it is an act of science."[94] Here, remarkably, Parsons lays the symbolic/technical dualism of the anthropological distinction between magic and religion onto the vertical and moral hierarchy of the traditional Neoplatonic magical universe, with gods asking for a subtle, erotic, and poetic art and the lower forces—elsewhere defined as "Goetia (Demonic)"—responding only to an exact science of technical protocols. The danger in the latter path is not, for Parsons, moral threat so much as a sort of naturalistic *goetic* blowback, such as the "side phenomena" he alludes to in another letter to Cameron, where he discusses the "Bornless Ritual" that Crowley adapted for his 1904 publication *The Goetia*: "It is a very ancient, potent & dangerous ritual, often used by bold magicians in the Guardian Angel Working. It is useful as a preliminary in almost any sort of work, causing a tremendous concentration of force. It is, however, liable to produce dangerous side phenomena and sometimes permanent haunting in an area where it is repeated, & is for this reason often avoided."[95] Though we should not confuse the "Bornless Ritual" with unadorned black magic, the attraction that sorcery and atavistic ritual held for Parsons is made clearer in light of the symbolic transfer from his experience with rocketry. The invocation of dangerous forces—what he calls in his occult lessons to Cameron the "sacrifice to the abysmal gods"—produces, through the mediation of proper ritual, a tremendous "concentration of force" useful to the magician's ascent but liable to go awry. Just as Parsons's animated recitation of Crowley's "Hymn to Pan" in some sense ritualized the rocket tests, here we might say that rocketry, and the instrumental causality that underlies it, "technologized" his understanding of *Goetia*. Playing against type, Crowley roundly criticized Parsons for his interest in the dark arts: "All this black magic stuff is 75% nonsense and the rest plain dirt," he wrote Parsons. "There is not even any point to it." Parsons wrote back, "I know that witchcraft is mostly nonsense, except where it is a blind."[96]

This qualification is somewhat obscure, but by "blind" I suspect that Parsons meant *deterministic*—lesser forces, we recall, are compelled by "exact" commands, by "science" rather than the "art" appropriate for higher forces.

This leads to a central question: what did Parsons want or expect to happen? In a letter to Crowley about the Babalon Working, Parsons noted, "I have been extremely careful and conscientious in this ritual, lending all my will and scientific training to its precision and preparation. Yet nothing seems to have happened."[97] Here, we cannot be comforted by the notion that Parsons sought results strictly on the symbolic side of magic's expressive/technical divide. Nor can his goals neatly be captured under the rubric of Crowley's "Spiritual Experience," by which Crowley primarily meant unitive mystical experience. Instead, Parsons wanted—and expected—actual things to happen in the physical world. When Parsons invoked Bartzabel, he wanted to attack L. Ron Hubbard, and he later judged the working a success when Hubbard's yacht was forced to return to shore. The Babalon Working, which Parsons called a "magical experiment," was designed—with a bit of wiggle room for more symbolic interpretations—to incarnate a goddess into an actual human womb. The same working also commenced with an operation to summon an "elemental," an operation that Parsons suggested was successfully realized in the (relatively) simultaneous entrance of Marjorie Cameron into his life. And in *The Book of Babalon*, Parsons's play-by-play account of the working, Parsons carefully includes half a dozen arguably paranormal events that he dubs "phenomena," which include relatively unremarkable instances of wind storms as well as more eerie eruptions of poltergeist activity, "metallic" voices, and, in one instance, the roof of an adjacent building catching fire. Though Parsons notes that such phenomena are potentially signs of "imperfect technique" and that only the "willed result" should obtain, he is still keen on recording them.

This is not the place to adjudicate Parsons's paranormal claims or to interpret the erratic and possibly pathological condition of his psyche in his final years, when deep conflicts and an ominous dissociative undertow mark both his actions and his writings.[98] Instead, I want to draw attention once again to the paradox of Parsons's attitude toward the efficacy of magical ritual in light of the two value spheres that haunt this chapter and that defined his universe of thought and practice: science and the sacral supernatural. Rather than favor a symbolic, performative, or psycho-spiritual account of magic's value, Parsons—a "real" scientist, recall—sought palpable physical results from his workings. Moreover, he seems to have been comparatively *more* interested in such materialist phenomena than his fellow magicians, who were, presumably, reasonably content with the dramatic, expressive, and subjective dimensions of their practice.

Parson's Frazerian spirit cuts against any attempt to accommodate ritual magic as an individually or socially meaningful practice whose value can be understood in symbolic terms alone. In fact, as William S. Sax reminds us in his discussion of ritual efficacy, the category of "ritual" is already predicated on the tacit assumption that the practice in question doesn't actually *do* anything: "To analyze rituals as 'expressing' inner states of feeling and emotion, or 'symbolizing' theological ideas or social relations, or 'representing' psychological states of the human organism, is to neglect the question of how they might be instrumental, how they might actually *do* things."[99] For Parsons, ceremonial magic was not a ritual—it was an "operation" or "experiment" with explicit, if sometimes vaguely characterized, instrumental aims. According to his own accounts, and to many of those who knew him, Parsons's rites actually "did" things, though whether he was fooling himself—in his (or our) terms—remains necessarily opaque. Still, Sax's question about ritual efficacy does encourage us to "do" something else with Parsons's workings: to use our understanding of those practices, and others before and after them, to probe, in a pragmatic manner that is not restricted to discursive intervention, the flickering phenomena that leap between the value spheres that organize modernity into Weber's "polytheistic" space of competing reality claims. By applying the "method of science" to occult experience with the aim of religion in mind, Parsons was most emphatically not attempting to collapse the difference between the two. Arrogantly, foolishly, heretically, experimentally, he was *probing the gap,* the excluded middle, that constitutes their division and that echoes across a number of homologous divides that rend the fabric of modern experience: the gaps between positivism and the holy, between magic as expression and magic as manipulation, between rationalism and romance.

The principal fissure here, of course, is the divide between a disenchanted world of deterministic causes operated on by instrumental actions and a symbolic, rhetorical, and dramatic domain of meaning and affect associated with human consciousness (and its unconscious margins). The fissure is easy to sense—it lies, for example, in the strong temptation to view Jack Parsons's paranormal magical claims as, in Weber's words again, "plain humbug or self-deception." Nonetheless, it is precisely in the extremity of those claims that one can glimpse the very operations that sustain modernity's theater of disingenuous disenchantment. As Randall Styers argues at the conclusion of his work on magic and social thought, "The instability of magic as a scholarly category, the palpable artifice required to conjure it, serves to illuminate the contrivance through which all rational objectivity is maintained."[100] In the half light of the occult, the operative concept of rational objectivity is revealed as the surface of an essentially magical operation that shapes the modern idea of science in the popular imagination. Bruno Latour asks the obvious question: "How can we speak of a 'modern world' when its efficacy depends upon idols: money, law, reason, nature, machines, organization, or linguistic structures? . . . Since the origins of the power of the 'modern world' are misunderstood and efficacy is attributed to things that neither move nor speak, we may speak of magic once again."[101] Latour points us to the value of restoring or reengaging the discourse of magic, whose very extravagance and liminal flicker destabilize the effort to clearly separate the world of human symbols and desires from the natural or fashioned world of objects.

In his critique of the term *magic*, discussed above, Jonathan Z. Smith complained about the logical contradiction implied in the fact that, in being opposed to both science and religion, which themselves stand in opposition, the anthropological discourse of magic breaks the law of the excluded middle. However, we might also say that *magic is the excluded middle*, the impossible simulacrum that haunts and modulates the relativistic gap between value spheres and that, in particular, confounds the Cartesian ruse that founds the modern subject in the divorce of mind and matter. "Despite so much scholarly insistence that subjectivity and desire must be cordoned away from the world of material causality," Styers argues, "magic illuminates the potency of their intermingling."[102] That said, even social scientists sympathetic to the immense complexity that characterizes the social and perceptual construction of reality quiver before the implications of this intermingling. At the close of Luhrmann's sensitive and sophisticated ethnographic study of modern British magical practitioners, she describes how the "interpretive drift" discussed above transformed her own experience. As she studied kabbalah, read tarot cards and astrology charts, and participated in "pathworkings," Luhrmann began to perceive the world quite differently: she began to have symbolically vivid dreams and imaginal experiences, felt energy moving through her body during ritual, and "began to use the word 'spiritual' to describe a fuzzy set of relatively new phenomenological states, experiences and responses." In Crowley's words, she did certain things and certain results followed. But, as a researcher, Lurhmann needed to draw a line for herself as well, to establish that point beyond which she could no longer consider herself an anthropologist. And that line was precisely the point of "asserting that rituals had an effect upon the material world."[103]

Jack Parsons—whose personality is almost a caricature of the "romantic rationalism" that Luhrmann analyzes—had no such qualms, and his passionate instrumentality reminds us that romance and rationalism are not simply balanced within the occult or kept in neat compartments. Modern magic, at least in the Thelemic current traced here, is a second-order phenomenon, an ambiguous fluctuation that appears sometimes as religion, sometimes as science, sometimes as an atavism, and sometimes as a postmodern pluralism. In this sense, the occult milieu is not simply another subculture pursuing religious or spiritual values in the multiplying margins of modernity's rationalized institutions, political ideologies, and dominant perceptual frameworks. Instead, the occult is a direct engagement, at once romantic and methodical, with the very ambivalences, contradictions, and ambiguous margins that characterize the reality field of modernity itself, with its polytheistic field of heterogeneous, dynamic, and disenchanted "gods." Properly speaking, such occult practice does not seek simply to "re-enchant" the world or to establish some integral holistic field of mystical science. As Crowley's powerful notion of "skeptical Theurgy" itself indicates, modern magic—or at least a vital strain of it—is already too disenchanted for that, too naturalistic, too self-reflexive. Instead, magic is an aggressive performance of pluralism, a playful and tricky theater of possibility whose "structured ambiguity rests upon a deconstructed notion of belief."[104] The "doubly double" character that Smith criticized in social-scientific accounts of magic is not, in this sense, a sign of conceptual weakness but rather a display of magic's furtive and phantasmic appearance, within the space of modernity, as a mischievous mediator or probe of overlapping reality claims. In this way, the method of science does indeed satisfy the aim of religion—a pluralistic and pragmatic religion of only relative enchantments.

NOTES

1. Parsons also went by the name John Whiteside Parsons and, as a child, Marvel Parsons; Jack is the name used most frequently in the accounts of those who knew him.

2. Crowley's signature spelling of "magick," the sexual and specifically Thelemite connotations of which Parsons avidly pursued, will not be retained in this chapter for the sake of clarity.

3. Max Weber, "Science as a Vocation," in From Max Weber: Essays in Sociology, ed. H. H. Gerth and C. Wright Mills (London: Psychology Press, 1991), 139, 154.

4. For some of these criticisms, see Peter Pels, "Introduction: Magic and Modernity," in Magic and Modernity: Interfaces of Revelation and Concealment, ed. Birgit Meyer and Peter Pels (Stanford: Stanford University Press, 2003), 26–29; for more on the enchantments of modern science and technology, see Erik Davis, Techgnosis: Myth, Magic, and Mysticism in the Age of Information (London: Serpent's Tail, 2004), esp. 164–224.

5. Weber, "Science as a Vocation," 143.

6. Ibid., 141.

7. Ibid., 154.

8. Max Weber, The Protestant Ethic and the Spirit of Capitalism, trans. Talcott Parsons (Mineola, N.Y.: Dover, 2013), 182.

9. Pels, "Introduction," 28–29; and Weber, "Science as a Vocation," 135.

10. Tanya M. Luhrmann, Persuasions of the Witch's Craft: Ritual Magic in Contemporary England (Cambridge: Harvard University Press, 1991), 337–44 (quotation at 337).

11. Randall Styers, Making Magic: Religion, Magic, and Science in the Modern World (New York: Oxford University Press, 2004), 8.

12. Jonathan Z. Smith, *Relating Religion: Essays in the Study of Religion* (Chicago: University of Chicago Press, 2004), 215–22 (quotation at 218). For example, Durkheim declared that magic was similar to religion but "more elementary"; more dichotomously, it derived its power by "profaning holy things" and performing "the contrary of the religious ceremony." See Émile Durkheim, *The Elementary Forms of the Religious Life* (New York: Free Press, 1965), 57. Similarly, Malinowski wrote that while religion does not produce the sort of specialists that magic claims, its mythology is nonetheless "more varied and more complex as well as more creative." See Bronislaw Malinowski, *Magic, Science, and Religion and Other Essays* (Whitefish, Mont.: Kessinger, 2004), 68.

13. Pels, "Introduction," 10. See also James George Frazer, *The Golden Bough* (Mineola, N.Y.: Dover, 2002), 50.

14. Stanley Jeyaraja Tambiah, *Magic, Science, Religion, and the Scope of Rationality* (New York: Cambridge University Press, 1990), 82.

15. My account of Parsons's story is drawn principally from John Carter, *Sex and Rockets: The Occult World of Jack Parsons* (Los Angeles: Feral House, 2005); and George Pendle, *Strange Angel: The Otherworldly Life of Rocket Scientist John Whiteside Parsons* (Orlando: Harcourt, 2005). Also highly worthwhile is *The Marvel*, an online comic-book biography written by Richard Carbonneau and drawn by Robin Simon, accessed October 31, 2010, http://www.webcomicsnation.com/rscarbonneau/parsons/toc.php.

16. Pendle, *Strange Angel*, 46, 44.

17. Carter, *Sex and Rockets*, 8, 18.

18. Pendle, *Strange Angel*, 157.

19. At least according to von Kármán. See Lawrence Sutin, *Do What Thou Wilt: A Life of Aleister Crowley* (New York: Macmillan, 2000), 396.

20. Carter, *Sex and Rockets*, 72.

21. In 2013, Aerojet merged with Pratt & Whitney Rocketdyne to form Aerojet Rocketdyne.

22. Quoted in Pendle, *Strange Angel*, 9.

23. Carter, *Sex and Rockets*, 86.

24. Ibid., 56.

25. Pendle, *Strange Angel*, 270.

26. A young actor and communist named Harry Hay was hired to play the organ for the lodge's Gnostic Mass. Though Hay could not resist adding ditties like "Barnacle Bill the Sailor" and "Yes! We Have No Bananas" to the accompaniment, Crowley remained an influence on the gay rights pioneer; announcing the first Spiritual Conference for Radical Faeries in 1979, Hay ended his exhortation to "dance in the moonlight" with a quotation from Crowley's *Book of the Law*. See Harry Hay, "A Call to Gay Brothers," in his *Radically Gay: Gay Liberation in the Words of Its Founder* (Boston: Beacon Press, 1997), 241.

27. Carter, *Sex and Rockets*, 55.

28. Quoted in Pendle, *Strange Angel*, 255.

29. While intimately related to the city Babylon, which in the guise of a whore plays a vital allegorical role in the book of Revelation, Crowley's "Babalon" replaces the *y* with an *a* for reasons most likely related to Kabbalistic *gematria* and the Enochian system of magic.

30. An influential figure in L.A.'s postwar bohemian and occult scenes and a good friend of Wallace Berman, Dennis Hopper, and George Herms, Cameron became a painter and occasional actress, upstaging Anaïs Nin as the Scarlet Woman in Kenneth Anger's 1954 film *Inauguration of the Pleasure Dome*. See Spencer Kansa, *Wormwood Star: The Magickal Life of Marjorie Cameron* (Oxford: Mandrake, 2010).

31. The reception of *Liber 49* provides a fruitful illumination of how the authenticity of modern occult revelation is constructed and resisted, at least within the OTO and Thelema-inspired communities. Parsons was a charismatic figure of some authority; nonetheless, his revealed text, which declares itself "the fourth chapter of the Book of the Law," has been widely rejected as such, on both substantial and stylistic grounds. Writing in a Typhonean

OTO publication, Michael Staley notes, "In terms of content, level of inspiration, and style, *Liber 49* is nothing like *The Book of the Law*; and on this basis alone, the claim can be looked at askance." Michael Staley, "Beloved of Babalon," *Starfire* 1, no. 3 (1989), accessed October 11, 2011, http://www.skeptictank.org/belovob.htm. In *The Red Goddess* (London: Scarlet Imprint, 2008), 163, Peter Grey describes the text as "a poor production with some howlingly bad lines only redeemed by a few shots of brilliant blood red clarity."

32. Pendle, *Strange Angel*, 240.

33. Melton's account can be found in his brazenly sympathetic treatment of Scientology. See J. Gordon Melton, *The Church of Scientology* (Salt Lake City: Signature, 2000), 7.

34. For Parsons's essays, see John Whiteside Parsons, *Freedom Is a Two-Edged Sword: Essays*, ed. Hymenaeus Beta and [Marjorie] Cameron (Las Vegas: Falcon Press, 1989); and John Whiteside Parsons, *Three Essays on Freedom* (York Beach, Maine: Teitan Press, 2008). For Parsons's letter (dated February 11, 1952, to Karl Germer), see Pendle, *Strange Angel*, 296.

35. In addition to Carter and Pendle, see Kenneth Grant, *The Magical Revival* (London: Starfire, 2010), 157–71; a more feverish account can be found in Kenneth Grant, *Outside the Circles of Time* (London: Frederick Muller, 1980), 45–52. See also Staley, "Beloved of Babalon"; Paul Rydeen, *Jack Parsons and the Fall of Babalon* (1994; electronic version copyright 2009); Richard Metzger, "The Crying of Liber 49: Jack Parsons, Antichrist Superstar," in *Book of Lies: The Disinformation Guide to Magick and the Occult*, ed. Richard Metzger (New York: Disinformation Company, 2008), 198–211; Nikolas Schreck and Zeena Schreck, *Demons of the Flesh: The Complete Guide to Left Hand Path Sex Magic* (San Francisco: Creation, 2002), 302–29; and Anthony Testa, *The Key of the Abyss: Jack Parsons, the Babalon Working, and the Black Pilgrimage Decoded* (Raleigh, N.C.: Lulu.com, 2006).

36. Pendle, *Strange Angel*, 330. Remarkably, at least a few scholars, among them James Lewis and J. Gordon Melton, consider the Church of Scientology account at least as plausible as the OTO account. The question of the influence of Thelema or Parsons on Dianetics/Scientology is controversial; while Melton insists that there is "no direct OTO influence," Hubbard spoke favorably of Crowley and his concept of will in 1952 (PDC Lecture 18). See J. Gordon Melton, "Birth of a Religion," in *Scientology*, ed. James R. Lewis (New York: Oxford University Press, 2009), 21.

37. Mike Davis, *City of Quartz: Excavating the Future in Los Angeles* (New York: Verso, 2006), 55–60 (quotation at 55).

38. Metzger, "Crying of Liber 49," 200. Parsons also makes a thinly disguised appearance as the occult scientist Hugo Chantrelle in Anthony Boucher's 1942 science-fiction roman à clef *Rocket to the Morgue*.

39. For a lively recent telling of Dee's life, see Benjamin Woolley, *The Queen's Conjurer: The Science and Magic of Dr. John Dee, Advisor to Queen Elizabeth I* (New York: Macmillan, 2002); see also Peter J. French, *John Dee: The World of an Elizabethan Magus* (London: Psychology Press, 1987). Parsons himself noted this correspondence a few years after the fact, writing to Cameron that "the parallel with my own Working with Ron is appalling." That said, Parsons overstates the similarities. See "Correspondence Between Jack Parsons and His 'Elemental,' Marjorie Cameron," ed. [Marjorie] Cameron and Hymenaeus Beta, January 25, 1950, accessed September 25, 2011, http://blacklies.xenu.ca/archives/3384.

40. Jack Parsons, *The Collected Writings of Jack Parsons* (a few versions of this widely circulated unpublished document exist), accessed September 25, 2011, www.hollywoodinsiders.net/texts/parsons.pdf.

41. Jeffrey J. Kripal, *Authors of the Impossible: The Paranormal and the Sacred* (Chicago: University of Chicago Press, 2010), 25, 34. Another echo of Kripal's thesis: during the initial phase of the Babalon Working, Parsons was woken up by nine loud, unexplained knocks. He noticed a lamp smashed on the floor. The Enochian word for "lamps" is, at least according to some Enochian dictionaries, HUBARDO. Benjamin Rowe, *Enochian Dictionary*, the Hermetic Library, accessed May 5, 2016, http://hermetic.com/norton/papers/endic.txt.

42. Quoted in Tambiah, *Magic, Science, Religion*, 23.

43. Carter, *Sex and Rockets*, 72.

44. Martin P. Starr, *The Unknown God: W. T. Smith and the Thelemites* (Bolingbrook, Ill.: Teitan Press, 2003), 254.

45. Quoted in Pendle, *Strange Angel*, 168.

46. Tambiah, *Magic, Science, Religion*, 92.

47. Parsons, *Collected Writings of Jack Parsons*, unpaginated (19).

48. Olav Hammer, *Claiming Knowledge: Strategies of Epistemology from Theosophy to the New Age* (Leiden: Brill, 2001), 323.

49. See Helena Petrovna Blavatsky, *Isis Unveiled: A Master Key to the Mysteries of Ancient and Modern Science and Theology* (San Diego: Aryan Theosophical Press, 1919), especially 310–22, 340–49, 393–97.

50. Hammer, *Claiming Knowledge*, 204.

51. See Luhrmann's brief but insightful discussion in *Persuasions of the Witch's Craft*, 123–25; see also Tambiah, *Magic, Science, Religion*, 140–54.

52. Hammer, *Claiming Knowledge*, 204.

53. Aleister Crowley, *The Confessions of Aleister Crowley: An Autohagiography*, ed. John Symonds and Kenneth Grant (London: Arkana, 1989), 399.

54. Quoted in Hammer, *Claiming Knowledge*, 222.

55. *Confessions of Aleister Crowley*, 296.

56. Egil Asprem, "Magic Naturalized? Negotiating Science and Occult Experience in Aleister Crowley's Scientific Illuminism," *Aries: Journal for the Study of Western Esotericism* 8, no. 2 (2008): 151.

57. Alex Owen, *The Place of Enchantment: British Occultism and the Culture of the Modern* (Chicago: University of Chicago Press, 2004), 239, 182.

58. Aleister Crowley, *Magick in Theory and Practice* (New York: Dover, 1976), 256.

59. For a discussion of testing spirits, see Nancy Caciola, *Discerning Spirits: Divine and Demonic Possession in the Middle Ages* (Ithaca: Cornell University Press, 2003), 274–98.

60. Asprem, "Magic Naturalized," 161–62.

61. Aleister Crowley, *Liber Aleph vel CXI: The Book of Wisdom or Folly, in the Form of an Epistle of 666, the Great Wild Beast to His Son 777, Being the Equinox, Volume III, Number VI* (York Beach, Maine: Samuel Weiser, 1991), 2.

62. Aleister Crowley and Samuel Liddell MacGregor Mathers, *The Goetia: The Lesser Key of Solomon the King* (Newburyport, Maine: Weiser, 1995), 15–20.

63. Quoted in James A. Eshelman, *The Mystical and Magical System of the A∴A∴* (Los Angeles: College of Thelema, 2008), 39. Also see Marco Pasi, "Varieties of Magical Experience: Aleister Crowley's Views on Occult Practice," *Magic, Ritual, and Witchcraft* 6, no. 2 (2011): 123–62. Qualifying Asprem's presentation of the "naturalized" Crowley, Pasi convincingly argues that Crowley, in order to ground his own prophetic aspirations as the founder of a new religion, created a "protected core where a 'disenchanted' vision of occult experience would not be allowed" (124).

64. Crowley, *Magick in Theory and Practice*, 247, 375.

65. Owen, *Place of Enchantment*, 248.

66. Quoted in Eshelman, *Mystical and Magical System*, 40.

67. Frank Malina, "On the GALCIT Rocket Research Project, 1936–38," in *First Steps Toward Space: Proceedings of the First and Second History Symposia of the International Academy of Astronautics at Belgrade, Yugoslavia, 26 September 1967, and New York, U.S.A., 16 October 1968*, ed. Frederick C. Durant III and George S. James (San Diego: American Astronautical Society, 1985), 113–24.

68. Ibid., 113; Pendle, *Strange Angel*, 63; and Carter, *Sex and Rockets*, 48.

69. Davis, *City of Quartz*, 57.

70. The scientific director of Aerojet was Frank Zwicky, a Caltech scientist who disliked Parsons. Against Parsons's strong advice, Zwicky, who was technically Parsons's superior,

ordered a batch of nitromethane for use as an oxidizer for liquid rocket fuel. When Parsons, who considered the material too volatile, came across the shipment, he intentionally detonated it on company property. Though Malina ultimately supported the action, the incident reflected Parsons's attitude toward institutional authority, if not his abiding compulsion to blow things up outside normal channels.

71. In "GALCIT Rocket Research Project," 113, Malina tips his hat to Jules Verne's *De la terre à la lune*, which he read as a boy in Czechoslovakia.

72. Ibid., 114.

73. Pendle, *Strange Angel*, 163.

74. Weber, "Science as a Vocation," 135, 136.

75. James Hillman and Wilhelm Heinrich Roscher, *Pan and the Nightmare* (New York: Spring Publications, 2000), 77.

76. Gilles Deleuze and Felix Guattari, *A Thousand Plateaus: Capitalism and Schizophrenia*, trans. Brian Massumi (Minneapolis: University of Minnesota Press, 1987), 408, 409.

77. Frank H. Winter, for example, characterizes the casting of solid fuel as a "breakthrough" but does not mention Parsons, calling Malina "the driving force" of a "small pool of scientists and other enthusiasts." See Frank H. Winter, *Prelude to the Space Age: The Rocket Societies, 1924–1940* (Washington, D.C.: Smithsonian Institution Press, 1983), 102–3.

78. Frank Malina, "The US Army Air Corps Jet Propulsion Research Project, GALCIT Project No. 1, 1939–1946: A Memoir," in *Essays on the History of Rocketry and Astronautics*, vol. 2, ed. R. C. Hall (Washington, D.C.: NASA, Scientific and Technical Information Office, 1977), 174, 172.

79. After leaving the United States and Aerojet in the 1950s, Malina became a kinetic artist and painter in France; he later founded the peer-reviewed arts journal *Leonardo*, which to this day focuses on the interaction between the arts, science, and technology.

80. Malina, "GALCIT Rocket Research Project," 114.

81. Weber, "Science as a Vocation," 148.

82. Parsons, *Freedom Is a Two-Edged Sword*, 12, 11.

83. Yves Lambert, "Religions in Modernity as a New Axial Age," *Sociology of Religion* 60, no. 3 (1999): 323; also see the discussion of such compartmentalization in modern occult thought in Luhrmann, *Persuasions of the Witch's Craft*, 283–386.

84. Quoted in Pendle, *Strange Angel*, 18, 168–69.

85. "Every man and every woman is a star." *Liber AL vel Legis*, 1.3, accessed October 10, 2011, http://www.sacred-texts.com/oto/engccxx.htm.

86. "Jack Parsons and His 'Elemental.'" These letters were prepared at the same time that Cameron and Hymenaeus Beta were editing *Freedom Is a Two-Edged Sword*, but they were never published. A complete edition of Parsons's writings and important correspondence is long overdue.

87. Theodor Adorno, *Minima Moralia: Reflections on a Damaged Life* (London: Verso, 1974), 243.

88. Parsons to Cameron, January 27, [1950], in "Jack Parsons and His 'Elemental.'"

89. Luhrmann also noted that "it was not so much that the ideas were being *tested*, but that they were being *used*." Luhrmann, *Persuasions of the Witch's Craft*, 142.

90. Quoted in Pendle, *Strange Angel*, 18.

91. Ibid., 219.

92. Carter, *Sex and Rockets*, 148.

93. Quoted in Pendle, *Strange Angel*, 258.

94. Parsons to Cameron, January 16, [1950?], in "Jack Parsons and His 'Elemental.'"

95. Ibid. The ritual was originally a Greco-Egyptian rite of exorcism, most recently translated by Hans Dieter Betz as "The Stele of Jeu the Hieroglyphist"; it was adapted for Crowley's 1904 publication *The Goetia* and later further altered by Crowley for inclusion in *Liber Samekh*. See Alex Sumner, "The Bornless Ritual," *Journal of the Western Mystery Tradition* 1, no. 7

(Autumnal Equinox 2004), accessed October 16, 2011, http://www.jwmt.org/v1n7/bornless.html.

96. Quoted in Pendle, *Strange Angel*, 257. Notably, it was in Crowley's introduction to *The Goetia* that the Beast produced his most positivist and naturalistic account of ceremonial magic.

97. Quoted in ibid., 257, 261.

98. Most notable here is Parsons's account of a magical working he described to Germer a few months before his death, using terms that mix psychoanalytic and "technical" language: "The operation began auspiciously with a chromatic display of psychosomatic symptoms, and progressed rapidly to acute psychosis. The operator has altered satisfactorily between manic hysteria and depressing melancholy stupor on approximately 60 (40?) cycles, and satisfactory progress has been maintained in social ostracism, economic collapse and mental disassociation." Parsons, *In the Continuum* 4, no. 9: 40.

99. William Sturman Sax, "Ritual and the Problem of Efficacy," in *The Problem of Ritual Efficacy*, ed. William Sturman Sax, Johannes Quack, and Jan Weinhold (New York: Oxford University Press, 2010), 6.

100. Styers, *Making Magic*, 225.

101. Bruno Latour, *The Pasteurization of France* (Cambridge: Harvard University Press, 1993), 209.

102. Styers, *Making Magic*, 226.

103. Luhrmann, *Persuasions of the Witch's Craft*, 319, 320.

104. Ibid., 336.

7

MANNING THE HIGH SEAT:

SEIÐR AS SELF-MAKING IN CONTEMPORARY NORSE NEOPAGANISMS

Megan Goodwin

Enn þic síþa koþo
Sámseyio í
oc draptv a vétt sem va/lor;
vitca líci
fórtv verþioþ yfir,
oc hvgða ec þat args aþal

But you once practiced *seiðr* on Samsey
And you beat on the drum as witches do
In the likeness of a wizard
you journeyed among mankind
And I thought that showed an *arg* [unmanly] nature

—*Lokasenna* 24

This passage illustrates the Norse god of mischief taunting Oðinn All-Father in the medieval Icelandic poem *Lokasenna*, "The Flyting of Loki."[1] *Flytings*, or insult battles, were a common literary device in medieval Norse poetic literature; the harshest and crassest of these insults were *nið*, slurs of a grossly sexual nature.[2] *Nið*-sayers meant to enrage their opponents and scandalize an audience, both goals manifesting a social hierarchy that prized hypermasculine virility. In the stanza above, Loki literally accuses Oðinn of having acted in an unmanly (*argr*)[3] manner by engaging in magical practices, or *seiðr*.[4] In short, Loki just called Oðinn a spell-casting faggot.[5]

As this epigraph shows, *seið*craft (Norse magical practice) has a complex historical relationship to gender. Traditionally, *seið* practitioners were women; the medieval Icelandic historian Snorri Sturluson recounted that the goddess Freyja brought *seiðr* to the Norse sky gods.[6] But the practice was never exclusively female; Snorri likewise chronicled Oðinn All-Father's using this magic both to foresee the future and to shape it. Despite the example of the All-Father, however, the literary and archaeological evidence for *seiðr* suggests not only that most *seið*workers were women but that *seiðr* was an inherently unmanly pursuit.[7] Contemporary Norse Neopagan and Heathens who reclaim or re-create *seiðr* must negotiate this tension between magical practice and gender identity. This chapter explores the ways in which trans- and cisgender men reconcile ambiguous textual evidence and contemporary gender norms through magical practice.[8]

Despite the historical unmanliness of oracular divination, Norse Neopagan men today are increasingly engaging in *seiðr*. Today's *seið*workers have reconstructed or reimagined the practice within *seiðr*'s gendered genealogy. Although conservative Heathenries discourage or forbid men from practicing oracular divination because of its historically unmanly connotations, more moderate Norse Neopaganisms accept *seiðr* as common practice while discarding or reinterpreting the historical taint of unmanliness. Northern Tradition Paganism, a northern European Neopagan tradition founded by female-to-male (FTM) transman Raven Kaldera, encourages *seiðr* and celebrates unmanliness as sacred service to a liminal religious community and to lesser-known gods. Contemporary Norse Neopagan men invested in establishing themselves as legitimate and authorized practitioners of *seiðr* must negotiate their identification *as men* through a historical precedent that identifies the practice as inherently unmanly.

Norse Neopagans glean information about their deities and notions of honorable behavior from "clues found in the Icelandic Sagas; the Poetic and Prose Eddas; Anglo-Saxon historical, legal, and medical texts; as well as modern archaeological, linguistic, and anthropological research."[9] Heathens (the designation many Norse Neopagans use to distinguish themselves from other Neopagans, particularly Wiccans, who they feel rely too heavily on individual gnosis) commonly refer to these clues simply as "the lore." Because Norse Neopagans place weighty emphasis on the historical and literary precedents for their contemporary beliefs and practices, and because the lore codes *seiðr* as a practice most (if not exclusively) appropriate for women, Norse Neopagan communities often challenge the legitimacy and propriety of male *seið*workers. For this reason, *seið*work requires male practitioners to negotiate—to defend or even discard—their masculine identities. Thus I argue that the high seat, the chair upon which the seeress sits and allows gods, ancestors, and spirits to speak through her, is for male *seið*workers a site of self-fashioning. Men who practice *seiðr* defend the legitimacy of their practice through negotiations of their own masculinity. If knowledge and full comprehension of the self is the ultimate goal of modernity, then *seiðr* emerges (despite its medieval roots) as a thoroughly modern practice: Norse magic serves as a vehicle through which *seiðmen* explore and expand their knowledge of themselves and their craft.

In what follows, I first briefly review the medieval literary sources that portray pre-Christian *seiðr* as an unmanly practice. I then explore contemporary examples of men as *seiðworkers*. Drawing on the ethnographic fieldwork of scholar and *seiðwoman* Jenny Blain, I show that many modern *seiðmen* reinterpret or reject the practice's unmanly connotations while maintaining a deep investment in identifying *as men*. For these men, legitimate *seiðr* need not be an unmanly undertaking, nor is the practice authoritative only when practiced by women and effeminate or queer men. By contrast, though, Northern Tradition shaman and transman Raven Kaldera embraces unmanliness not only as a condition of magic practice but also as an essential element of his religio-magical identity. For Kaldera, *seiðr* is part of a larger magical project of deconstructing and ultimately discarding traditional masculinity as a stable or desirable identity. Instead, unmanliness, for Kaldera, is a position of power and a liberating expansion of religious and gendered possibility. I conclude that *seiðr* is best understood as thoroughly modern magic, in that contemporary practitioners both expand authorized access to the practice and deeply engage their own gendered identities.

Gender and Pre-Christian *Seiðr*

Seiðcraft has long fascinated historians, scholars of Scandinavian literature, and enthusiasts of Viking culture. But the Sagas and Eddas—poetic and prosaic recounting of the deeds of Norse gods and heroes—provide only glimpses into how and why pre-Christian *seiðworkers* might have engaged in this kind of magic.[10] Most tales of *seið*-magic follow a similar formula: the *querent* (often a hero or a god/dess) asks for the insight of a *völva* (seeress), who reveals occult knowledge. The initial question is the protagonist's, but thereafter the *seið*-worker drives the exchange. She tells of past, present, and future events, always challenging, almost taunting her audience: would you know more?

As noted above, medieval accounts of pre-Christian *seiðr* usually relate stories of female practitioners. Three sections of Snorri's *Poetic Edda* chronicle the practices of *seiðwomen*.[11] In *Völuspá*, or "The Speaking of the Seeress," Oðinn asks a *seiðwoman* "born of giants" for "the ancient histories of men and gods, those which [she] remember[s] from the first."[12] *Baldrsdraumr* narrates Oðinn's journey to a grave mound on the borders of Hel, upon which he raises a *völva*, or seeress, from the dead. And in *Hyndlujöð*, the seeress Hyndla foretells the doom of the gods and the destruction and renewal of the world (*Ragnarök*).

However, there is demonstrable literary evidence of pre-Christian *seið*men, though the accounts are unclear as to the social standing of men who practiced *seiðr*.[13] The poem *Hyndlujöð*, for instance, refers to male *seið*workers not as *seiðmaðr* (*seið*men) but as *seiðberendur*. Queer theorist Brit Solli translates *berendur* here as "a very coarse word for female genitalia."[14] Blain argues for a more ambiguous reading of *seiðberendur*: citing the historian Gunnora Halla-karva, Blain notes that *berendi* (from the verb *bera*, to give birth) refers specifi-cally to "the sexual parts of a female animal, particularly a cow." While Blain acknowledges that *berendi* might be "an extreme insult," she also suggests that the term might imply a male practitioner's "actively giving birth to the *seiðr*," allowing the magic passage through the *seið*man's body.[15] Men's role in pre-Christian *seiðr*, then, was at best ambiguous and at worst grossly denigrated.

Given the warrior culture's social organization around a hypervirile mascu-line ideal, it follows that Vikings would have regarded magic (or any other weakness or anxiety not pursuant to feats of physical potency) with marked suspicion.[16] The Sagas nevertheless tell of *seið*men, male practitioners of magi-cal workings.[17] *Lokasenna* and other tales suggest that Viking men of the Saga age—even the All-Father himself—practiced oracular divination despite the culturally transgressive implications of the practice.[18]

Snorri explained the bias against men working *seiðr* in his commentary on *Ynglinga Saga,* which provides the only detailed account of a *seið*man: that of Oðinn himself.

> Oðinn understood also the art in which the greatest power is lodged, and which he himself practised; namely, what is called magic [*seiðr*]. By means of this he could know beforehand the predestined fate of men, or their not yet completed lot; and also bring on the death, ill-luck, or bad health of people, and take the strength or wit from one person and give it to another. But after such witchcraft followed such weakness and anxiety [*ergi*], that it was not thought respectable for men to practise it; and therefore the priestesses were brought up in this art.[19]

Here, Snorri directly connected magic (*seiðr*) and unmanliness (*ergi*). This link is not surprising: a warrior culture might well be suspicious of nonphysical practices that left one weak or anxious. Snorri's commentary on the *Ynglinga Saga* thus underscores pre-Christian Viking anxiety about masculinity while illustrating the gendered nature of *seið*work.

In addition to the discussion in the *Ynglinga Saga*, *Lokasenna* also narrates a link between gender anxieties and magical practices. In response to Oðinn's accusation that Loki bore children, showing an *"argr* nature," Loki suggests that Oðinn behaved in an *argr* manner for having "practiced *seiðr* on [the island of] Samsey."[20] Medieval Norse literature clearly demonstrates prevailing attitudes about the unmanliness of magic.

The work of Däg Strömbäck, Peter Buchholz, Folke Ström, and Preben Meulengracht Sørensen has directly influenced present-day Norse Neopagan thinking on the presumed unmanliness of *seiðr*. In his 1935 dissertation "Sejd: Textstudier i nordisk religionshistoria" (*Seiðr*: Textual Studies in Norse Religious History), Strömbäck argues that pre-Christian *seiðr* "was originally a masculine technique, tied to the god Oðinn which only in later stages transferred to women and thus became subject to contempt."[21] For Strömbäck, then, the unmanliness of *seiðr* was a degradation of an originally masculine ritual practice. By contrast, Buchholz suggested not only that *seiðr* was an unmanly practice but also that unmanliness was an asset to *seiðr*workers: in his 1968 *Schamanistische Züge in der altislädndischen Überlieferung* (Shamanic Features in the Old Icelandic Tradition), Buchholz "assumes that 'sexual perverts' (*sexuell Abartige*) are more receptive to a state of [religious] ecstasy, since they unite the characteristics of man and woman."[22]

In his 1974 *Nid, Ergi, and Old Norse Moral Attitudes*, Folke Ström designated *seiðr* "the element in the *ergi* complex related to sorcery and magic." For Ström, then, *seiðr* was a subset of unmanly behaviors. Ström suggested that the "sexually obscene" connotations of *ergi* were specifically related to "the female role in a homosexual act" (that of being sexually penetrated), and therefore that *seiðr*, as a form of spiritual penetration by gods or ancestors, was likewise "a role that was regarded as specifically female." Ström thus concluded that "the performance by an individual man of a role normally belonging to the female sex which constitutes perversity in his action and causes it to be branded as *ergi*" applies equally to "a sexual relationship" or "the carrying out of a magical function."[23] In short, Ström argued that pre-Christian Viking society drew no meaningful distinction between the shame of a man being sexually penetrated and the shame of a man working *seiðr*.

Finally, Sørensen's *The Unmanly Man: Concepts of Sexual Defamation in Early Northern Society* cites Snorri to suggest that "the practice of heathen witchcraft, sorcery, included . . . sexual activities and taboo-breaking . . . men appeared as women." Understanding *seiðr* as unmanly, Sørensen explained, linked this sort of magic to effeminacy, cross-dressing, and passive homosexuality.[24] While their readings of the practice's social function vary broadly,

Sørensen, Ström, and Buchholz all suggested that *seiðr* either required or was equivalent to sexual passivity, gender transgression, or effeminacy.

More recent scholarship has attempted to add nuance to the language of previous studies, shying away from anachronistic notions of Viking homo-sexuality[25] and offering alternative readings of the unmanliness of *seiðr*.[26] Jenny Blain, herself a scholar of Viking lore and a *seiðw*orker, offers a nuanced reading of these materials. Blain emphasizes that translating *ergi* in terms of sexual receptivity or passivity relies on a heteronormative understanding of "active male / passive female" gender norms, an understanding strongly cri-tiqued by scholars of gender and sexuality. Blain suggests that "it may be more useful to regard *ergi* primarily as an insult, that can be used to convey the meaning (pejoratively) . . . of 'acted upon sexually,' or simply 'coward,'" without necessarily indicating sexual penetration.[27] Indeed, as both Sørensen and Ström note, accusations of sexual passivity or "perversion" are secondary char-acteristics of gendered insults—even suggesting that a "tendency or inclina-tion" toward being used sexually by a man still falls under the category of *ergi*, which can also imply cowardice or poverty.[28] Blain's glossing of *ergi* as simply "insult," then, gestures toward the inherent gender ambiguity of the term.

Ergi is, however, a very specific and severe form of insult: many scholars categorize *ergi* as *nið*, "the most spectacular . . . form of sexual defamation" in Viking society.[29] The complexities of *nið* exceed the scope of this chapter, but it should be noted that the severity of the insult lies not so much in implications of sodomy or sexual passivity but rather in culturally specific understandings of gender.[30] The ambiguities of *ergi* included sexual transgression; as Ström suggested, sodomy might have served as a "symbolic presentation" of the larger concern, unmanliness.[31]

If Viking masculinity required the constant performance of masculinity, and *seiðr* was considered unmanly, pre-Christian *seiðr* would have served as a form of negative masculinity. *Seiðm*en had knowingly to behave in a manner otherwise antithetical to their cultural conditioning. The Sagas and Eddas shed little insight into the motivation behind so transgressive a gender perfor-mance.[32] *Seiðm*en might have invoked the power of transgression to authorize deliberate performances of negative masculinity. They might have read their own "unmanly" bodies as a sign of other forms of power or spiritual authority or responsibility. Pre-Christian *seiðm*en might have desired occult knowledge and risked scorn to access that knowledge, or they might have felt called by gods, or spirits, or ancestors to speak to their communities, simply accepting unmanliness as a consequence of that duty. The literary evidence demonstrates only that Viking culture placed great weight upon performances of a masculine ideal and that some Viking men acted in ways that contradicted that masculine ideal by performing *seiðr*.

Norse Neopagan *Seiðr* and Rethinking Masculinity

Contemporary North American and British *seiðr*workers face the not inconsiderable task of re-creating practices from fourteenth-century post-Christian descriptions of eleventh- and twelfth-century pre-Christian practices translated into English by nineteenth- and twentieth-century British and American scholars. It is no wonder, then, that present-day *seiðr* is a contested practice, particularly given the weight that contemporary Heathenry places on written sources.

Contemporary practitioners negotiate tensions between a historically masculine religiosity and a historically unmanly magical practice. These men often seek to divorce unmanliness from *seiðr*, insisting that this magic is not the sole province of women and effeminate or queer men. Notably, these *seiðr*men maintain a deep investment in identifying as male while insisting on their legitimacy as practitioners; masculinity remains for these men a stable (if elastic) and desirable identity.

Ethnographic inquiries into contemporary *seiðr* suggest that many Norse Neopagan *seiðr*men are consciously negotiating the gendered genealogy of the practice. Jenny Blain's fieldwork suggests that many contemporary *seiðr*men are rethinking the discursive construction of *seiðr* as inherently unmanly, preferring to reconstruct or reimagine the practice as "a means of resistance to today's dominant gender paradigms."[33]

Contemporary Norse Neopaganisms emerged in the early 1970s as an adamantly polytheistic and demonstrably masculine new religious movement.[34] Heathens also tend to be more politically and socially conservative than other Neopagans.[35] Scholars have noted a tendency among Heathens to distance themselves from Wiccans and other less textually informed paganisms, for reasons of perceived legitimacy and connection with spiritual ancestors.[36]

This concern for adherence to textual evidence, legitimacy, and spiritual heritage directly contributes to the heavy emphasis Heathens place on historical precedents for their beliefs and practices—"the lore." Religious studies scholar and "free range tribal Heathen" Galina Krasskova suggests that Heathens depend so heavily on the lore "to ensure that our practices are as logically consistent with the practices of our ancestors as possible."[37] Heathens sometimes make changes and additions to their beliefs and practices, but Krasskova argues that these alterations are made "within a coherent historical and lore-based framework," so that "our modern religion remains attuned to the spirit of the original practice."[38] Again, a sense of historical and spiritual continuity with pre-Christian Viking religiosity is vital to contemporary Heathenry.

What might be termed "orthodox Heathenries" (Theodism and Odinism) attempt a strict interpretation of the ethics, rituals, and theology contained in the lore.[39] In contrast, more moderate Heathenries claim inspiration from and creatively interpret the lore to create new religiosities. Ásatrú is by far the largest sect of Norse Neopagan Heathenry. Ásatrú literally means "true to the Æsir," Norse sky gods like Oðinn, Frigga, Thor, and Baldr, though many practitioners of Norse Neopaganisms often also revere the Vanir, the Norse earth gods like Frey and Freya. Norse Neopagans demonstrate varying degrees of focus on, but a broadly marked interest in, the history and culture of medieval Scandinavian and Germanic areas, particularly the activities of the Vikings.

Heathenry is a votive religion, which is to say that it places far greater emphasis on honoring the gods than on any form of magical practice.[40] While "many Heathens do not attempt magic," Blain suggests that those "in need . . . will go to those who do, including seiðworkers." For some, seiðr provides a connection with the gods and spirits of their ancestors for the purposes of individual and community protection, healing, and divination.[41]

Since 1990, seiðr has been an increasingly common Heathen practice. Norse Neopagans broadly credit Diana Paxson and her group *Hrafnar* with popularizing contemporary seiðr in the United States, though the Swedish group *Yggdrasil* has engaged in the practice since 1982.[42] Blain notes that while seiðworkers remain "somewhat marginalized," seiðr has become "an expected part of Heathen gatherings."[43]

Despite growing acceptance, seiðr remains a contested practice. There is widespread disagreement regarding precisely what practices seiðr encompasses and whether it can be considered benevolent, for "in the Sagas [seiðr] is usually described as performed against the hero of the story."[44] Given the relative paucity of medieval descriptions of the practice, many seiðworkers draw on scholarship about comparable circumpolar shamanic and shamanistic practices.[45] Others rely on fellow seiðworkers, personally intuit deeper knowledge about seiðr, or understand themselves to be spirit taught. As Blain suggests, "the learning [of seiðr] is not only from human seiðworkers. The teachers are 'the spirits,' especially ancestors and Landwights, and including the deities who themselves perform seiðr, Freyja and Óðinn."[46]

Knowledge gained from personal relationships with the gods or spirits is commonly referred to among Heathens as UPG ("unverified personal gnosis").

UPG refers to "those experiences and spiritual epiphanies that, while very powerful on an individual level, are completely unverifiable in surviving Heathen lore."[47] Given the emphasis Norse Neopagans place upon textual primacy, it is perhaps not surprising that more conservative Heathenries regard UPG (and thus *seiðr*) with marked suspicion.[48]

The medieval literary precedent for the gender and sexual ambiguity implicit in *seiðr* has further contributed to conservative resistance to the practice. As with Snorri's account of pre-Christian seiðr, contemporary *seiðr* also began, at least in the United States, as women's magic. Blain notes that American oracular *seiðr* emerged "when Diana Paxson went looking for 'something for the women to do' while men were involved in performing 'viking games' and drinking beer, playing out the gendered, non-*ergi* stereotype of the macho warrior."[49] Heathen *seið*workers are still primarily women; male *seið*workers remain anomalous.[50] Some in the Norse Neopagan community still feel that "*seiðr* is for women and gay men," owing in large part to the continued connotations of *seið*craft as unmanly.[51]

More stringently textual Heathenries recall the references in the lore to the unmanliness of *seiðr* and thus disparage men who engage in spell work. As Blain reminds us, "heathenism is not immune to the homophobia of the wider society"; some conservative Norse Neopagans have suggested that *seið*men must necessarily be gay.[52] Here, as in the discussion above of the insulting nature of *ergi*, we see gendered ambiguity elided with sexual nonconformity.[53] Blain and her collaborator and co-practitioner Robert J. Wallis suggest that "those people who are most uncomfortable with *seiðr* and '*ergi*' also tend often to be those who are most 'folkish' or right-wing and farthest politically from the mainstream."[54] Despite the *seiðr*'s "unmanly" genealogy and fraught status among Heathenry writ large, increasing numbers of Heathens, "women and men, straight and gay," are performing oracular divination.[55]

Blain, often in conversation with Wallis, has interpreted the male practice of *seið*work in several ways, usually offering a liberatory reading of the practice. She acknowledges that *ergi* is still used as an insult, particularly to impugn the *seið*man's sexuality, yet she observes that "some *seið*men are now reclaiming it to describe their construction of self."[56] Wallis and Blain categorize *seiðr* as gendered practice as a "means of resistance" to contemporary gender paradigms, as "empowering and life-transforming" for "individuals and communities," and as "facilitat[ing] the alteration of normative Western gender stereotypes."[57] Blain thus locates *seiðr* as a site of performative potentiality for embodied religious practice: unmanly *seiðr* creates space for variable instantiations of Norse Neopagan masculinity: "These *seið*men perform their variant masculinities through the 'active accomplishment of meaning' by mediating among people and spirits to create both community and knowledge."[58] According to Blain's fieldwork, seiðmen instantiate their masculinities in several ways. Some deny that the practice of seiðr is unmanly, while others deliberately adopt and reinterpret unmanliness. Some seiðmen align their unmanliness with their gay identities, though Blain insists that "gay male seiðworkers ... do not define the field." Blain's interlocutor Malcolm interprets ergi as beyond the sexual implications of the term; for Malcolm, the unmanliness of seiðr should be understood "in terms of rejection of conventional masculine ideology, including, today, rejection of violence as a first line approach to dealing with interpersonal problems."[59] Others among Blain's interlocutors understand ergi as a loss of ego or an "abnegation of self" or of personal privilege, which these seiðmen feel is necessary in service to their communities.[60] In short, "practitioners use the terms of the past within today's narrative constructions, to recreate or subvert hegemonic practice and to shape new meanings for themselves and directions for their communities."[61] Blain's accounts of her interlocutors' experiences, then, indicate a transformative and liberating potential in the unmanliness of seiðr.

In theorizing the multiple masculinities of contemporary seiðmen, Blain makes an important contribution to the scholarship of gender and magic. Her consideration of gendered magic is nevertheless incomplete. Blain never moves beyond binary understandings of sex/gender and sexuality: she speaks in terms of "male and female, gay and straight." Her dichotomization of terms both elides sex/gender and sexuality and occludes the rich and varied multiplicity of queer identities. I discuss the challenge of transgender identity to Blain's theorization of argr seiðr below, but transgender issues are not the only lacuna in her work. Perhaps Blain's largest omission is the exclusion of women from conversations of unmanliness. Blain privileges the perspective and subjectivity of queer men, leaving little space for lesbian or masculine female subjectivity in her thinking about unmanliness and magic.[62]

These criticisms notwithstanding, Blain correctly notes the emergence of multiple masculinities among Norse Neopagan seiðmen. But while Blain's ethnographies show contemporary seiðmen willing to reinterpret, challenge, or embrace unmanliness in order to serve their communities (which include ancestors, spirits, and gods), Blain's interlocutors do not cite unmanliness as a reason for engaging in magical practice. It is not clear from the ethnographic evidence she presents that gender is as central a concern to her interlocutors as it is to Blain's analysis. Indeed, her interlocutors demonstrate a deep and persistent investment in retaining the category of masculinity, even as they struggle to authorize themselves as legitimate male practitioners of seiðr.

"Power/Blessing/Curse/Wiring/Energy/Sacredness":
Kaldera's Rejection of Masculinity

By contrast, Northern Tradition shaman and transman Raven Kaldera understands unmanliness not only as a condition or consequence of *seiðr* but as one
key reason for performing *seiðr*. Kaldera's understanding of his role as shaman
requires a constant performance of unmanliness, in which the performing of
seiðr forms a key element.

Unmanliness informs not only Kaldera's practice of *seiðr* but also his identity and responsibilities as a shaman. For Kaldera, unmanliness is not a condition for or consequence of accessing occult knowledge but rather a crucial
element of Kaldera's shamanic identity and authority, a religious vocation.
More so than with previous examples, Kaldera uses *seiðr* to rethink and redo
gender. For Kaldera, the high seat is a site for dismantling traditional gender
roles, and traditional masculinity in particular.

Raven Kaldera, a female-to-male transperson, transgender and intersex
activist, and founder of Northern Tradition Paganism, notes that transgender
individuals do not have the luxury of taking gender for granted.[63] Many
transfolk do not experience gender transgression as voluntary, and Kaldera
emphatically refutes the notion of choice in transgenderism throughout his
writings and interviews: "Those of us who 'do' gender . . . twist it and play with
it and transform it into something quite different from what society intends,"
he writes. "*We don't get the privilege of living an unquestioned life*" (emphasis
added).[64] In another work, Kaldera asserts, "Some of us are living in that sacred
space [between genders] right now. . . . *We did not choose to be what we are, and
we cannot unchoose it*. But being what we are has given us choices, choices the
likes of which you can only hope to imagine" (emphasis added).[65] The margin-
ality of trans existence is, as Kaldera demonstrates, not based solely on choice.
It is a fact of trans life—a matter of knowing and living in one's body.

Kaldera also suggests that a calling by the spirits to serve as shaman further
complicates the notion of voluntarism in gender identity.[66] While mundane
transfolk can hide or refuse to acknowledge being differently gendered, the
third-sex shaman's first duty is to resolve hir own gender confusions.[67] Transgender spirit workers, those "called by the Gods and/or spirits to destroy [their
lives] and be reborn to serve others, to be ridden by spirits, to lose everything
and gain this knowledge," do not have the option of concealing a gender-
ambiguous identity, Kaldera explains. "We [transgender spirit workers] must
deal fully and completely with our gender issues, as quickly and as honestly as
possible. . . . If you are not dealing with—and fully living—your sacred gender,
then everything that the Gods and spirits will do to you will be about forcing

you to come to terms with this [identity.]"[68] Kaldera describes his religious identity as shaman and his bodily identity as transgender as inextricably entwined. He is not alone in this belief: of the roughly thirty members of what Kaldera calls his "tribe," approximately 80 percent are transgender. According to one such member, if we expand the definition of unmanliness to include "atypical gender presentation . . . third gender, androgyne, or any degree of gender dysphoria, or simple gender transgression . . . that percentage rises to 99%."[69]

Kaldera's "third-sex shamanism" combines spirit-taught knowledge with medieval literary evidence of *seiðr* and scholarship regarding subarctic circumpolar shamanisms.[70] In his essay "Ergi: The Way of the Third," Kaldera indicates that he did not initially connect his transgender identity with shamanism. Rather, he says, Hela, the Norse goddess of death who "owns [him] body and soul," ordered him to change his gender. Only during his postsurgery research on historical shamanisms did Kaldera connect this transformation with shamanism. "When I began to read up on shamanism, the transgender issue hit me like a shock wave. These things weren't separate, they were part and parcel of the same system."[71]

Here, Kaldera is referring to the prevalence of gender-ambiguous or gender-fluid shamans among the Sáami, Inuit, Chukchi, and similar circumpolar tribes. Kaldera suggests that many such shamans historically transgressed gender roles and engaged in unusual sexual practices. "If an ordinary person of the tribe decided to change their gender, they might be shunned," Kaldera explains, "but if a shaman did it, it was a sacred thing done by the spirits to give them extra power." Kaldera cites archaeological findings, anthropological accounts, and historical documents to present a broad narrative history for what he labels his third-sex shamanism.

Kaldera explains that the third-sex shaman today must transgress gender and sexual norms as an inherent part of the shaman's identity. What is more, the shaman must be public about both gender-queering behaviors and transgressive sexual activities. The shaman's gender queering can range from cross-dressing in ritual context or deliberately transgressive sexual acts and object choices to a full surgical gender change, according to what the gods demand. Kaldera further clarifies that transgressive sex need not necessarily be homosexual. Rather, Kaldera places primary emphasis on the need for public performance of these transgressive behaviors. "It isn't enough to be third-gendered internally. You have to be visibly different in that way as well, whether it's only that your ceremonial costume has strong elements of clothing that is socially acceptable only for a sex different from the one that you most appear, or that you must act in a way that is deliberately gender-inappropriate. Your gender transgressing has to be evident to everyone who comes to see you in your professional capacity, and you may never deny it when asked."

Publicly breaking gender and sexual norms sets the third-sex spirit worker apart and allows hir gods and honored dead to speak through hir, specifically through oracular divination. Kaldera retains the term *ergi*, or unmanliness, in his third-sex spirit work because, he says, "we need a word for this thing that we are and do (for it's both something we are and something we do), and we see the echo of this same power/blessing/curse/wiring/energy/sacredness in those brief glimpses of the ones called *ergi*." Thus, for Kaldera, unmanliness is not limited to *seiðr* but is a necessary element of shamanic identity. In Kaldera's Northern Tradition, shamans derive their authority and magical power from deliberate performances of unmanliness.

Kaldera directs his own *seið*work toward serving his tribe, including spirits and ancestors—the honored dead of the transgender community, those killed for doing and speaking gender wrong: "Our Dead are angry, and they demand this of us: that as much as we are able, we will do what has to be done to make sure that there are no more fallen in this war. In order to save each other, we must band together and take care of each other, because alone we go down."[72] Kaldera's *seið*work relays the pain and fury of the transgender dead, their pleas for community building, their calls to action. For Kaldera, the doing of gender and the doing of magic cannot be divided.

More so than with Blain's interlocutors, Kaldera's *seiðr* works deliberately with and on cultural constructions (and deconstructions) of masculinity. Kaldera's intention is clear: third-sex shamanism attempts a radical restructuring of broader understandings of sex/gender within Norse Neopaganisms and beyond. For Kaldera, unmanliness is a sacred duty. Ultimately, he suggests, the unmanly *seið*worker turns "the world upside down. We are living, walking catalysts, and this is the first mystery of our existence. We turn everything that people think they know about gender—that supposedly safe ground beneath their feet—upside down. We change worlds."[73] For Kaldera and his tribe, then, sitting in the high seat creates space not only for contact between the mundane and divine but also for deploying a historically unmanly magical practice to dismantle traditional masculinity.

Modern Unmanliness

I have shown that the high seat upon which *seið*men work their magic can serve as a site of self-fashioning: the unmanly genealogy of *seiðr* facilitates—indeed, requires—male practitioners to negotiate their own masculinities as they defend the legitimacy of their magical practice. Medieval Icelandic literature provides historical and cultural evidence for pre-Christian *seiðr* as unmanly practice in a society invested in and demonstrably anxious about constant performances of manliness. The Sagas and Eddas testify to the existence of early *seið*men and to cultural tensions surrounding their practices. Blain's interlocutors detailed the ways in which contemporary *seiðr*men negotiate the unmanly genealogy of *seiðr* while relying on the Sagas and Eddas to reconstruct or reimagine the practice. Some disregard the connotations of unmanliness, while others conceptualize unmanliness in terms of a refusal of violence or male privilege. Blain thus identifies *seiðr* as a site for the emergence of "multiple masculinities" within Norse Neopagan traditions; at the same time, her interlocutors demonstrate an abiding investment in continuing to identify as male. Finally, Raven Kaldera deliberately performs and embodies unmanliness not merely as a consequence or condition of magical practice but as an integral part of his shamanic role. For Kaldera and his community, *seið*work does not merely redefine traditional masculinity, but rather speeds its demolition.

Norse Neopagan *seiðr* is a vivid example of magic as an exercise in making and understanding the self through contact with the divine and supernormal.[74] In her 2004 *Place of Enchantment*, Alex Owen suggests that the "elaboration and full comprehension of the self" is the quintessential modern pursuit, and that modern magicians negotiate gender as part of their "broader quest of self-knowledge."[75] Inasmuch as *seiðr* is a vehicle for the negotiation, reformation, and understanding of the self, it must then be understood as a thoroughly modern magical practice. The unmanly genealogy of the practice requires contemporary *seið*men to interrogate their own gendered identities even as they insist on the legitimacy of their magical work.

NOTES

1. Given Jenny Blain's attention to the ambivalence of unmanliness in this passage, I rely here on her translation. Jenny Blain, *Nine Worlds of Seið-Magic: Ecstasy and Neo-Shamanism in North European Paganism* (London: Routledge, 2002), 123.

2. On *flytings*, particularly the sexual/gendered nature thereof, see Carol J. Clover, "Regardless of Sex: Men, Women, and Power in Early Northern Europe," *Speculum* 68, no. 2 (1993): 373; and Stefanie V. Schnurbein, "Shamanism in the Old Norse Tradition: A Theory Between Ideological Camps," *History of Religions* 43, no. 2 (2003): 124.

3. *Argr* is the adjectival form of *ergi*. Thus, in this chapter, *argr* should be understood as "unmanly," whereas *ergi* should be read as "unmanliness." According to Blain, *ergi* extended well beyond *seið*workers and was applicable to both women and men. Blain, *Nine Worlds of Seið-Magic*, 111.

4. With regard to *seiðr*, while most Neopagan *seið*workers restrict themselves to oracular divination, medieval accounts of the pre-Christian practice also encompassed manipulation of present and future events. Ibid., 16. As Blain and Wallis note, "There have been considerable

arguments within Heathenry about *seiðr*, on what the term covers, and notably on whether it is 'good' magic: in the Sagas it is usually described as performed against the hero of the story." Jenny Blain and Robert J. Wallis, "Heathenry," in *Handbook of Contemporary Paganism*, ed. James R. Lewis and Murphy Pizza (Leiden: Brill, 2009), 427.

5. That is, Loki can be understood as calling Odin a "faggot" if we understand "faggot" here in terms of sexual behavior (i.e., sodomy) rather than sexual identity. As Blain notes and as I discuss later in this chapter, notions of sexual identity would not have been operant in pre-Christian Viking societies. The point here is to recognize that in Old Norse literature even the masculinity of the pantheon's high god is not sacrosanct. See Clover, "Regardless of Sex," 387.

6. Snorri recounted that Freyja, goddess of love, fertility, and death, first brought *seiðr* to the Æsir, chief gods of the Norse pantheon. "The Ynglinga Saga, or The Story of the Yngling Family from Odin to Halfdan the Black," Online Medieval and Classical Library, accessed November 22, 2014, http://omacl.org/Heimskringla/ynglinga.html.

7. Blain, *Nine Worlds of Seið-Magic*, 17, 100.

8. Social justice advocate Sam Killerman uses the term trans as "an umbrella term that refers to all of the identities within the identity gender spectrum," including transgender, genderqueer, and genderless persons. See Sam Killerman, "What Does the Asterisk in Trans* Stand For?," accessed November 22, 2014, http://itspronouncedmetrosexual.com/2012/05/what-does-the-asterisk-in-trans-stand-for/. It is worth noting, however, that trans activists have criticized Killerman for allegedly appropriating and commodifying trans-created resources. See "The Genderbread Plagiarist," accessed June 13, 2016, https://storify.com/cisnormativity/the-gender bread-plagiarist.

9. Galina Krasskova, *Exploring the Northern Tradition: A Guide to the Gods, Lore, Rites, and Celebrations from the Norse, German, and Anglo-Saxon Traditions* (Pompton Plains, N.J.: Career Press, 2005), 12.

10. Written by the thirteenth-century Icelandic historian Snorri Sturluson, the Poetic and Prose Eddas were mythological guides for young poets. The Eddas serve as the principal source for the pre-Christian mythology and cosmology of northern Europe. The Sagas of the Icelanders (*Íslendingasögur*) are histories, primarily family histories, written in the post-Christian thirteenth and fourteenth centuries about events of the (pre-Christian) tenth and eleventh centuries. Although, as Blain notes, these sources are "set within a *euhemerized*-Christianized framework," northern European Neopaganisms rely heavily on the Sagas and the Eddas to reimagine and reconstruct Viking religiosity. See Blain, *Nine Worlds of Seið-Magic*, 18.

11. Ibid., 34.

12. Carolyne Larrington, trans., *The Poetic Edda* (Oxford: Oxford University Press, 1999), 147. Blain notes that the Larrington translation is "currently the most accessible translation to practitioners," which is to say that contemporary practitioners are most familiar with this translation and thus this articulation of unmanliness. For this reason, I rely on Larrington's translations unless otherwise noted. See Blain, *Nine Worlds of Seið-Magic*, 161.

13. Regarding male *seiðworkers* in the Sagas, see also *Gísla saga Súrssonar*, Icelandic Saga Database, http://sagadb.org/gisla_saga_surssonar; *The Story of the Laxdalers*, trans. Robert Proctor from the original *Laxdæla saga*, ibid., http://sagadb.org/laxdaela_saga.en2; and *The Saga of Cormac the Skald*, trans. W. G. Collingwood and J. Stefansson from the original *Kormáks saga*, ibid., http://sagadb.org/kormaks_saga.en, all accessed November 22, 2014. See also Blain, *Nine Worlds of Seið-Magic*, 114.

14. Brit Solli, "Queering the Cosmology of the Vikings: A Queer Analysis of the Cult of Odin and 'Holy White Stones,'" *Journal of Homosexuality* 54, no. 1 (2008): 197. From this line in the *Shorter Völuspa*, Solli extrapolates the existence of a third-gendered category in pre-Christian Norse societies. While Blain does not dismiss this possibility, she suggests that *seiðberendur* need not refer to a third-gendered magician but rather "potentially link[s] gender and magic with action, agency, performance." *Nine Worlds of Seið-Magic*, 133. Nevertheless, Solli's argument for *seiðberendur* as a discrete gender category owes more to a liberatory

queer reading of the text and an overreliance on a universalized (and decidedly Eliadean) category of shamanism than the evidence might allow, particularly given Carol Clover's compelling argument for a one-sex model operant in pre-Christian Viking societies. See Schnurbein, "Shamanism in the Old Norse Tradition," 122.

15. Blain, *Nine Worlds of Seið-Magic*, 132, 133.

16. See Clover, "Regardless of Sex," on masculinity as guarantor of meaning/worth in Viking society. Blain also suggests that Vikings might have considered *seiðr*/magic, if it did constitute an attempt to change worldly events, unmanly precisely because magic attempts to change things without the use of physical force. See Blain, *Nine Worlds of Seið-Magic*, 109.

17. Neil S. Price, *The Archaeology of Shamanism* (London: Routledge, 2001), 110. As the primary evidence for *seið*work is literary, I restrict myself here to discursive analysis of the practice. However, Price notes both that material evidence (grave goods, including staffs and masks) corroborates literary accounts of the practice and that the archaeological record demonstrates an "overwhelming predominance of [*seiðr*] objects from female graves" (119). Nevertheless, Price acknowledges that given "the numerous descriptions of men performing *seiðr*, the situation may not have been so simple," and he thus concludes that "both sexes were involved in sorcery, with evidence for different and precise social roles for men and women, together with the existence of complex sexual, social and gender constructions" (119, 121).

18. On Oðinn as unmanly *seið*worker, see in particular Solli, "Queering the Cosmology of the Vikings."

19. *Ynglinga Saga*, part of the *Heimskringla* (or "Chronicle of the Kings of Norway"), is an account of medieval Scandinavian history written by Snorri Sturluson. As noted above, Snorri was an Icelandic historian and, in addition to the *Heimskringla*, author of the Poetic and Prose Eddas, mythological guides for young poets. On this magic as an inherently unmanly pursuit, see also Price, *Archaeology of Shamanism*, 115.

20. Blain's translation, in *Nine Worlds of Seið-Magic*, 123. Larrington's rendering is even more sexually explicit. She renders "oc hvgða ec þat args aþal" as "I thought that the hallmark of a pervert." Larrington, *Poetic Edda*, 88.

21. Quoted in Schnurbein, "Shamanism in the Old Norse Tradition," 121.

22. Quoted in ibid., 121–22; Schnurbein credits Buchholz as "the most comprehensive study on [the] shamanic elements [of *seiðr*] to date" (120). In a later article, Buchholz noted that "the direct meaning of the word *ergi* (*argr* adj.) is passive homosexuality, perhaps an effeminate behavior. The close connection between *ergi* and magic, which gives a quite negative denotation to the term, may entitle us to regard *ergi* as the negative aspect of sexual ecstasy in its totality. Heterosexuality was after all the only legitimate and accepted form of sexuality in Scandinavian culture." Peter Buchholz, "Shamanism in Medieval Scandinavian Literature," in *Communicating with the Spirits: Christian Demonology and Popular Mythology (Demons, Spirits, and Witches)*, ed. Eva Pocs and Gábor Klaniczay (Budapest: Central European University Press, 2005), 241.

23. Folke Ström, *Nid, Ergi, and Old Norse Moral Attitudes* (London: Viking Society for Northern Research, 1974), 9–10. It should be noted that Ström did not necessarily insist that *seiðr* required sexual receptivity from its male practitioners or that those *seið*men accused of unmanliness were necessarily accused of being sodomites. Rather, suggestions of sexual penetration might serve as a "symbolic presentation" of a deeper and "more contemptible" character flaw, unmanliness.

24. Preben Meulengracht Sørensen, *The Unmanly Man: Concepts of Sexual Defamation in Early Northern Society* (Odense: Odense University Press, 1983), 19, 85. Like Strom, Sørensen suggests that while *ergi* could imply sodomy, the two terms are not interchangeable. Rather, "the idea of passive homosexuality was so closely linked with notions of immorality in general that the sexual sense could serve to express the moral sense." "Sexual perversion," then, is beside the point. The *argr* man's true failing lay not in having been used sexually by another man but rather in having failed to perform his masculinity appropriately (see also Clover on this point). Sørensen, *Unmanly Man*, 20. As I mentioned at the beginning of the chapter,

notions of pre-Christian Viking homosexuality are grossly anachronistic, as notions of sexual identity would not have been operant at this time.

25. This is to say that where allegations of *ergi* pertain to sexual impropriety or passivity, it should be read as sodomy (a sexual act) rather than homosexuality (a sexual identity). As Foucault demonstrated, sexual identity—and in particular the understanding of sexuality as the core of identity—emerged as a condition of possibility concurrently with psychoanalysis (that is, not until the nineteenth century). Michel Foucault, *The History of Sexuality, Volume 1: An Introduction*, trans. Robert Hurley (New York: Pantheon Books, 1978). See also Blain, *Nine Worlds of Seið-Magic*, 125. To refer to pre-Christian *seið*men as homosexual is grossly anachronistic and renders much scholarship on the "queer" potentialities of pre-Christian *seiðr* problematic from a sexuality studies perspective. See also Solli, "Queering the Cosmology of the Vikings," 195.

26. Though beyond scope of this study, scholarly explanations of *seiðr*'s unmanliness are not limited to gender or sexuality. See, for example, Blain's suggestion that *seiðr* was considered *argr* because it was based on foreign (*Sáami*) practices. *Nine Worlds of Seið-Magic*, 137. See also Ronald Grambo, "Unmanliness and *Seiðr*: Problems Concerning the Change of Sex," in *Shamanisms Past and Present,* ed. Mihály Hoppál and Otto J. von Sadovszky (Budapest: International Society for Oceanic Research, 1989), 103–14.

27. Blain, *Nine Worlds of Seið-Magic*, 124.

28. Clover, "Regardless of Sex," 381. Regarding *ergi* as a tendency or inclination, see Blain, *Nine Worlds of Seið-Magic*, 18.

29. Clover, "Regardless of Sex," 381. Regarding the inclusion of *ergi* as *nið*, see the work of Ström, Clover, Solli, and Sørensen, among others.

30. As Clover notes, modern understandings of sex and gender are not directly applicable in pre-Christian Norse contexts: pre-Christian Norse society, she insists, "is a world in which gender, if we can even call it that, is neither coextensive with biological sex, despite its dependence on sexual imagery, nor a closed system, but a system based to an extraordinary extent on winnable and losable attributes." If a binary were operant in pre-Christian Norse societies, Clover suggests that it would have been "between strong and weak, powerful and powerless or disempowered, swordworthy and unswordworthy, honored and unhonored or dishonored, winners and losers." Clover, "Regardless of Sex," 376. Nevertheless, for the sake of expediency, I use "gender" as shorthand for this analytical concept.

31. Ström, *Nid, Ergi, and Old Norse*, 9.

32. The categorization of *seiðr* within the context of Saami and/or circumpolar shamanic practices might lend some insight, though whether *seiðr* can be understood as shamanic or merely shamanistic has been cause for much debate among scholars and is well beyond the scope of this inquiry. See, in this regard, the work of Blain, Schnurbein, and Wallis.

33. Jenny Blain and Robert J. Wallis, "The '*Ergi*' *Seið*man: Contestations of Gender, Shamanism, and Sexuality in Northern Religion Past and Present," *Journal of Contemporary Religion* 15, no. 3 (2000): 396.

34. Margot Adler, *Drawing Down the Moon: Witches, Druids, Goddess-Worshippers, and Other Pagans in America* (New York: Penguin Books, 2006), 298.

35. Helen A. Berger, Evan A. Leach, and Leigh S. Shaffer, *Voices from the Pagan Census: A National Survey of Witches and Neo-Pagans in the United States* (Columbia: University of South Carolina Press, 2003), 17. As I noted above, Norse Neopaganisms include a number of different approaches to re-creating or reimagining Viking religiosity. There is some contention about which Norse Neopaganisms do or do not constitute Heathenism or Heathenry. For the purposes of this chapter, I group Odinism, Theodism, and "Asatru" under the banner "Heathen." While Raven Kaldera's Northern Tradition Paganism draws on many texts that Heathens use to reconstruct or reimagine Viking religious praxis, Kaldera takes some pains to distance himself from the title "Heathen" in order to emphasize the Northern Tradition's openness to personal experience.

36. Ibid. See also Krasskova, *Exploring the Northern Tradition*, 13.

37. Berger, Leach, and Shaffer, *Voices from the Pagan Census*. On Krasskova's religious affiliations, see "About Galina Krasskova," accessed November 22, 2014, http://krasskova.weebly.com/about-galina-krasskova.html.

38. Krasskova, *Exploring the Northern Tradition*, 13.

39. Although the particularities of ultraconservative (or "folkish/völkisch") Norse Neopaganisms exceed the scope of this chapter, these groups provide rich fodder for religious studies and scholars of sex, gender, and sexuality alike. Several such groups have gained notoriety among Neopagans and beyond for claims to racial purity and white supremacy. On this point, see Mattias Gardell, *Gods of the Blood: The Pagan Revival and White Separatism* (Durham: Duke University Press, 2003).

40. Adler, *Drawing Down the Moon*, 298.

41. Jenny Blain, "Heathenry, the Past, and Sacred Sites in Today's Britain," in *Modern Paganism in World Cultures: Comparative Perspectives*, ed. Michael Strmiska (Santa Barbara, Calif.: ABC-CLIO, 2005), 191.

42. Schnurbein, "Shamanism in the Old Norse Tradition," 133.

43. Blain, "Heathenry, the Past," 191; and Blain, *Nine Worlds of Seið-Magic*, 143.

44. Blain and Wallis, "Heathenry," 427; and Blain, *Nine Worlds of Seið-Magic*, 143.

45. See, for example, Robert J. Wallis, "Queer Shamans: Autoarchaeology and Neo-Shamanism," *World Archaeology* 32, no. 2 (2000): 252–62.

46. Blain, *Nine Worlds of Seið-Magic*, 149.

47. Krasskova, *Exploring the Northern Tradition*, 13. Blain glosses UPG as "unusual personal gnosis." *Nine Worlds of Seið-Magic*, 14.

48. Krasskova, *Exploring the Northern Tradition*, 13.

49. Blain, *Nine Worlds of Seið-Magic*, 143.

50. Blain and Wallis, "'Ergi' Seiðman," 404.

51. Ibid., and Blain and Wallis, "Heathenry," 427–28.

52. Blain and Wallis, "'Ergi' Seiðman," 401; and Blain, "Heathenry, the Past," 204.

53. Blain, "Heathenry, the Past," 206.

54. Blain and Wallis, "'Ergi' Seiðman," 407. See also Schnurbein, "Shamanism in the Old Norse Tradition," 135.

55. Blain and Wallis, "Heathenry," 401.

56. Blain and Wallis, "'Ergi' Seiðman," 395.

57. Ibid., 407, 396.

58. Blain, *Nine Worlds of Seið-Magic*, 26 (emphasis in original), 155.

59. Ibid., 402.

60. Blain and Wallis, "'Ergi' Seiðman," 404.

61. Blain, *Nine Worlds of Seið-Magic*, 6.

62. On this point, see Judith Halberstam, *Female Masculinity* (Durham: Duke University Press, 1998). Halberstam's work explores the embodied experiences of "women who feel themselves to be more masculine than feminine," while noting that American culture seems far more concerned with male femininity (xi).

63. I do not intend to place the burden of performativity upon transfolk. However, Kaldera explicitly emphasizes the performativity of his role as unmanly shaman; he insists that "*ergi* is something we are and something we do."

64. Raven Brangwyn Kaldera, *Hermaphrodeities: The Transgender Spirituality Workbook* (Bloomington, Ind.: Xlibris Corporation, 2002), 58.

65. Raven Kaldera, "Feminist on Testosterone: The View from an Intersexual FTM," accessed November 22, 2014, http://www.ravenkaldera.org/gender-archive/feminist-on-testosterone.html.

66. Raven Kaldera, "For Transgendered Spirit-Workers," accessed October 18, 2016, http://www.ravenkaldera.org/gender-archive/for-transgendered-spirit-workers.html.

67. "Hir" in this instance is the possessive form of a gender-neutral pronoun.

68. Kaldera, "For Transgendered Spirit-Workers."

69. Quoted by Galina Krasskova, e-mail to author, October 29, 2008.

70. Much ink has been spilled over whether historical or contemporary *seiðr* constitutes shamanic or shamanistic practice (see the work of Blain, Schnurlbein, and others). I have no position on this argument; I use the term "shaman" to describe Kaldera because that is how Kaldera describes himself.

71. Raven Kaldera, "Ergi: The Way of the Third," accessed November 22, 2014, http://www.northernshamanism.org/shamanic-techniques/gender-sexuality/ergi-the-way-of-the-third.html. The quotations in the next three paragraphs are from this online source.

72. Kaldera, "For Transgendered Spirit-Workers."

73. Kaldera, "Ergi." Regarding *seiðworkers* "turning the world upside down" in *Vatnsdœla saga*, see also Blain, *Nine Worlds of Seið-Magic*, 98.

74. Following Kripal, I use "supernormal" to indicate phenomena experienced as unusual but not outside natural systems or processes. Jeffrey J. Kripal, *Authors of the Impossible: The Paranormal and the Sacred* (Chicago: University of Chicago Press, 2010), 67.

75. Alex Owen, *The Place of Enchantment: British Occultism and the Culture of the Modern* (Chicago: University of Chicago Press, 2004), 13, 113.

8

REVIVING DEAD NAMES:
STRATEGIES OF LEGITIMIZATION IN THE *NECRONOMICON*
OF SIMON AND THE DARK AESTHETIC

Dan Harms

Magic, as a term, has long been synonymous with supernatural beliefs and practices that have fallen outside the realm of the socially acceptable and sanctioned.[1] Within such a framework, people who undertake actions that might be described as magical often find themselves justifying their activities through the use of accepted philosophies, tropes, and signifiers of their particular sociocultural milieu. Simultaneously, one way for a magical incantation or collection to gain legitimacy has been through transgression of the norms and values of the dominant discourses. Such transgression allows it to meet needs (whether tangible or psychological) that the discourses are unable to address, yet it must accommodate those discourses lest those who encounter magical practices reject them entirely. The question becomes which discourses should be engaged and how they should be accommodated or flouted in order for magic to serve its role as part of a culture's intellectual, psychological, and spiritual life.

For centuries, books of magic in western Europe have justified their legitimacy in religious terms, drawing upon the scriptures, literature, and folklore of Judaism and Christianity.[2] Among these claims of legitimacy are the common attribution of books and incantations to figures from Judeo-Christian tradition, such as Solomon, Moses, Saint Christopher, and Paul.[3] Through these attributions, practitioners negotiated justifications for goals that were outside the dominant religious paradigms, including acquiring wealth, learning the future, and compelling sexual acts. Shifts in these legitimizing strategies occurred over time with changes in societal paradigms; for instance, the Protestant rhetoric linking Catholicism with superstition led authors to claim that their books were "discovered" in monasteries or that they had purported links to the Dominicans and Jesuits.[4]

As science became a dominant paradigm in the later nineteenth century, practitioners of magical practice began to employ a new, quasi-scientific language with which to legitimize itself. Theories of psychoanalysis, Jungian archetypes, and quantum physics have been appropriated and decontextualized for these purposes through a process that Olav Hammer refers to as "scientism," in order to justify magical practice to a more secular and humanistic audience.[5]

More recently, however, globalization, immigration, and mass communication technologies have done much to destabilize many religious, spiritual, scientific, economic, and philosophical paradigms. Within this milieu, magical writings and practices employ complex and variegated strategies for legitimization, in which different spiritualities, ideologies, scientific discoveries, and cosmologies, both fictional and imaginary, compete for the attention of consumers. Perhaps the best example of such a bricolage is *The Necronomicon*, attributed to a mysterious figure known as Simon and first published in New York City in 1977. Unlike previous grimoires, the *Necronomicon* did not appear at a time when a single religious tradition could be used to legitimize its existence. An examination of the text, its milieu, its promotional material, and its introduction shows that Simon relied upon multiple strategies, some more successful than others, to establish his project's legitimacy and link it to broader trends in the areas of occultism, publishing, archaeology, and popular entertainment.

The *Necronomicon*

Although originally published in hardcover by the publisher Schlangekraft, the *Necronomicon* has become perhaps the most popular modern grimoire through the paperback editions of HarperCollins's Avon imprint, a house mainly known for romance novels. Anyone who has browsed the occult literature section of a chain bookstore has no doubt seen a black paperback with bold white letters on the spine and a curious sigil on the cover, the artist Khem Caigan's recombination of three seals found inside the book. The book has had at least seventy printings (it first appeared in paperback in 1980), with the author claiming in 2006 that eight hundred thousand copies had been sold. At least four translations have appeared (an authorized one in Spanish and three unauthorized ones, in German, Russian, and French).[6] A pirated electronic edition was released by "The Coroner" in December 1985 and circulated through the bulletin board systems of the time. Today, a number of electronic versions are available through both the Internet and for purchase at print-on-demand sites. To follow up on his success, Simon himself has written *Report on the Necronomicon* (retitled *Necronomicon Spellbook*), *Dead Names: The Dark History of the Necronomicon,* and *Gates of the Necronomicon,* while other publishers have released their own guides to the book. In 2008, a new hardcover edition was issued, with an exclusive leather-bound run selling for $275. That a publisher can charge such a price for a book that is available in paperback for $7.99 says a great deal about the work's wide-ranging popularity.

"Simon" is a mysterious individual who has been the subject of a great deal of speculation. One name often associated with him is Peter Levenda, an author on occultism and conspiracy theories who was a member of a loose circle centered around the Magickal Childe shop (which was founded as the Warlock Shop in Brooklyn in 1972 but changed its name when it moved to Manhattan in 1976).[7] Levenda and Simon have both denied this, but the copyright record for *Gates of the Necronomicon* clearly identifies both men as the same.[8] In addition, at least one member of the Magickal Childe circle has claimed that they are identical, and no one else present at the time has corroborated Levenda's denials. Others could have been involved in the process of creating the *Necronomicon,* or the pseudonym could have been used by different people at different times.[9] Even if he is not Simon, Levenda was, by the accounts of "Simon" and others, heavily involved in the book's creation, and at times his statements can illuminate choices made during the text's composition that are baffling otherwise.

Purporting to be a translation of a Greek manuscript from the tenth century, the *Necronomicon* describes magical techniques uncovered by a "mad Arab." This unnamed individual starts with a tale of how he began to delve into sorcery. As a young shepherd visiting the Mountains of Masshu (a probably mythical location mentioned in the *Epic of Gilgamesh*), he unwittingly became part of a ceremony in which black-robed cultists called up a tentacled beast from beneath a great rock bearing a magical seal. Escaping when the creature apparently destroyed his captors, the shepherd wandered about the world gathering the knowledge that propelled him into becoming a great sorcerer.

Central to the book is a battle between the forces of the Zonei (the planetary gods of the Sumerians and Babylonians who protect humanity) and the Azonei (the demonlike forces beyond the stars and in the underworld). The main magical component of the book is a ritual in which the magician walks through seven symbolic gates, each corresponding to a planet in the solar system, thus gaining authority over the forces of the cosmos. Lengthy procedures for calling up the "Watcher" (or guardian spirit), creating the seals and vestments, and other ritual tasks occupy much of the book. An individual who undergoes initiation by passing through these gates might summon up the names of the god

Marduk (the names are seen as autonomous beings in their own right), the dead, and even the Azonei, though this is a dangerous process. Despite possessing numerous amulets and rites of protection, the book's magic is unable to protect its author, whose writing trails off amid portents of doom.

The *Necronomicon* itself provides no information on the manuscript's origins, save only that Simon is prevented by agreements with the manuscript's owner from showing the manuscript or revealing its source. In later publications, Simon tells the reader that two monks from the Autocephalous Slavonic Orthodox Catholic Church came across this work in the course of a series of thefts, handing it off to Andrew Prazsky, the archbishop of that denomination. Simon claims that he discovered the manuscript in Prazsky's library, the bulk of which was later destroyed. Prazsky passed away in 1984, leaving his version of events untold. Even decades later, Simon has denied any suggestion that the work could be a modern invention.[10]

Such statements provide a challenge to criticism of the book, although one not unfamiliar to historians of esotericism. It is fair to say that, at this time, no manuscript, reproductions of the manuscript, notes or documentation of the translation, or corroborating statements from those who worked with the manuscript have emerged to validate Simon's account. Even without such evidence, it is still useful to explore what appear to be, or in any case function as, the textual strategies used to legitimize the *Necronomicon*.

Indeed, the sheer number of the legitimizing strategies enlisted in the text of the *Necronomicon*, its introduction, and its advertisement and dissemination are truly impressive. The author took what we might call a "kitchen sink" approach to legitimacy: instead of seeking to adhere to tropes from Judeo-Christian faiths, as books did in the past, or from science, as many more recent books on occult topics have done, he chose as many sources as possible, including the horror fiction of H. P. Lovecraft, various religious traditions, archaeology, and the theme of Satanism in popular culture.

Olav Hammer identifies two rhetorical techniques that New Age authors use to reference materials from different times and backgrounds in order to gain legitimacy. The first is reduction, through which complex traditions, cultures, and philosophies are simplified to create a set of pared-down items between which comparisons can more easily be justified. The second is pattern recognition, in which the basic capacity of the human mind allows a presenter to allow his or her ideas to be "spuriously corroborated by adducing carefully selected and skewed data."[11] Both of these tendencies are at work in the *Necronomicon*, though, as I will argue, they are not sufficient to explain the book's self-legitimization. The process here is much more convoluted, with appeals to multiple authorities and elements of tradition that create a bricolage of mysticism, religion, history, and fiction.

The Book Is Born

The *Necronomicon* appeared in the alternative spirituality scene of New York City in the mid-1970s, especially that surrounding the Warlock Shop and Magickal Childe bookshop. The Warlock Shop was founded by Herman Slater and Ed Buczynski in Brooklyn in 1972. The shop moved to 35 West 19th Street in Manhattan in February 1976, and its name was changed to Magickal Childe that August. The store was widely known for its extensive stock of books and occult supplies, and it became a meeting point for New York's alternative spiritual community. Slater described it as follows in a letter in a 1972 issue of *Green Egg*: "The shop has become a gathering ground for Traditionalists, Gardnerians, pagans, ceremonial magicians and Church of Satanists, etc. We are completely unbiased and have met and been visited by such as Dr. Leo Martello, Ray Buckland, Terry of Pagan Way, Lilith of Church of Satan, and Ed the High Priest of the New England Traditionalists."[12] An advertisement for upcoming events from 1984 is a veritable who's who of the occultists of the time: Raymond Buckland, Grady McMurtry, Brad Steiger, Migene González-Wippler, Gavin Frost, and Simon himself.[13] Many of these figures were authors, and some who were even better known for their creative work, such as filmmaker Kenneth Anger and *X-Men* creator Chris Claremont, were connected with the scene.

There were at least three distinct groups that had considerable importance in this milieu. The first was composed of the ceremonial magicians, the most prominent among them being the local chapter of the Ordo Templi Orientis, an occult organization popularized decades before by the infamous Aleister Crowley. The second comprised Wiccans and representatives of other witchcraft traditions, including Gardnerians, Alexandrians, Strega, Welsh Traditionalists, the Minoan Brotherhood founded by Buczynski, and the Pagan Way (a more open organization that was used to recruit for others). The third group was made up of Satanists, mainly associated with Anton LaVey's Church of Satan, although they had a much smaller impact on the Magickal Childe scene for reasons that will be discussed shortly.

These divisions should only be seen as the beginning of understanding the Magickal Childe circle, though, and not as a rigid set of boundaries. Considerable overlap existed at this time among groups both in membership and in philosophy. Slater, for instance, was an initiate not only of the Gardnerian and

Welsh witchcraft traditions but also of the OTO.[14] Within this setting, the *Necronomicon*'s creator could find a wide variety of knowledge bases from which his subject matter could be drawn and individuals to whom it could be marketed.

The *Necronomicon* and the Grimoires

One important strategy of legitimization for the *Necronomicon* was to associate it with the older grimoire tradition and the ceremonial magic tradition it drew from. Much of Western magical practice has derived from a small number of magical texts dating from the medieval period onward, including such titles as the *Key of Solomon*, the *Lemegeton*, the *Fourth Book of Occult Philosophy*, attributed to Agrippa, the *Book of the Sacred Magic of Abramelin the Mage*, and others.[15] Levenda became familiar with these books during his later high school years through their repackaging in the work of Arthur Edward Waite:

> During my last two years at Columbus [High School], I was friendly with a number of people who lived in and near Pelham Bay Park. . . . These individuals were very involved in ritual practices, as they understood them. (Some were even teachers at the local high school.) We held séances together in Pelham Bay, near where Co-Op City now stands; some of us even tried summoning demons. As a text, we relied upon A. E. Waite's *Book of Ceremonial Magic* (or, in its more ominous incarnation, *The Book of Black Magic and of Pacts*). . . . We scrupulously copied down arcane ceremonies and mispronounced Greek and Hebrew incantations (although we could be counted upon to get the Latin right, altar boys as some of us had been before the days of Vatican II and the vernacular Mass). We made our own instruments and tools "of Art": wands, knives, swords, robes, and censers. . . . This was the Bronx in 1968.[16]

Waite's *Book of Black Magic and of Pacts*, or *The Book of Ceremonial Magic*, has been a staple of magical libraries since it was first published in 1898. Ironically, according to the author, this compilation of translated rituals from many grimoires was composed "to place within reach of those persons who are inclined to such a subject the fullest evidence of the futility of Ceremonial Magic as it is found in books."[17] Nonetheless, the unavailability of many of the original texts in translation until recently has ensured the book's popularity, and several editions have been published since.

That these books were very much part of the New York City occult scene is clear in a full-page advertisement in *Earth Religion News* from 1973, providing a list of books that could be purchased from the Warlock Shop. Under the heading "Practice" on its "Ceremonial Magick—Basic Reading List," the shop listed two different editions of Waite's book, *The Book of Black Magic and of Pacts* and *The Book of Ceremonial Magic.* The rest of the list displayed a wide variety of grimoires and related works, including the *Key of Solomon, The Black Pullet, The Book of the Sacred Magic of Abramelin the Mage,* and *The Sword of Moses.*[18]

Even if we set aside the likely Simon-Levenda equation, there is no question that Simon had personal knowledge of the grimoire tradition. In fact, he translated two grimoires with the intent of publishing them. The first of these, *Le dragon rouge* (or *Red Dragon*), is a work possibly dating from the seventeenth century and infamous in the French countryside.[19] A translation by Simon was advertised in *Books in Print* as a Magickal Childe release slated for April 1992, though it never appeared. More recently, Simon's translation of the *Grimoire du Pape Honorius,* a work dating to the seventeenth century, appeared in a book on occultism in the Catholic Church.[20] Simon was thus deeply involved with the texts of older grimoires.

Given this background, the similarities between the *Necronomicon* and previous grimoires are impressive. The magical illustrations in the book, especially those of the names of Marduk, are very similar to those from late-period grimoires such as the seventeenth-century *Lemegeton,* or *Lesser Key of Solomon,* many seals of which are shown in Waite's book. Striking similarities exist between the gate-walking ceremony in the *Necronomicon* and the ritual "Another rite more easie to perform for calling forth spirits" in the *Fourth Book of Occult Philosophy,* attributed to Heinrich Cornelius Agrippa.[21] Likewise, a diagram for one of the *Necronomicon* gates bears a striking resemblance to a talisman from the *Key of Solomon.*[22] By incorporating ritual processes and iconography from older works, Simon could legitimize the new book within this tradition, providing familiar ground that would encourage readers who practiced ceremonial magic to try the rituals.[23]

The introduction to the *Necronomicon* makes these linkages even more explicit. Addressing the reader's presumed doubts about the authenticity of the *Necronomicon,* Simon uses the tradition of rare books of magic as a legitimizing device for the book: "Such books have existed in fact, and do exist. Idries Shah tells us of a search he conducted for a copy of the *Book of Power* by the Arab magician Abdul-Kadir (see: *The Secret Lore of Magic* by Shah), of which only one copy was ever found. The *Keys* of Solomon had a similar reputation [for rarity] as did *The Magus* by Barrett, until all of these works were eventually reprinted in the last fifteen years or so."[24] This strategy is also visible in the book's initial marketing, via the aforementioned ad in *Earth Religion News*. Following the long list of historical books of ceremonial magic, the last item on the list is the *Necronomicon* itself. This association with older grimoires was clearly intended to lend the *Necronomicon* legitimacy in the eyes of potential buyers.

The Dreamer from Providence

The grimoires might have provided the template for Simon's book, but the title itself requires another line of inquiry, leading us away from musty tomes of forbidden magic and into the realm of speculative fiction. The term *necronomicon* was the creation of Howard Phillips Lovecraft (1890–1937), a horror and science fiction author from Providence, Rhode Island. Lovecraft's life and work have been dealt with thoroughly by a number of recent authors.[25] Lovecraft is best known for the creation of his own mythology of terror, built around the "Old Ones," beings described in different stories as gods or aliens that once ruled the universe and will do so again after humanity is destroyed or goes extinct. The most infamous of these figures is Cthulhu, a winged octopoid monstrosity trapped beneath the Pacific Ocean in a city called R'lyeh. Other members of the pantheon include Azathoth (the chaotic progenitor of the universe), Yog-Sothoth (who opens the gateways to other times, places, and dimensions), and Shub-Niggurath (a female deity associated with fertility).[26] For the most part, Lovecraft steered clear of conventional notions of good and evil; his Old Ones are indifferent and uncaring manifestations of a cosmos in which humanity is ephemeral and alone.

The first recorded instance of the term *necronomicon* appears in Lovecraft's short story "The Hound," published in the February 1924 issue of *Weird Tales* magazine. The book continued to appear throughout Lovecraft's oeuvre with different contents, but always as a collection of dire knowledge about topics beyond the ken of human civilization. Lovecraft went so far as to draw up a "History of the Necronomicon," a two-page pseudohistorical essay describing the book's history, from its original composition, under the title "Al Azif," in Yemen in 730 (by the "mad Arab Abdul Alhazred"), to the few copies kept locked away at the British Library, Harvard University, and Lovecraft's own fictional Miskatonic University.[27]

By the time the Warlock Shop opened, Lovecraft's work was entering the public consciousness. As S. T. Joshi puts it:

The first half of the 1970s was an extraordinarily fertile period, both in terms of the publication of Lovecraft's stories and criticism of his life and work. Beagle Books (later subsumed by Ballantine) began an extensive publication of Lovecraft in paperback in 1969. . . . The various Beagle/Ballantine editions sold nearly a million copies, and definitively made Lovecraft a posthumous member of the counterculture. He became fashionable reading amongst high school and college students, and rock musicians began making covert allusions to him.[28]

To this list we might add Lovecraft's appearances in other media. The radio program *Black Mass* produced audio dramas based upon his stories "The Rats in the Walls" (1964) and "The Outsider." Movies based on his works, such as *The Haunted Palace* (1963), *Die, Monster, Die!* (1965), and *The Dunwich Horror* (1970), had gained attention, if not acclaim, among cinemagoers. *The Dunwich Horror* is notable for its prominent use of the *Necronomicon*, as Dean Stockwell uses its incantations to summon up the alien god Yog-Sothoth, using a swooning Sandra Dee as a lectern.

Lovecraft's fiction certainly did play a role in at least the presentation of Simon's book. The *Necronomicon*'s introduction begins by noting the proximity between the Warlock Shop in Brooklyn and a former address of Lovecraft's, during his brief sojourn to the city in 1925–26. The introduction refers to Lovecraft several times, and the bibliography contains four references to his works.[29] At the same time, Simon claims not to have read Lovecraft until late 1972, when he presented the manuscript to Warlock Shop owner Herman Slater, who had read Lovecraft during his recovery from tuberculosis in 1971.[30] Nonetheless, another Lovecraft-inspired source was probably the precursor for the work.

The most likely and immediate impetus for Simon's *Necronomicon* seems to have been an earlier work, one that Simon mentions in none of his accounts. This was the *Al Azif,* published by Owlswick Press in 1973 with an introduction by noted author and Lovecraft commentator L. Sprague de Camp. *Al Azif* was, according to Lovecraft's "History of the Necronomicon," the original title for the *Necronomicon.*[31] De Camp's version consisted of more than a hundred pages of fake Arabic-like calligraphy, which he later admitted was a hoax.[32] The *Al Azif* was not unknown in the New York occult scene; I have seen a copy of the book belonging to the Earthstar Temple, which met in the back of Magickal Childe. In addition, the advertisement in the first issue of *Earth Religion News* (Yule 1973), cited above, offered preorders for the Simon *Necronomicon* "translation" just under another *Necronomicon* in the "original script" written by "Abdul Alhazred" (for $30). It would appear that Simon's *Necronomicon* was originally intended to be presented as a translation of the Owlswick Press work and that other accounts of its provenance were constructed when that one faltered.

Although Simon pays considerable tribute to Lovecraft in the introduction to his work, Lovecraft's creations play only walk-on roles as the "evil" creatures opposed to the "good" gods of the heavens. Simon appears to insert their names at dramatic intervals or at lacunae in the Mesopotamian texts that he quotes. The most prominent discussion of Lovecraft's figures in the *Necronomicon* appears in the Urilia Text, a section of the book dedicated to evil spirits. Here, such figures as Kutulu (Cthulhu),[33] Azag-Thoth (Azathoth),[34] and Xastur (Hastur)[35] brush up against listings of Mesopotamian demons such as Pazuzu, Lilith, and the Akhkharu. It is likely that the names of Lovecraft's creations were changed—or, in the case of Alhazred, omitted—in order to avoid the risk of lawsuit. Arkham House, the publisher that had staunchly maintained its ownership of Lovecraft, had given up on controlling his creations' use by this time.[36] The Lovecraft fan community knew about this change, but this knowledge might not have reached the Warlock Shop.

Lovecraft's status as an occult celebrity had already been cemented in the early 1970s. A less likely individual could hardly be imagined, as Lovecraft himself was a mechanistic materialist who railed against all types of spiritual belief. Nonetheless, even during his lifetime, his correspondent William Lumley believed that Lovecraft was channeling messages from the beyond, and he has been reinterpreted and appropriated by many practitioners in the field of magic as a prophet and seer.[37] For the particular cultural milieu of the *Necronomicon*, Lovecraft became known in connection with another important figure, Aleister Crowley.

The Beast and the Book: Aleister Crowley and the *Necronomicon*

The English magician and poet Aleister Crowley (1875–1947) was perhaps the most influential individual in twentieth-century magic. Crowley has gained this status in the occult community for two reasons: first, because of his magical philosophy and practice as epitomized in his writings and the workings of the magical organizations he headed, the A∴A∴ and the Ordo Templi Orientis, and second, and more prominently, owing to his reputation as an antinomian, hedonistic, drug-using individual who dubbed himself the "Beast 666."[38]

Crowley and his books had a considerable impact on the New York occult scene. When it came time to change the name of the Warlock Shop, Slater deliberately picked a name that would evoke Crowley's proposed ritual workings to create a spiritual entity.[39] Magickal Childe's catalogue included thirty of Crowley's works, ranging from his metaphysical novel *Moonchild* ($1.25) to a complete set of his periodical the *Equinox* ($200), outstripping every other author listed in sheer quantity. The Ordo Templi Orientis was an influential group around the Magickal Childe shop, making it a key part of the intellectual milieu with which Simon would have been in contact there.

Based upon this background, it is not surprising that Crowley is invoked as a key figure in the *Necronomicon*. Simon quotes four of Crowley's works in the bibliography—the most by any one author, save Lovecraft—and gives special thanks to "the demon PERDURABO" (one of Crowley's magical names) in the acknowledgments.[40] The introduction refers repeatedly to Crowley's infamous reputation and his prophecies of the bloody start to an Age of Horus as presented in *Liber AL vel Legis,* drawing on Crowley as the next stage in the transmission of ancient lore. At one point, Simon explicitly draws together Crowley, the grimoire tradition, and his own work: "Therefore it was (and is) insanity for the tyro to pick up a work on ceremonial Magick like the *Lesser Key of Solomon* to practice conjurations. It would also be folly to pick up Crowley's *Magick in Theory and Practice* with the same intention. . . . Unfortunately, perhaps, the dread NECRONOMICON falls into this category."[41] We will return to Crowley later, to address the second aspect of his reputation as the Beast 666, in the section below on the dark aesthetic. What is immediately relevant is the role played by the works of Kenneth Grant in bringing together Crowley and Lovecraft, whom Grant portrayed as two mystics on parallel tracks to enlightenment.

As a young man, Grant (1924–2011) became interested in the occult, and even served as a secretary to Crowley himself for a short period.[42] After Crowley's death, Grant became a founder of one of the competing groups presenting themselves as the heirs of the Ordo Templi Orientis. According to his accounts in *Hecate's Fountain,* Grant conducted rituals drawing on Lovecraft's symbolism and creations as part of his New Isis Lodge from 1955 to 1962. In 1972, he released the first volume of his Typhonian trilogies, *The Magical Revival.* This book discussed Lovecraft and his supposed connections with Aleister Crowley.

Grant saw Lovecraft's materialism as a mask for fear and as the sign of a failed spiritual journey: "But Lovecraft seems not to have passed the final pylons of Initiation, as evidenced by his stories, and particularly his poems, in which, at the last dreadful encounter, he invariably recoiled. . . . Understandably terrified of crossing the Abyss, he forever recoiled on the brink, and spent his life in a vain attempt to deny the potent Entities that moved him. Little wonder the tales he wrote are among the most hideous and powerful ever penned."[43] Grant's book (likely in the Samuel Weiser reprint edition) was for sale in the Warlock Shop, and Simon later cited Grant in the bibliography of the *Necronomicon*. Simon even adapted a chart in Grant's *Magical Revival* showing the correspondences between Lovecraft and Crowley, and added another column purporting to show the correspondence between the two authors and Sumerian religion.[44]

Pagans Old and New

Simon's introduction did not stop with the practitioners of ceremonial magic. It also sought to legitimize the work in the eyes of Wiccans, witches, and other members of the pagan community. Simon's introduction notes the importance of the Goddess, the moon, and other topics of interest to such individuals. Nonetheless, he drew upon a different symbol set, previously little used within contemporary paganism: that of Sumerian belief.

Some debate still occurs as to the origin of Sumerian civilization, but it seems likely that it arose from the earlier Ubaid culture in the region.[45] In the 1970s, however, its origin was hotly disputed, even as Sumer's reputation had begun to reach the popular consciousness through works such as Samuel Noah Kramer's *History Begins at Sumer* (1959). Information on Sumer was prominent in local media; for example, while Simon was working on the *Necronomicon*, the Metropolitan Museum of Art heralded the reassembly of a statue of a Sumerian official's son with missing pieces brought from the Louvre.[46]

Two aspects of Mesopotamian myth entered popular consciousness in striking ways at this time. The first, based upon depictions of the Assyrian demon Pazuzu, will be addressed below. The second was a growing interest in figures such as Inanna, Ishtar, and Tiamat among advocates of feminist spirituality. A prime example from the same milieu as Simon's *Necronomicon* is the second volume of *Earth Rites,* edited by Sherry Mestel and published in Brooklyn in 1978. This work of feminist Goddess spirituality contains both a prayer to the goddess Ishtar and a song in honor of Tiamat.[47]

When Simon discusses the "Sumerian" nature of the *Necronomicon,* he uses the term as a touchstone for many elements taken from the Sumerian, Babylonian, and Assyrian cultures, as well as later systems such as Gnosticism and Greco-Egyptian religion. One cannot help but notice the close correspondences between the text of the *Necronomicon* and such sources as Knut Tallqvist, James Pritchard, and R. Campbell Thompson, with prayers and incantations extracted and reworded to fit Simon's conception of a grimoire.[48] Likewise, Khem Caigan, the artist for the book, has observed the parallels between the sevenfold initiatory structure of the gates and similar works from the gnostic tradition, especially the Books of Jeu.[49] Simon's bibliography reveals that his sources range not only through time but also from the realms of the scholarly to the popular and beyond. The more scholarly monographs mentioned above are found alongside more popular works by authors such as Kramer and Hooke.

One source bears particular notice, because it is clearly far removed from the scholarly corpus. This is *The Sumer-Aryan Dictionary,* a highly speculative work by Lieutenant Colonel Laurence Austine Waddell (1854–1938), which postulated that the Sumerians were pale-skinned individuals responsible for the rise of Egypt and for all the notable achievements of civilization.[50] One would think that the title, let alone the introduction, would be sufficient to exclude it from Simon's consideration, but he quotes from it repeatedly and even refers to the "Aryan Race" as an uncontroversial fact.[51] Why this argument would appear in the book remains a mystery.[52] Although no sign exists that such an attitude was prevalent among the members of the Magickal Childe community, it bears noting that James H. Madole, head of the racial purity-endorsing National Renaissance Party, was part of the local occult scene.[53] Madole, with whom Levenda was acquainted, was not only an advocate of theosophical and satanic philosophy but also a fan of science fiction who once debated LaVey about the *Necronomicon* itself, according to one former member of the Church of Satan's Council of Nine.[54] Simon's "Sumer," like many other lands of the past appropriated by Western esotericism,[55] is meant to send messages of antiquity, and possibly racial purity, relevant to his potential audience.

Having established this framework, Simon set out to bring together the ancient pagan religion of Sumer with the beliefs of pagans from the 1970s. This was no mean feat, given the vast gaps between the massive priestly institutions of the ancient Middle Eastern city-states and the individualized, nature-revering faiths typifying late twentieth-century paganism. Using the techniques of reduction and pattern recognition that Hammer describes, Simon brought the two together by selecting particular aspects of each faith—either very broad or very minor—and suggesting that they were comparable: "The Witches of today, however, while acknowledging the importance of the Male element of telluric Power, generally prefer to give the greater honor to the Female Principle. . . . That TIAMAT [the Babylonian monster whose body formed the world] was undoubtedly female is to the point. . . . Another hallmark of the Craft of the Wise is evident within the NECRONOMICON, as well as in general Sumerian literature, and that is the arrangement of the cross-quarter days, which make up half of the Craft's official pagan holidays."[56] The latter indicates a contemporary creation; as Ronald Hutton observes, the calendar of cross-quarter days appears in only one witch trial account, from which Margaret Murray took the classic calendar now followed by modern witches and pagans, and it seems to have few or no Sumerian parallels.[57] Thus the strategy here is to turn to Wicca for justification for the book's contents and to elide the dissimilarities between the twentieth-century religion and that of the Mesopotamians.

In another passage, Simon draws on rhetoric regarding the "Burning Times," the period of the witch trials, compares it to an Assyrian ritual for warding off evil, and then draws it back to Lovecraft:

> The word "maklu" or "maqlu" itself is controversial, but Tallqvist seems to think that it does, indeed, mean "burning"; especially so as the incantations to be found therein invariably entail burning something, usually a doll made in the likeness of a witch or evil sorcerer that the magician wished to dispose of. Hence, we have here probably the archetype of the Great Burning Times of the Inquisition, when people were condemned to a fiery death as Witches and Pagans. The chant "burn, witch! burn!" can be found in the Maklu text, in all its pristine glory. Indeed, Cthulhu calls.[58]

The Maqlû text is, in fact, a nightlong ritual in which a practitioner seeks to ward off for his client the bad fortune caused by a witch.[59] What Simon gives us here is a conflation of the popular conception of the "Burning Times," in which practitioners of magic were burned at the stake, and Mesopotamian magical practices in which practitioners of magic burn witches symbolically through the image of a doll. Bizarre as the link might seem, it served as a means, via reduction and pattern recognition, for Simon to connect the material he used in the *Necronomicon* with one of the most compelling foundation stories of modern paganism.

Simon was also familiar with a "forbidden tome" from the pagan Book of Shadows tradition. This book, a key element of many witchcraft traditions, is a collection of witches' incantations, rules, and rituals not shown to outsiders. Individual editions vary considerably between traditions and even between practitioners in the same tradition, with new material being added to keep up with changing times or to serve particular purposes. Despite admonitions about secrecy, it is not uncommon for such works to be circulated outside a group's membership, whether in manuscript or published form.[60] Herman Slater was an initiate of two traditions, the Gardnerian and the Welsh, which maintained separate Books of Shadows, making their existence very much part of the local milieu. His one-time partner, Eddie Buczynski, is said to have taken much of the Book of Shadows for the Welsh tradition he founded from those of another organization, leading to tensions in the local witch community.[61]

Simon also became embroiled in the controversies over such works. In 1973, he was accused of presenting material from the Welsh Traditionalist book in a paid lecture. Simon responded by stating that while he had indeed seen pages of the Welsh book and others of the genre, he had not incorporated them into his lecture.[62] He also admitted to being involved in another controversy regarding the Gardnerian tradition's Book of Shadows: "I attended coven meetings all over New York, and eventually began to understand that the Gardnerian Book of Shadows was essentially a Golden Dawn manual mixed with elements of the OTO and a lot of poetry by Kipling. I admit I caused a bit of a stir when I handed one Gardnerian high priest a copy of poems taken from Kipling's 'Puck of Pook's Hill,' poems which contained some of the Gardnerian invocations! The HP went ashen white, and asked to be excused so he could make a few phone calls."[63] Simon was thus familiar with both the deep respect that these traditions had for their holy scriptures and the constructed nature of those scriptures, perhaps inspiring him to make a "rediscovery" of another "forbidden" book of pagan magic. Given this background, it is unsurprising that Simon refers to the "Book of Shadows" in passing, in the introduction of the *Necronomicon,* as another tome of forbidden lore.[64]

Simon seems to have seen his role not merely as an emulator of pagan tradition but as a creator of it as well. Before the *Necronomicon* was released, he wrote a series of articles that not only to refer to both paganism and ceremonial magic but also present a conscious fusion of the two traditions. Simon had a semiregular feature in Slater's *Earth Religion News* titled "A Short Primer on Pagan Ceremonial Magick." He introduced the series in the second issue as follows: "I have been asked to present a course of instruction on ceremonial magick as practice, and practice-able, by 'pagans.' . . . The course will examine both the essential similarities and the various differences between all of the Pagan Cults aforementioned . . . with examples of their rites and ceremonies, and suggestions for performing them, and celebrating them, for any interested pagans at heart; and all this from the point of view of Ceremonial Magick."[65] The second installment dealt extensively with Sumerian religion, presenting a reinterpretation of the Wiccan watchtower ritual using gods and phrases from Mesopotamian mythology.[66] When it came time to market the *Necronomicon,* the same conceptual marriage is clearly visible—the book is presented as "a complete Sumerian High Magick Grimoire of archaeologically pre-Flood Magick."[67]

Simon did not stop with ties to ceremonial magic and paganism, however. The *Necronomicon* is perhaps one of the few books in history intended to be integrated into the belief systems of at least three different spiritual traditions, the third of which was Satanism.

Satanism and the Dark Aesthetic

Another potential market for the book would have been the satanic community. The local satanic scene was quite dynamic at the time, with a great deal of interest in Anton LaVey's *Satanic Bible* and visits by the author to the New York area. Slater carried books on Satanism and even spoke up in its favor so often that some of his Wiccan patrons boycotted his shop.[68]

Nonetheless, the role of Satanists in the Magickal Childe scene was not as great as one might think. Many Satanists found their own source of occult supplies in the Magician, a shop in Greenwich Village run by Church of Satan member Ronald K. Barrett until 1974. LaVey himself seems never to have visited the Childe and even privately expressed the opinion that it should be avoided because of its Wiccan ownership, although his lieutenant Jay Solomon was an occasional visitor.[69] Some around the Childe returned the sentiment. In perhaps his first piece of writing under his pseudonym, "Simon" published an editorial "To Hell in a Breadbasket" in the first issue of *Earth Religion News* (Yule 1973). The article was highly critical of LaVey's motives and statements regarding pagans, and of the occult knowledge of the Magician's proprietors.[70] Nonetheless, the display ad in the same issue, discussed above, shows that the Warlock Shop carried LaVey's works alongside a full stock of books for ceremonial magicians, witches, and pagans.

The satanic community also contributed another possible source of inspiration for the *Necronomicon,* Anton LaVay's *Satanic Rituals* (1972), which included two rituals, the "Ceremony of Nine Angles" and the "Call to Cthulhu," written by Church of Satan member Michael Aquino and based on the works of Lovecraft.[71] In "To Hell in a Breadbasket," Simon showed himself to be familiar with the book's contents, including these rituals. The rituals in the *Necronomicon* are not similar to Aquino's, but *The Satanic Rituals* was nonetheless the first work to step from theoretical linkages between Lovecraft and occultism to use of the author's concepts in a ritual setting. As such, it might have given Simon an example of the actual infusion of Lovecraftian elements into religious ritual, a process that occurs throughout the *Necronomicon.* It is notable that both of LaVey's works were published in paperback by Avon, the same imprint responsible for the mass-market version of the *Necronomicon.*

A greater influence than any satanic philosophy was what we might call the "dark aesthetic" prominent in the popular media at this time. Crucial to the dark aesthetic is that it does not map onto any particular faith or tradition, though particular faiths may gain legitimacy from it through either endorsing or condemning it. Instead, this aesthetic reflects popular anxieties regarding alternative spiritualities. It includes a bricolage of concepts and images from surface perceptions of various faiths (centering on Satanism and witchcraft in modern society), reports of criminal acts with ritual overtones, and the entertainment media. The popular portrayal of this aesthetic is visible in a piece by Andrew Greeley published in the *New York Times* on February 4, 1973.

> "Rosemary's Baby" and "The Exorcist" are best sellers. Dennis Wheatley's novels of Satanism are airport paperback-rack favorites. In a cemetery in Florida heads have been stolen from six graves, perhaps to be used in a witches' ceremony. . . . According to Time, one of the "Council of Nine" in LaVey's Church of Satan, a fourth-degree Satanic "priest," is also a U.S. Army officer. . . . In various suburban basements around the country young marrieds peel off their clothes (thus becoming "sky clad") and jump within a nine-foot circle to celebrate a witches' sabbat.[72]

This passage is a prime example of the dark aesthetic: popular films and novels conflated with speculation on motivations for criminal acts (e.g., skulls being used in rituals), the rituals of various religious traditions (most notably Wicca, Satanism, and Voudon), and a hint (or more) of sex. The passage does not provide an in-depth or nuanced examination of these phenomena, but instead creates a delicious frisson in the reader. Another contemporary example would be the 1970 film *Sex Ritual of the Occult,* which conflates Satanism, witchcraft, Voudon, orgies, BDSM, and the gay and lesbian community.

The dark aesthetic could be harmful to the communities it represented or misrepresented, but it could also be appropriated for publicity. No doubt, the best-known example is Anton LaVey, but the New York occult scene saw other notable examples. In 1971, Wiccan author and Magickal Childe regular Leo Martello held court before a cauldron in the lobby of a theater showing the Hammer picture *Blood on Satan's Claw,* and the Childe itself appeared in movies and documentaries in the late 1980s.[73] Indeed, five of Wheatley's novels were advertised in *Earth Religion News* under the heading "Devotional Material."

Likewise, the *Necronomicon* played to this dark aesthetic through its allusions and associations. Simon's introduction refers prominently to the film *Rosemary's Baby* (1968), the Rolling Stones' 1968 hit "Sympathy for the Devil," and the works of Dennis Wheatley. Though inspired more by entertainment than by doctrine, the dark aesthetic was very much part of the scene and a topic on which Simon sought to capitalize.

Legitimization of the *Necronomicon* through these links to Lovecraft seems to have been a double-edged sword. Even before its original appearance, it appears that there was a backlash against the book because many potential buyers saw it as fictional. A promotional flyer from the Magickal Childe assures customers that even though "H. P. Lovecraft's private journal states the 'Book' never existed," it is now available and is certainly "not a phoney [sic], or a cleverly composed forgery."[74] As mentioned above, the occult world had already been presented with several pseudo-*Necronomicons*. Let us examine how this invocation of a fictional title played out in the long term.

Another key source for Simon's dark aesthetic was Aleister Crowley. Although Crowley operated largely in a tradition that mixed ceremonial magic with yoga, the *Tao Te Ching*, and other forms of Eastern mysticism, his identification with the Beast 666, misunderstandings regarding his maxim "Do what thou wilt shall be the whole of the Law," and his statements about the overthrow of other faiths in the "New Aeon" in his *Liber AL* have given him a dark reputation that does not reflect the complexity of his philosophy. To associate his book with the dark aesthetic, Simon introduces Crowley by quoting blatantly inaccurate newspaper coverage regarding Crowley's Abbey of Thelema in Cefalù (1920–23), alluding to stories of "satanic rituals, black masses, animal sacrifice, or even human sacrifice" that "were simply not true or fanciful exaggeration."[75] It appears that Simon presents material that he knows to be inaccurate in order to create a specific mood. Simon goes on to mention that Crowley was known as "The Beast 666" before discussing his ceremonial work and *Liber AL*. In doing so, Simon evokes Crowley's dark reputation for his own ends without being held to any definite statement on Crowley's philosophy.

Another of the key touchstones of Simon's dark aesthetic is the 1973 film *The Exorcist*, based on William Peter Blatty's novel. Given the popularity of the film and sensational stories circulating about its veracity, the movie stirred up considerable controversy during the period in which the *Necronomicon* was being written. The demonic statue in the opening sequence of *The Exorcist* is actually a depiction of the Assyrian wind and plague demon Pazuzu, and Simon was quick to connect this demon with the movie, Sumer, and the *Necronomicon*. Simon reviewed the movie in *Earth Religion News*, playing up its use of Pazuzu and (inaccurately) tying it to the Sumerian civilization, while dismissing the movie as a whole.[76] Nonetheless, *The Exorcist*, Pazuzu, and the concept of exorcism played important roles in the book. One promotional flyer for the book prominently features the movie,[77] and Simon repeatedly refers to Pazuzu in passages like the following: "there was fear of the Demon, PAZUZU; a genie so amply recreated in the book and the movie by Blatty, *The Exorcist*, and similarly recognized as the Devil Himself by the Church. PAZUZU, the Beast, was brought to life by Aleister Crowley, and the Demon walked the earth once more. With publicity provided by H. P. Lovecraft."[78] I have yet to find any comments on Pazuzu in Lovecraft, Crowley, or the Roman Catholic Church. By eliding the differences between demonic figures from different traditions, Simon sought to create a tradition drawing on fiction, magic, and religion to legitimize his book.

The Reception of *The Necronomicon*

Any examination of a strategy of legitimization must address the question of how well it succeeded. In the broadest possible terms, the book seems to have done quite well. In his 2006 publication *Dead Names,* as noted above, Simon states that eight hundred thousand copies had been sold, and the *Necronomicon* has become a staple of occult and New Age sections in chain bookstores. The question, however, is who bought it, and can any of its strategies of legitimacy account for its sales?

As we have already seen, the book's attempt at legitimacy through its title backfired even before it appeared, with even the advertising having to deny that the book was a fiction. Since its appearance, the ridicule has only increased, both in print and on the Internet. The *Necronomicon*'s various incarnations, by Simon and other authors, are the subject of Eric Hoffman and Poke Runyon's song "There Ain't No Necronomicon," which has circulated on the Internet since 1992. Even William S. Burroughs, who wrote a glowing blurb that still adorns the back cover of the book, referred ironically to "the Necronomicon, a highly secret magical text released in paperback."[79] For the most part, however, the book has been dismissed and ignored in works aimed at scholars and practitioners alike. Given this reception, it is not surprising that many in the occult community have distanced themselves from the book as much as possible.

At the same time, though, we should not conclude that the fictional nature of the book was necessarily an insurmountable barrier to its acceptance. When the *Necronomicon* was released, pagans were already open to inspiration from science fiction. The Zell's Church of All Worlds, heavily inspired by Heinlein's *Stranger in a Strange Land,* was very visible in the pagan community. The influential pagan magazine *Green Egg* included an article by a pagan group that used Star Trek as the basis for its rituals, and among the offerings of the Warlock Shop were such works as *The Hobbit.*[80] A great deal of attention has been paid to the fusion of media tropes with religious belief in the neopagan realm, but an examination of how such traditions are legitimized and enter into the broader discourse of the community as a whole has yet to be conducted. What is clear is that many modern pagans do not view texts as authoritative, but rather as living entities to be interpreted, reinterpreted, performed, and transformed.[81] Perhaps if Simon had framed the *Necronomicon* in a more playful manner, the text would have gained greater influence in the pagan scene.

An additional factor affecting the *Necronomicon*'s popularity seems to have been the shift in paganism between the book's composition circa 1973 and its appearance in mass-market format in 1980. The 1970s saw a transformation in the witchcraft movement. First, most witches came to see themselves less as adherents of a particular path dedicated to magical practices than as members of a religion comparable to any of the great world faiths. Second, the burgeoning environmental movement in the 1970s, coupled with the lack of a desire to re-create an indigenous religion, caused American paganism to redefine itself in opposition to lineages and reconstructions of older faiths and toward an environmental consciousness and a focus on the sacrality of nature. Third, through the efforts of Z. Budapest and Starhawk, many Wiccans found common ground with advocates of feminism and the women's movement. This is not to say that these changes were universal or uncontroversial within the movement, but the basic character of the people defining themselves as pagans changed substantially during this period. The *Necronomicon* was geared toward magical operations, with few references to the environment and with a distinctly masculine outlook, putting it very much out of step with these changes.[82] Even J. Gordon Melton, in a contemporary review of the *Necronomicon*, pointed out that the book "differs from most that have been published in recent years," many of which were "concerned with the feminine nature deities of the witches."[83]

Another obstacle to the widespread acceptance of the book has been the relative lack of interest in Mesopotamian religion among today's alternative spiritualities. Though a few pagan groups have adopted the gods of the ancient Near East, these groups are relatively marginal in the modern scene. The only exception to this overall trend is the figure of Inanna or Ishtar, whose descent into the underworld has been framed as a triumph over adversity that has been inspirational to many contemporary pagans, forming the basis for many visualizations, spiritual exercises, and rituals. Even this cannot be said to be a reconstruction of the Sumerian religion, however, as the figure of Inanna in modern feminist spiritual practice bears little resemblance to the ancient goddess.[84] The same is true of Pazuzu, whose star turn in *The Exorcist* gave him a public profile that has grown with no hint of his historic origins.[85] As such, Simon's work has gained little from an association with Mesopotamian culture.

Nonetheless, it should be noted that the *Necronomicon* has attracted some spiritual seekers who have incorporated it into their practices. For example, it has seen some usage by Chicago occultist Michael Bertiaux, who sees in its Sumerian roots a way to access modes of consciousness not previously available and to bring humanity closer to its roots in Lemuria, a lost continent in the Indian Ocean.[86] In the works of Kenneth Grant, the matter has come full circle; the author who himself inspired the Lovecraftian magic of the *Necronomicon* occasionally quoted from the "Schlangekraft recension," a term for Simon's work referring to its publisher.[87] Gerald Messadié notes that his survey of satanic groups in California in the 1980s revealed that many of them used the *Necronomicon* as part of their practice.[88] Later examinations have turned up a number of small, geographically limited groups using the Simon *Necronomicon* as the source for their doctrines.[89] In the past few years, a small online community whose members call themselves "Gatewalkers" has dedicated itself to using and expanding upon the rituals in the book. Its first published work appeared recently, and it is likely that others will follow.[90]

Although these links show that Simon's *Necronomicon* has had some influence on magical practice, it is surprising that it has not had more impact on contemporary esoteric thought. With sales of a few thousand copies considered a midlist success in occult publishing, Simon's claim of eight hundred thousand copies sold is a simply amazing figure, even more so when we include sales of pirated foreign translations and numerous copies circulated on the Internet. Even more astounding is how few signs of its presence are visible on the esoteric scene as a whole. Other works, including Starhawk's *Spiral Dance*, Harner's *The Way of the Shaman*, and LaVey's *Satanic Bible*, have been the basis for movements, group formation and splintering, books by imitators, and workshops that continue to have an influence on spirituality on an international basis. Although acknowledged by some authors in passing, the *Necronomicon* has not achieved the influence of other titles. If any aspect of the book's strategy has been successful, it has been tapping into the dark aesthetic. Though perhaps not as strong as it was in the early 1970s, this particular brand of media-delivered diabolism is still a prominent portion of our cultural landscape. But this hardly means that the satanic community has embraced the book; the Church of Satan has gone so far as to deny any link to the Simon or other *Necronomicons* that have appeared recently.[91]

The *Necronomicon*'s chief realm of influence has been its own appropriation as a portion of the same dark aesthetic in multiple media. Musical groups such as Morbid Angel and Fields of the Nephilim refer to concepts from the *Necronomicon* in their lyrics,[92] and sigils from the book decorate the cover of Rob Zombie's 2001 album *The Sinister Urge*. In the realm of digital entertainment, the sigils from the *Necronomicon* turn up in a secret level of the computer game *Doom II*. Simon's book has also influenced popular cinema; the *Necronomicon ex Mortis* that appears in the films *Evil Dead II* and *Army of Darkness* is said to be Sumerian in origin (though Lovecraft never made a statement to that effect).

A recent made-for-television adaptation of Lovecraft's story "The Dunwich Horror" used artificially aged pages from Simon's book as a prop, and a recent episode of *South Park* featured the Necronomicon's seal on the robes of the cult of Cthulhu fought by the child superhero group Coon and Friends.[93] Thanks largely to Simon's book, the *Necronomicon* has become a pop culture phenomenon, even to the extent that Guillermo del Toro decided not to create a fictional *Necronomicon* quote at the beginning of the 2004 movie *Hellboy* for fear that the title had been overused.[94]

The *Necronomicon* presents us with a curious and illuminating case when it comes to thinking about legitimizing magical practice. Simon sought to legitimize the text by appealing to a broad set of theologies and bodies of knowledge. Yet its popularity seems due less to any appeal to a particular belief system or science than to its ability to tap into a media-saturated society's fears and thrills as expressed in a particular type of entertainment. Indeed, the *Necronomicon* sought to establish its authority not through reference to magic itself but through our postmodern conceptions of what magic should be. In this way, it performs a valuable role in highlighting the varied ways in which magic, its practitioners, and its critics both align with and distinguish its practice from their cultural contexts.

NOTES

For previous discussions of this topic, see Daniel Harms and John Wisdom Gonce, *The Necronomicon Files: The Truth Behind Lovecraft's Legend* (Boston: Weiser Books, 2003), and Simon, *Dead Names: The Dark History of the Necronomicon* (New York: Avon, 2006). Thanks to John Wisdom Gonce III for all of his assistance and encouragement.

1. This chapter will not attempt to create a detailed definition of magic. On that topic, see Jonathan Z. Smith, "Trading Places," in *Ancient Magic and Ritual Power*, ed. Marvin Meyer and Paul Mirecki (Leiden: Brill, 1995), 13–27; Jonathan Z. Smith, "Great Scott! Thought and Action One More Time," in *Magic and Ritual in the Ancient World*, ed. Paul Allan Mirecki and Marvin W. Meyer (Leiden: Brill, 2002), 73–91; Christopher I. Lehrich, *The Language of Demons and Angels: Cornelius Agrippa's Occult Philosophy* (Leiden: Brill, 2003); and Christopher I. Lehrich, *The Occult Mind: Magic in Theory and Practice* (Ithaca: Cornell University Press, 2007).

2. See Owen Davies, *Grimoires: A History of Magic Books* (Oxford: Oxford University Press, 2009).

3. See E. M. Butler, *Ritual Magic* (Cambridge: Cambridge University Press, 1949).

4. Or both, as in the case of the *Grimorium Verum*, which claims to be written by a "Jesuite Dominicain." See Joseph H. Peterson, ed. and trans., *Grimorium Verum* (Scotts Valley, Calif.: CreateSpace, 2007).

5. Olav Hammer, *Claiming Knowledge: Strategies of Epistemology from Theosophy to the New Age* (Leiden: Brill, 2001), 205–6.

6. Simon, *Dead Names*, 246, 5.

7. The store's name change during the *Necronomicon*'s creation and publication has led to some uncertainty regarding terminology. References in this chapter to the "Magickal Childe community" apply also to the community surrounding the Warlock Shop.

8. U.S. Copyright Office, Form TX 6-458-891, filed November 13, 2006; see also Alan Cabal, "The Doom That Came to Chelsea," *New York Press*, June 10, 2003; Ian Punnett, *Coast to Coast with Ian Punnett: Guest, Simon*, August 13, 2006, radio broadcast; Tracy R. Twyman, *Plus Ultra Podcast Episode 1: Interview with Peter Levenda, Part 1*, May 1, 2007, podcast broadcast, https://youtu.be/54FdHyb1IPY.

9. The copyright form for *Report on the Necronomicon*, for instance, lists two individuals as sharing the pseudonym "Simon," and it has been reported that other individuals signed copies of the *Necronomicon* on Simon's behalf.

10. The defense and the details of his narrative are available in Simon, *Dead Names*. A useful counterpoint to these arguments is Michael Lloyd's *Bull of Heaven: The Mythic Life of Eddie Buczynski and the Rise of the New York Pagan* (Hubbardston, Mass.: Asphodel Press, 2012).

11. Hammer, *Claiming Knowledge*, 159-62.

12. Herman Slater, letter to the editor, *Green Egg*, Samhain 1972, 9-10.

13. American Religions Collection, ARC MS 1, Department of Special Collections, Davidson Library, University of California, Santa Barbara.

14. Charis, "Herman Slater: Thee Magickal Childe, Part 2," *Behutet: Modern Thelemic Magick and Culture* (Autumn Equinox 2001): 10.

15. See Davies, *Grimoires*.

16. Peter Levenda, *Sinister Forces: A Grimoire of American Political Witchcraft*, vol. 3 (Walterville, Ore.: TrinDay, 2005), 175-76.

17. Arthur Edward Waite, *The Book of Ceremonial Magic* (Secaucus, N.J.: Citadel, 1911; reprint, 1997), xxvii.

18. Earth Religion Supplies, "Looking for a Good Book? Start Here," *Earth Religion News*, Yule 1973, 6.

19. "Le dragon rouge," in *Grimoires et rituels magiques*, ed. François Ribadeau Dumas (Paris: P. Belfond, 1972), 95-131. For commentary, see John Tedeschi, "The Question of Magic and Witchcraft in Two Unpublished Inquisitorial Manuals of the Seventeenth Century," *Proceedings of the American Philosophical Society* 131, no. 1 (1987): 92-111; and Judith Devlin, *The Superstitious Mind: French Peasants and the Supernatural in the Nineteenth Century* (New Haven: Yale University Press, 1976), 165-71.

20. Simon, *Papal Magic: Occult Practices Within the Catholic Church* (New York: Harper, 2007).

21. Heinrich Cornelius Agrippa von Nettesheim, *Armatae militiae eqvitis avrati et ivris vtrivsqve ac medicinae doctoris, opera omnia* (Lyon: Per Beringon, ca. 1600), 1:434-35.

22. Compare Simon, *The Necronomicon* (New York: Avon, 1980), 89; and S. Liddell MacGregor Mathers, ed., *The Key of Solomon the King (Clavicula Salomonis)* (York Beach, Maine: Weiser, 2000), plate 11.

23. Simon's own explanation for these similarities is that these books are themselves derived from the *Necronomicon*. See *Dead Names*, 231.

24. Simon, *Necronomicon*, xv.

25. See, for example, S. T. Joshi, *I Am Providence: The Life and Times of H. P. Lovecraft* (New York: Hippocampus Press, 2010).

26. See Daniel Harms, *The Cthulhu Mythos Encyclopedia* (Lake Orion, Mich.: Elder Signs Press, 2008).

27. H. P. Lovecraft and Willis Conover, *Lovecraft at Last: The Master of Horror in His Own Words* (Arlington, Va.: Carrollton Clark, 1975), 104-5.

28. Joshi, *I Am Providence*, 1034-35.

29. Simon, *Necronomicon*, xi, lv-lvi.

30. Simon, *Dead Names*, 100-101; and Lloyd, *Bull of Heaven*, 652-53.

31. Lovecraft and Conover, *Lovecraft at Last*.

32. L. Sprague de Camp, "Preface to the Necronomicon," *Crypt of Cthulhu* 3, no. 7 (1984): 17. This paper will not discuss the broader range of Necronomicon-related hoaxes that have

appeared over the past half century. For more discussion on this topic, see Harms and Gonce, *Necronomicon Files*.

33. This term is a corruption of "Cthulhu" that Simon asserted meant "Man of Kutu," but that is probably incorrect.

34. The "asag" in Sumerian myth was a monster, probably in tree form, that lived in the mountains. See Thorkild Jacobsen, *The Harps That Once . . . : Sumerian Poetry in Translation* (New Haven: Yale University Press, 1997), 234. Simon's translation of the term as "magician" (*Necronomicon*, xix) probably derives from the work of L. A. Waddell, *A Sumer-Aryan Dictionary: An Etymological Lexicon of the English and Other Aryan Languages, Ancient and Modern, and the Sumerian Origin of Egyptian and Its Hieroglyphs* (London: Luzac, 1927), 22. Waddell's work will be discussed below.

35. This term is probably derived from Ambrose Bierce's "Hastur," in his story "Haïta the Shepherd," as later developed by Robert W. Chambers and August Derleth. See Harms, *Cthulhu Mythos Encyclopedia*, 128.

36. "With respect to the Cthulhu Mythos, I wish to advise that there is nothing to stop you from using it. Originally, the use of this literary material was restricted, but it is now [so] widely used that no restrictions have been placed upon it." Forrest D. Hartmann to E. P. Berglund, November 22, 1971 (unpublished letter provided to author by E. P. Berglund, August 7, 2011).

37. H. P. Lovecraft, *Selected Letters, 1932–1934*, ed. August William Derleth and James Turner (Sauk City, Wisc.: Arkham House, 1976), 270–71; Wouter J. Hanegraaff, "Fiction in the Desert of the Real: Lovecraft's Cthulhu Mythos," *Aries* 7 (2007): 85–109; and Justin Woodman, "Alien Selves: Modernity and the Social Diagnostics of the Demonic in 'Lovecraftian Magick,'" *Journal for the Academic Study of Magic* 2 (2004): 13–47.

38. On Crowley, see Richard Kaczynski, *Perdurabo: The Life of Aleister Crowley* (Berkeley: North Atlantic Books, 2010); Henrik Bogdan and Martin P. Starr, eds., *Aleister Crowley and Western Esotericism* (New York: Oxford University Press, 2012); and Marco Pasi, *Aleister Crowley and the Temptation of Politics* (Durham, UK: Acumen, 2014).

39. Lloyd, *Bull of Heaven*, 355; and Ordo Templi Orientis and Francis King, *The Secret Rituals of the O.T.O.* (London: Daniel, 1973), 233–39.

40. Simon, *Necronomicon*, lv, iv.

41. Ibid., xvi. This concern would soon be overcome. In 1981, Simon released the *Report on the Necronomicon* (later released as the *Necronomicon Spellbook*), which promised "a neat, simple method of using the ancient and awesome forces of the NECRONOMICON to gain wisdom, power, love and protection in these troubled times." Simon, *Necronomicon Spellbook* (New York: Avon Books, 1998), 3.

42. See Kenneth Grant, *Remembering Aleister Crowley* (London: Skoob Books, 1991).

43. Kenneth Grant, *The Magical Revival* (London: Skoob Books, 1991), 99.

44. Ibid., 115–17; and Simon, *Necronomicon*, xxxix.

45. See Harriet E. W. Crawford, *Sumer and the Sumerians* (Cambridge: Cambridge University Press, 2004).

46. Murray Illson, "Met (Head) and Louvre (Torso) Unite Pieces of Rare Sumerian Statue for Rotating Exhibitions," *New York Times*, August 12, 1974, 12.

47. Sherry Mestel, ed., *Earth Rites*, vol. 2 (Brooklyn: Earth Rites Press, 1978), 115–19.

48. Knut Leonard Tallqvist, *Die assyrische Beschwörungsserie Maqlû nach den Originalen im British Museum* (Helsinki: Officina Typographica Societatis Litterariae Fennicae, 1895); James B. Pritchard, *Ancient Near Eastern Texts Relating to the Old Testament* (Princeton: Princeton University Press, 1969); R. Campbell Thompson, *The Devils and Evil Spirits of Babylonia. . . .*, 2. vols. (London: Luzac, 1903–4). See Harms and Gonce, *Necronomicon Files,* 46–48.

49. Carl Schmidt, ed., and Violet MacDermot, trans., *The Books of Jeu and the Untitled Text in the Bruce Codex* (Leiden: Brill, 1978).

50. For more on Waddell, see Christine Preston, *The Rise of Man in the Gardens of Sumeria: A Biography of L. A. Waddell* (Brighton, UK: Sussex Academic Press, 2009).

51. Simon, *Necronomicon*, xviii, xxxiii, xxxix.

52. Simon's response to criticism on this front conflates the linguistic, historical, and racial definitions of the term "Aryan" and thus fails to address the connotations of the term. Simon, *Dead Names*, 277. I have raised the question directly with Simon, and he has chosen not to answer.

53. Nicholas Goodrick-Clarke, *Black Sun: Aryan Cults, Esoteric Nazism, and the Politics of Identity* (New York: New York University Press, 2002), 72–87. Some of Goodrick-Clarke's details have been disputed; see Lloyd, *Bull of Heaven*, 353.

54. Peter Levenda, *Unholy Alliance* (New York: Avon Books, 1995), 319–20; Tani Jantsang, "Did I Ever Meet Anton LaVey? Tani Jantsang Relates Her Meeting with Anton LaVey," accessed August 17, 2011, http://www.luckymojo.com/esoteric/religion/satanism/first-churchofsatan/cosfiles/DID_I_EVER_MEET_ANTON_LAVEY.html.

55. See Hammer, *Claiming Knowledge*, 98–139; and Lehrich, *Occult Mind*, 1–17.

56. Simon, *Necronomicon*, xxiii–xxiv.

57. Ronald Hutton, *The Triumph of the Moon: A History of Modern Pagan Witchcraft* (Oxford: Oxford University Press, 1999), 194.

58. Simon, *Necronomicon*, xlv.

59. I. Tzvi Abusch, *The Magical Ceremony Maqlû: A Critical Edition* (Leiden: Brill, 2016), xiv.

60. For information on the Gardnerian Book of Shadows and its origins, see Aidan A. Kelly, *Crafting the Art of Magic, Book I: A History of Modern Witchcraft, 1939–1964* (St. Paul, Minn.: Llewellyn, 1991); and Hutton, *Triumph of the Moon*, 226–36. For an analysis of the Book of Shadows tradition, see Shawn Krause-Loner, "Be-Witching Scripture: The Book of Shadows as Scripture Within Wicca/Neopagan Witchcraft," *Postscripts: The Journal of Sacred Texts and Contemporary Worlds* 2, nos. 2–3 (2006): 273–92. On the circulation of Books of Shadows, see Lloyd, *Bull of Heaven*, 131–32.

61. Lloyd, *Bull of Heaven*, 126.

62. Simon, "Letters: Ecce!," *Earth Religion News*, Yule 1973, 2.

63. Frater Inominadum, "Simon Speaks, Part II," *Behutet: Modern Thelemic Magick and Culture* 17 (2003): 16–17.

64. Simon, *Necronomicon*, xxviii.

65. Simon, "A Short Primer on Pagan Ceremonial Magick I," *Earth Religion News*, Imbolc 1974, 7, 26.

66. Simon, "A Short Primer on Pagan Ceremonial Magick II," *Earth Religion News*, Spring Equinox 1974, 13.

67. Promotional flyer, American Religions Collection, ARC MS 1, Department of Special Collections, Davidson Library, University of California, Santa Barbara.

68. Lloyd, *Bull of Heaven*, 349.

69. Ibid., 353; and Michael Aquino, *The Church of Satan*, 5th ed. (San Francisco: Michael Aquino, 2002), 225, 242.

70. Simon, "To Hell in a Breadbasket," *Earth Religion News*, Yule 1973, 3, 12. To give an idea of the overlap between occultism and Lovecraft fandom at the time, the response to the piece in the next issue was written under the pseudonym Eric Zann. Erich Zann was the title character in one of Lovecraft's most famous stories, "The Music of Erich Zann." See Eric Zann, "In Answer to This Papers [sic] Attack on the Church of Satan Yule Issue," *Earth Religion News*, Imbolc 1974, 1; and Lovecraft, *The Thing on the Doorstep and Other Weird Stories* (New York: Penguin, 2001). See also Aquino, *Church of Satan*, 223.

71. See Michael Aquino, "Lovecraftian Ritual: Ceremony of the Nine Angles, the Call to Cthulhu," *Nyctalops* 13 (1977): 13–15.

72. Andrew M. Greeley, "The Devil, You Say," *New York Times*, February 4, 1973, 256. Interestingly enough for our examination of the *Necronomicon*'s milieu, Greeley also devotes a few sentences to Pazuzu and Tiamat.

73. Lloyd, *Bull of Heaven*, 250, 353, 454.

74. Lovecraft's "diaries" were unpublished at this time and contain nothing about the *Necronomicon*. H. P. Lovecraft, "Diary: 1925" and "Diary: 1937," in *Collected Essays*, ed. S. T. Joshi, vol. 5 (New York: Hippocampus Press, 2007), 149–79 and 241–42, respectively. Lovecraft makes statements in the diaries similar to those in a number of his letters. See, for example, Lovecraft, *Selected Letters*, 285–86.

75. Simon, *Necronomicon*, xii.

76. Simon, "The Exorcist—Satan 2, Christ 0," *Earth Religion News,* Spring Equinox 1974, 18.

77. I saw this flyer in the private collection of Khem Caigan.

78. Simon, *Necronomicon*, xxvii.

79. William S. Burroughs, *The Burroughs File* (San Francisco: City Lights Books, 1984), 110.

80. Garret M. Hayes, "The Society of What?," *Green Egg,* May 1975, 31–32.

81. Jenny Blain and Robert J. Wallis, "Sites, Texts, Contexts, and Inscriptions of Meaning: Investigating Pagan 'Authenticities' in a Text-Based Society," *Pomegranate: The International Journal of Pagan Studies* 6, no. 2 (2004): 231–52.

82. For example: "Thou must abstain from spilling thy seed in any manner for like period of time, but thou mayest worship at the Temple of ISHTAR, provided thou lose not thine Essence." Simon, *Necronomicon*, 37.

83. J. Gordon Melton, "New Books," *Fate*, September 1978, 101.

84. Paul Thomas, "Re-Imagining Inanna: The Gendered Reappropriation of the Ancient Goddess in Modern Goddess Worship," *Pomegranate: The International Journal of Pagan Studies* 6, no. 1 (2004): 53–69.

85. See especially Nils P. Heessel, *Pazuzu: Archäologische und philologische Studien zu einem alt-orientalischen Dämon* (Leiden: Brill, 2002), 87–90. Heessel's investigation of modern uses of the spirit seems to have missed the *Necronomicon* entirely.

86. Michael Bertiaux, "The Necronomicon: Review of Magical Literature," Technicians of the Sacred, accessed September 10, 2007, http://www.techniciansofthesacred.com/new_page_38.htm.

87. See Kenneth Grant, *The Ninth Arch* (London: Starfire, 2002), xii.

88. Gerald Messadié, *A History of the Devil* (New York: Kodansha International, 1996), 319.

89. Harms and Gonce, *Necronomicon Files*, 201–7.

90. Warlock Asylum, *Atlantean Necronomicon* (New York: Warlock Asylum, 2010).

91. Peter Gilmore, "Necronomicon: Some Facts About a Fiction," Church of Satan, accessed August 19, 2011, http://www.churchofsatan.com/Pages/FAQnecronomicon.html.

92. See, for example, Morbid Angel, *Blessed Are the Sick* (Earache Records, 1995), and Fields of the Nephilim, *Elizium* (Beggars Banquet Records, 1990).

93. "Mysterion Rises," *South Park,* season 14, episode 12, directed by Trey Parker, aired November 3, 2010, on Comedy Central.

94. Guillermo del Toro, "Director's Commentary," *Hellboy,* DVD (Culver City, Calif.: Columbia TriStar Home Entertainment, 2004).

SELECTED BIBLIOGRAPHY

Abusch, I. Tzvi. *The Magical Ceremony Maqlû: A Critical Edition.* Ancient Magic and Divination 10. Boston: Brill, 2016.

Adams, Gretchen A. *The Specter of Salem: Remembering the Witch Trials in Nineteenth-Century America.* Chicago: University of Chicago Press, 2008.

Adler, Margot. *Drawing Down the Moon: Witches, Druids, Goddess-Worshippers, and Other Pagans in America.* New York: Penguin Books, 2006.

Adorno, Theodor W. *The Stars Down to Earth and Other Essays on the Irrational in Culture.* Edited by Stephen Crook. New York: Routledge, 1994.

Anderson, Jeffrey E. *Conjure in African American Society.* Baton Rouge: Louisiana State University Press, 2005.

Aquino, Michael. *The Church of Satan.* 5th ed. San Francisco: Michael Aquino, 2002.

Asprem, Egil. *Arguing with Angels: Enochian Magic and Modern Occulture.* Albany: State University of New York Press, 2012.

———. "False, Lying Spirits and Angels of Light: Ambiguous Mediation in Dr Rudd's Seventeenth-Century Treatise on Angel Magic." *Magic, Ritual, and Witchcraft* 3, no. 1 (2008): 54–80.

———. "Magic Naturalized? Negotiating Science and Occult Experience in Aleister Crowley's Scientific Illuminism." *Aries: Journal for the Study of Western Esotericism* 8, no. 2 (2008): 139–65.

Bell, Karl. *The Magical Imagination: Magic and Modernity in Urban England, 1780–1914.* Cambridge: Cambridge University Press, 2012.

Berger, Helen A., Evan A. Leach, and Leigh S. Shaffer. *Voices from the Pagan Census: A National Survey of Witches and Neo-Pagans in the United States.* Columbia: University of South Carolina Press, 2003.

Berman, Morris. *Coming to Our Senses: Body and Spirit in the Hidden History of the West.* New York: Simon & Schuster, 1989.

Bever, Edward. *The Realities of Witchcraft and Popular Magic in Early Modern Europe: Culture, Cognition, and Everyday Life.* Basingstoke: Palgrave, 2008.

Blain, Jenny. "Heathenry, the Past, and Sacred Sites in Today's Britain." In *Modern Paganism in World Cultures: Comparative Perspectives,* edited by Michael Strmiska, 181–208. Santa Barbara, Calif.: ABC-CLIO, 2005.

———. *Nine Worlds of Seið-Magic: Ecstasy and Neo-Shamanism in North European Paganism.* London: Routledge, 2002.

Blain, Jenny, and Robert J. Wallis. "The 'Ergi' Seiðman: Contestations of Gender, Shamanism, and Sexuality in Northern Religion Past and Present." *Journal of Contemporary Religion* 15, no. 3 (2000): 395–411.

———. "Heathenry." In *Handbook of Contemporary Paganism,* edited by James R. Lewis and Murphy Pizza, 413–32. Leiden: Brill, 2009.

Bordo, Susan R. *The Flight to Objectivity: Essays on Cartesianism and Culture.* Albany: State University of New York Press, 1987.

Boudet, Jean-Patrice. *Entre science et "nigromance": Astrologie, divination et magie dans l'Occident médiéval (XIIe–XVe siècle).* Paris: Publications de la Sorbonne, 2006.

Brooke, John L. *The Refiner's Fire: The Making of Mormon Cosmology, 1644–1844.* Cambridge: Cambridge University Press, 1994.

Buchholz, Peter. "Shamanism in Medieval Scandinavian Literature." In *Communicating with the Spirits: Christian Demonology and Popular Mythology (Demons, Spirits, and Witches),* edited by Eva Pocs and Gábor Klaniczay, 234–45. Budapest: Central European University Press, 2005.

Butler, E. M. *Ritual Magic.* Cambridge: Cambridge University Press, 1949.

Cameron, Euan. *Enchanted Europe: Superstition, Reason, and Religion, 1250–1750.* Oxford: Oxford University Press, 2010.

Carter, John. *Sex and Rockets: The Occult World of Jack Parsons.* Los Angeles: Feral House, 2005.

Casaubon, Meric, ed. *A True and Faithful Relation of What passed for many Yeers Between Dr. John Dee and some Spirits.* London, 1659.

Chireau, Yvonne P. *Black Magic: Religion and the African American Conjuring Tradition.* Berkeley: University of California Press, 2003.

Clark, Stuart. "One-Tier History." *Magic, Ritual, and Witchcraft* 5, no. 1 (2010): 84–91.

————. *Thinking with Demons: The Idea of Witchcraft in Early Modern Europe.* Oxford: Oxford University Press, 1997.

Clover, Carol J. "Regardless of Sex: Men, Women, and Power in Early Northern Europe." *Speculum* 68, no. 2 (1993): 363–87.

Cole, John. *The Olympian Dreams and the Youthful Rebellion of René Descartes.* Urbana: University of Illinois Press, 1992.

Collins, Harry, and Trevor Pinch, eds. *The Golem: What You Should Know About Science.* Cambridge: Cambridge University Press, 1998.

Cook, James W. *The Arts of Deception: Playing with Fraud in the Age of Barnum.* Cambridge: Harvard University Press, 2001.

Crowley, Aleister. *Magick in Theory and Practice.* New York: Dover, 1976.

Crowley, Aleister, with Victor B. Neuburg and Mary Desti. *The Vision and the Voice, with Commentary and Other Papers.* Edited by William Breeze. York Beach, Maine: Weiser Books, 1998.

Daston, Lorraine, and Katharine Park. *Wonders and the Order of Nature, 1150–1750.* New York: Zone Books, 1998.

Davies, Owen. *Grimoires: A History of Magic Books.* Oxford: Oxford University Press, 2009.

————. *Magic, Witchcraft, and Culture, 1736–1951.* Manchester: Manchester University Press, 1999.

Davis, Mike. *City of Quartz: Excavating the Future in Los Angeles.* New York: Verso, 2006.

Dear, Peter. *Discipline and Experience: The Mathematical Way in the Scientific Revolution.* Chicago: University of Chicago Press, 1995.

Dee, John. *The Heptarchia Mystica of John Dee.* Edited by Robert Turner. Edinburgh: Magnum Opus Hermetic Sourceworks, 1983.

————. *John Dee's Five Books of Mystery: Original Sourcebook of Enochian Magic.* Edited by Joseph Peterson. York Beach, Maine: Red Wheel/Weiser Books, 2003.

Deleuze, Gilles, and Felix Guattari. *A Thousand Plateaus: Capitalism and Schizophrenia.* Translated by Brian Massumi. Minneapolis: University of Minnesota Press, 1987.

Domhoff, William. *The Scientific Study of Dreams: Neural Networks, Cognitive Development, and Content Analysis.* Washington, D.C.: American Psychological Association, 2003.

Eslea, Brian. *Witch Hunting, Magic, and the New Philosophy: An Introduction to Debates of the Scientific Revolution, 1450–1750.* Brighton, UK: Harvester Press, 1980.

Flanagan, Owen. *Dreaming Souls: Sleep, Dreams, and the Evolution of the Conscious Mind.* Oxford: Oxford University Press, 2000.

Foucault, Michel. *The History of Sexuality, Volume 1: An Introduction.* Translated by Robert Hurley. New York: Pantheon Books, 1978.

Frazer, James George. *The Golden Bough: A Study in Magic and Religion.* Abr. ed. New York: Macmillan, 1922.

Gardell, Mattias. *Gods of the Blood: The Pagan Revival and White Separatism.* Durham: Duke University Press, 2003.

Gaukroger, Stephen. *Descartes: An Intellectual Biography.* Oxford: Clarendon Press, 1995.

"The Genderbread Plagiarist." Accessed August 31, 2016. https://storify.com/cisnormativity/the-genderbread-plagiarist.

Gísla saga Súrssonar. Icelandic Saga Database. Accessed August 31, 2016. http://sagadb.org/gisla_saga_surssonar.

Gould, Philip. "New England Witch-Hunting and the Politics of Reason in the Early Republic." *New England Quarterly* 68, no. 1 (1995): 58–82.

Grambo, Ronald. "Unmanliness and *Seiðr*: Problems Concerning the Change of Sex." In *Shamanisms Past and Present,* edited by Mihály Hoppál and Otto J. von Sadovszky, 103–14. Budapest: International Society for Oceanic Research, 1989.

Halberstam, Judith. *Female Masculinity.* Durham: Duke University Press, 1998.

Hall, G. Stanley. *Adolescence: Its Psychology and Its Relations to Physiology, Anthropology, Sociology, Sex, Crime, Religion, and Education.* 2 vols. New York: D. Appleton, 1905.

Hammer, Olav. *Claiming Knowledge: Strategies of Epistemology from Theosophy to the New Age.* Numen Book Series 90. Leiden: Brill, 2001.

Hanegraaff, Wouter. "Beyond the Yates Paradigm: The Study of Western Esotericism Between Counterculture and New Complexity." *Aries: Journal for the Study of Western Esotericism* 1, no. 1 (2001): 5–37.

———. "How Magic Survived the Disenchantment of the World." *Religion* 33 (2003): 357–88.

Harkness, Deborah. *John Dee's Conversations with Angels: Cabala, Alchemy, and the End of Nature.* Cambridge: Cambridge University Press, 1999.

Harms, Daniel, and John Wisdom Gonce. *The Necronomicon Files: The Truth Behind Lovecraft's Legend.* Boston: Weiser Books, 2003.

Hazen, Craig James. *The Village Enlightenment in America.* Urbana: University of Illinois Press, 2000.

Hillman, James, and Wilhelm Heinrich Roscher. *Pan and the Nightmare.* New York: Spring Publications, 2000.

Hobson, J. Allan. *The Dream Drugstore: Chemically Altered States of Consciousness.* Cambridge: MIT Press, 2001.

Hume, David. *Writings on Religion.* Edited by Antony Flew. La Salle, Ill.: Open Court, 1992.

Hutton, Ronald. *The Triumph of the Moon: A History of Modern Pagan Witchcraft.* Oxford: Oxford University Press, 1999.

Jahoda, Gustav. *The Psychology of Superstition.* London: Allen Lane/Penguin Press, 1969.

James, Geoffrey. *The Enochian Evocation of Dr. John Dee.* Gillette, N.J.: Heptangle Books, 1984.

Joshi, S. T. *I Am Providence: The Life and Times of H. P. Lovecraft.* New York: Hippocampus Press, 2010.

Kaldera, Raven Brangwyn. "Ergi: The Way of the Third." Accessed November 22, 2014. http://www.northernshamanism.org/ergi-the-way-of-the-third.html.

———. "Feminist on Testosterone: The View from an Intersexual FTM." Accessed November 22, 2014. http://www.ravenkaldera.org/gender-archive/feminist-on-testosterone.html.

———. "For Transgendered Spirit-Workers." Accessed October 18, 2016. http://www.ravenkaldera.org/gender-archive/for-transgendered-spirit-workers.html.

———. *Hermaphrodeities: The Transgender Spirituality Workbook.* Bloomington, Ind.: Xlibris Corporation, 2002.

Kant, Immanuel. *Religion Within the Limits of Reason Alone*. Translated by Theodore M. Green and Hoyt H. Hudson. New York: Harper Torchbooks, 1960.

Kieckhefer, Richard. *Magic in the Middle Ages*. Cambridge: Cambridge University Press, 1989.

Killerman, Sam. "What Does the Asterisk in Trans* Stand For?" Accessed November 22, 2014. http://itspronouncedmetrosexual.com/2012/05/what-does-the-asterisk-in-trans-stand-for/.

Klaniczay, Gábor. *The Uses of Supernatural Power: The Transformation of Popular Religion in Medieval and Early Modern Europe*. Princeton: Princeton University Press, 1990.

Krasskova, Galina. "About Galina Krasskova." Accessed November 22, 2014. http://krasskova.weebly.com/about-galina-krasskova.html.

———. *Exploring the Northern Tradition: A Guide to the Gods, Lore, Rites, and Celebrations from the Norse, German, and Anglo-Saxon Traditions*. Pompton Plains, N.J.: Career Press, 2005.

Kripal, Jeffrey J. *Authors of the Impossible: The Paranormal and the Sacred*. Chicago: University of Chicago Press, 2010.

Kuhn, Thomas. "History of Science." In *International Encyclopedia of the Social Sciences*, vol. 14, edited by David L. Sills and Robert K. Merton, 74–83. New York: Macmillan, 1968.

Küntz, Darcy, ed. *The Enochian Experiments of the Golden Dawn: The Enochian Alphabet Clairvoyantly Examined*. Sequim, Wash.: Holmes, 1996.

Lambert, Yves. "Religions in Modernity as a New Axial Age." *Sociology of Religion* 60, no. 3 (1999): 303–33.

Landy, Joshua, and Michael Saler. "Introduction: The Varieties of Modern Enchantment." In *The Re-Enchantment of the World: Secular Magic in a Rational Age*, edited by Joshua Landy and Michael Saler, 1–14. Stanford: Stanford University Press, 2009.

Láng, Benedek. *Unlocked Books: Manuscripts of Learned Magic in the Medieval Libraries of Central Europe*. University Park: Pennsylvania State University Press, 2008.

Larrington, Carolyne, trans. *The Poetic Edda*. Oxford: Oxford University Press, 1999.

LaVey, Anton Szandor. *The Satanic Bible*. New York: Avon Books, 1969.

Laycock, Donald C. "Enochian: Angelic Language or Mortal Folly?" In *The Complete Enochian Dictionary*, edited by Donald C. Laycock, 19–64. Boston: Weiser Books, 1994.

Lehoux, Daryn. "Tropes, Facts, and Empiricism." *Perspectives on Science* 11 (2003): 326–44.

Leuba, James H. *A Psychological Study of Religion: Its Origin, Function, and Future*. 1912. Reprint, New York: AMS Press, 1969.

Lewin, Bertram. *Dreams and the Uses of Regression*. New York: International Universities Press, 1958.

Lloyd, Michael G. *Bull of Heaven: The Mythic Life of Eddie Buczynski and the Rise of the New York Pagan*. Hubbardston, Mass.: Asphodel Press, 2012.

Luhrmann, Tanya M. *Persuasions of the Witch's Craft: Ritual Magic in Contemporary England*. Cambridge: Harvard University Press, 1991.

MacLachlan, James. "A Test of an 'Imaginary' Experiment of Galileo's." *Isis* 64 (1973): 374–79.

Marciniak, Vwadek P. *Towards a History of Consciousness: Space, Time, and Death*. New York: Peter Lang, 2006.

Maritain, Jacques. *The Dream of Descartes, Together with Some Other Essays*. Translated by Mabelle L. Andison. Port Washington, N.Y.: Kennikat Press, 1969.

Mavromatis, Andreas. *Hypnagogia: The Unique State of Consciousness Between Wakefulness and Sleep*. London: Routledge & Kegan Paul, 1987.

Merchant, Carolyn. *The Death of Nature: Women, Ecology, and the Scientific Revolution*. San Francisco: Harper San Francisco, 1990.

Owen, Alex. *The Place of Enchantment: British Occultism and the Culture of the Modern*. Chicago: University of Chicago Press, 2004.

Partridge, Christopher. *The Re-Enchantment of the West*. Vol. 1. London: T&T Clark International, 2004.

Pasi, Marco. "Varieties of Magical Experience: Aleister Crowley's Views on Occult Practice." *Magic, Ritual, and Witchcraft* 6, no. 2 (2011): 123–62.

Pasi, Marco, and Philippe Rabaté. "Langue angélique, langue magique, l'énochien." *Politica Hermetica* 13 (1999): 94–123.

Pels, Peter. "Introduction: Magic and Modernity." In *Magic and Modernity: Interfaces of Revelation and Concealment,* edited by Birgit Meyer and Peter Pels, 1–38. Stanford: Stanford University Press, 2003.

Pendle, George. *Strange Angel: The Otherworldly Life of Rocket Scientist John Whiteside Parsons.* Orlando: Harcourt, 2005.

Porter, Roy. "Witchcraft and Magic in Enlightenment, Romantic, and Liberal Thought." In *Witchcraft and Magic,* vol. 5, *The Eighteenth and Nineteenth Centuries,* edited by Bengt Ankarloo and Stuart Clark, 191–282. Philadelphia: University of Pennsylvania Press, 1999.

Price, Neil S. *The Archaeology of Shamanism.* London: Routledge, 2001.

Pritchard, James B. *Ancient Near Eastern Texts Relating to the Old Testament.* Princeton: Princeton University Press, 1969.

Quinn, D. Michael. *Early Mormonism and the Magic World View.* Salt Lake City: Signature Books, 1998.

Regardie, Israel, ed. *The Golden Dawn: The Original Account of the Teachings, Rites, and Ceremonies of the Hermetic Order of the Golden Dawn.* St. Paul, Minn.: Llewellyn Publications, 1989.

Rock, Andrea. *The Mind at Night: The New Science of How and Why We Dream.* New York: Basic Books, 2004.

The Saga of Cormac the Skald. Translated by W. G. Collingwood and J. Stefansson from the original *Kormáks saga.* Icelandic Saga database. Accessed November 22, 2014. http://sagadb.org/kormaks_saga.en.

Sax, William Sturman. "Ritual and the Problem of Efficacy." In *The Problem of Ritual Efficacy,* edited by William Sturman Sax, Johannes Quack, and Jan Weinhold, 3–16. New York: Oxford University Press, 2010.

Schmidt, Leigh Eric. *Hearing Things: Religion, Illusion, and the American Enlightenment.* Cambridge: Harvard University Press, 2000.

Schnurbein, Stefanie V. "Shamanism in the Old Norse Tradition: A Theory Between Ideological Camps." *History of Religions* 43, no. 2 (2003): 116–38.

Sebba, Gregor. *The Dream of Descartes.* Carbondale: Southern Illinois University Press, 1987.

Simon. *Dead Names: The Dark History of the Necronomicon.* New York: Avon, 2006.

———. *The Necronomicon.* New York: Avon, 1980.

———. "A Short Primer on Pagan Ceremonial Magick I." *Earth Religion News,* Imbolc 1974, 7, 26.

———. "A Short Primer on Pagan Ceremonial Magick II." *Earth Religion News,* Spring Equinox 1974, 13.

Skinner, B. F. "'Superstition' in the Pigeon." *Journal of Experimental Psychology* 38 (1948): 168–72.

Smith, Jonathan Z. *Relating Religion: Essays in the Study of Religion.* Chicago: University of Chicago Press, 2004.

Solli, Brit. "Queering the Cosmology of the Vikings: A Queer Analysis of the Cult of Odin and 'Holy White Stones.'" *Journal of Homosexuality* 54, no. 1 (2008): 192–208.

Solms, Mark. *The Neuropsychology of Dreams: A Clinico-Anatomical Study.* Mahwah, N.J.: Lawrence Erlbaum, 1997.

Sørensen, Preben Meulengracht. *The Unmanly Man: Concepts of Sexual Defamation in Early Northern Society.* Odense: Odense University Press, 1983.

Starr, Martin P. *The Unknown God: W. T. Smith and the Thelemites.* Bolingbrook, Ill.: Teitan Press, 2003.

The Story of the Laxdalers. Translated by Robert Proctor from the original *Laxdœla saga.* Icelandic Saga database. Accessed November 22, 2014. http://sagadb.org/laxdaela _saga.en2.

Ström, Folke. *Nid, Ergi, and Old Norse Moral Attitudes.* London: Viking Society for Northern Research, 1974.

Sturluson, Snorri. "Ynglinga Saga, or The Story of the Yngling Family from Odin to Halfdan the Black." Online Medieval and Classical Library. Accessed November 22, 2014. http://omacl.org/Heimskringla/ynglinga.html.

Styers, Randall. *Making Magic: Religion, Magic, and Science in the Modern World.* New York: Oxford University Press, 2004.

Subbotsky, Eugene. *Magic and the Mind: Mechanisms, Functions, and Development of Magical Thinking and Behavior.* Oxford: Oxford University Press, 2010.

Tallqvist, Knut Leonard. *Die assyrische Beschwörungsserie Maqlû nach den Originalen im British Museum.* Helsingforsiae: Officina Typographica Societatis Litterariae Fennicae, 1895.

Tambiah, Stanley Jeyaraja. *Magic, Science, Religion, and the Scope of Rationality.* New York: Cambridge University Press, 1990.

Taylor, Alan. "The Early Republic's Supernatural Economy: Treasure Seeking in the American Northeast, 1780–1830." *American Quarterly* 38, no. 1 (1986): 6–34.

Thomas, Keith. *Religion and the Decline of Magic.* New York: Scribner, 1971.

Thompson, R. Campbell. *The Devils and Evil Spirits of Babylonia, Being Babylonian and Assyrian Incantations Against the Demons, Ghouls, Vampires, Hobgoblins, Ghosts, and Kindred Evil Spirits, Which Attack Mankind.* 2 vols. London: Luzac, 1903–4.

Tylor, Edward Burnett. *Primitive Culture: Researches into the Development of Mythology, Philosophy, Religion, Language, Art, and Custom.* 3rd American ed. Vol. 1. New York: Henry Holt, 1889.

Vyse, Stuart A. *Believing in Magic: The Psychology of Superstition.* New York: Oxford University Press, 1997.

Waddell, L. A. *A Sumer-Aryan Dictionary: An Etymological Lexicon of the English and Other Aryan Languages, Ancient and Modern, and the Sumerian Origin of Egyptian and Its Hieroglyphs.* London: Luzac, 1927.

Waite, Arthur Edward. *The Book of Ceremonial Magic.* Secaucus, N.J.: Citadel, 1911.

Wallis, Robert J. "Queer Shamans: Autoarchaeology and Neo-Shamanism." *World Archaeology* 32, no. 2 (2000): 252–62.

Weill-Parot, Nicolas. *Les "images astrologiques" au Moyen Âge et à la Renaissance: Speculations intellectuelles et pratiques magiques (XIIe–XVe siècle).* Paris: Honoré Champion, 2002.

Young, William. *A debate proposed in the Temple Patrick Society . . . whether witches, wizards, magicians, sorcerers, &c. had supernatural powers.* Philadelphia: Young, 1788.

CONTRIBUTORS

Egil Asprem is an assistant professor in the history of religions at Stockholm University. His research interests include the history of Western esotericism, contemporary alternative spiritualities, and the cognitive science of religion. He is the author of *Arguing with Angels: Enochian Magic and Modern Occulture* and *The Problem of Disenchantment: Scientific Naturalism and Esoteric Discourse, 1900–1939*, and the co-editor (with Kennet Granholm) of *Contemporary Esotericism*.

Edward Bever is a professor of history at the State University of New York College at Old Westbury and director of its School of Professional Studies. His research interests include early modern history, the history of magic and witchcraft, and the relationship of cognitive science to magical beliefs and practices. He is the author of *The Realities of Witchcraft and Popular Magic in Early Modern Europe: Culture, Cognition, and Everyday Life,* and he has published numerous shorter works on early modern witchcraft and popular magic as well.

Erik Davis is an author, award-winning journalist, and podcaster based in San Francisco. His work encompasses academic and popular writing and focuses on the intersection of alternative religion, media, and the cultural imagination. He is the author of *Nomad Codes: Adventures in Modern Esoterica, The Visionary State: A Journey Through California's Spiritual Landscape,* and *TechGnosis: Myth, Magic, and Mysticism in the Age of Information* (which has been recently reissued by North Atlantic Books). He graduated magna cum laude from Yale University, and he recently earned his PhD in religion at Rice University.

Megan Goodwin is a visiting assistant professor in race, religion, and politics in the Department of Religion at Syracuse University. She recently completed an Andrew W. Mellon Postdoctoral Fellowship for creative and innovative pedagogy in the humanities at Bates College. Her research focuses on race, gender, sexuality, and minority religions in the contemporary United States. She has recently published in the *Muslim World* and *Nova Religio.*

Dan Harms is an author and a librarian at SUNY Cortland. His research interest is in texts of ritual magic as they relate to the history of the book and publishing. He has been published in *Abraxas,* the *Journal of Scholarly Communication,* the *Journal for the Academic Study of Magic, Old Cornwall,* and elsewhere. He is the co-author of *The Necronomicon Files,* a book on the legends and hoaxes surrounding the infamous creation of H. P. Lovecraft, edited *The Long-Lost Friend: A Nineteenth-Century American Grimoire,* and co-edited *The Book of Oberon: A Sourcebook of Elizabethan Magic.*

Adam Jortner is an associate professor of history at Auburn University. His work focuses on the rise of new religions in the early U.S. Republic and the history of church-state relations. He is the author of *The Gods of Prophetstown: The Battle of Tippecanoe and the Holy War for the American Frontier,* and the forthcoming *Blood from the Sky: Miracles and Politics in the Early American Republic.*

Benedek Láng is a professor and chair of the Department of Philosophy and History of Science at the Budapest University of Technology and Economics. In 2012–13, he held a fellowship at the Collegium de Lyon. A historian of science and medievalist, he specializes in late medieval manuscripts of learned magic and early modern secret communication (artificial languages and cipher systems). His *Unlocked Books: Manuscripts of Learned Magic in the Medieval Libraries of Central Europe* was published by the Pennsylvania State University Press in 2008.

Randall Styers is an associate professor and chair of the Department of Religious Studies at the University of North Carolina at Chapel Hill. His research and teaching focus on the position of religion in modern Western culture, including such themes as supernaturalism in contemporary culture, critical approaches to the study of religion, and religion in American law and politics. He is the author of *Making Magic: Religion, Magic, and Science in the Modern World* and a number of articles on modern constructions of magic.

INDEX